WOMEN & CHILDREN FIRST

WOMEN& CHILDREN FIRST

The Contribution of the Children's Bureau to Social Work Education

Edited by Alice Lieberman and Kristine Nelson

PRESS

COUNCIL ON SOCIAL WORK EDUCATION

Alexandria, Virginia

Library of Congress Cataloging-in-Publication Data
Women and children first : the contribution of the Children's Bureau to social
work education / edited by Alice Lieberman and Kristine Nelson.
     pages cm
  Includes bibliographical references and index.
  ISBN 978-0-87293-150-3
  1. United States. Children's Bureau. 2. Child welfare—United States. 3. Social
work with children—United States. 4. Social work with women—United States.
5. Women—United States—Social conditions. I. Lieberman, Alice A. editor of
compilation. II. Nelson, Kristine E. editor of compilation.

  HV741.W686 2013
  361.3071′173--dc23

                                                                  2013003124

Printed in the United States of America on acid-free paper that meets the
American National Standards Institute Z39-48 standard.

Council on Social Work Education, Inc.
1701 Duke Street, Suite 200
Alexandria, VA 22314-3457
www.cswe.org

CONTENTS

ACKNOWLEDGMENTS

I want to gratefully acknowledge all of the people who have worked so hard to bring this book to life under rather unusual circumstances. The authors of each chapter are established, successful scholars who took a detour from their usual pursuits to write their chapters. Kristi and I asked each of them to write because we wanted the best, most knowledgeable in our field to be part of this book, and we were thrilled when they said yes.

Our colleagues on the Council on Publications, including Elaine Congress and Carol Tully, the current and previous chairs respectively, and Sondra Fogel, our liaison to the Council, have worked with us each step of the way. Sondra's comments and the comments of two anonymous reviewers were extremely helpful. Given their thoughtful feedback, we are very hopeful that they will like the finished product.

I remain grateful to the goddesses that I was hired at the University of Kansas. The School of Social Welfare remains the same repository of great work, great ideas, and great colleagues that it was a quarter-century ago when I first got here. In particular, my husband, Tom McDonald, and our dean, Mary Ellen Kondrat, have been especially supportive.

Within days after the transmittal of the first draft of this book to CSWE, Kristine (Kristi) Nelson, its guiding force, died. Through all of her treatments, and through all of her bad days, she worked on the manuscript, hoping to be able to see the end product. I am grateful that she knew the work was substantially done at the time of her death, and grateful that I knew this tireless advocate for kids.

In gratitude, then, for her life and her work, we dedicate this book to Kristine Nelson.

Alice Lieberman

FOREWORD

I want to thank the social work education community for both its enthusiastic participation in our Children's Bureau centennial celebrations and for allowing me to say a few words about an insightful, educational, and important book.

President William Howard Taft appointed Julia Lathrop the first Children's Bureau chief one century ago, when the Bureau resided within the Department of Commerce and Labor. It was a most appropriate "home" given that the problem of child labor, often under harsh and impoverished conditions, ranked among the most serious social problems of the day. As a social worker and reformer, Lathrop, who could rightly be called a pioneer of sorts in a nascent urban America, saw her role as one of advocacy. During her time with the Bureau, she expanded her portfolio beyond the effective abolition of the worst abuses of children in the workforce and also confronted the problems of infant mortality, poor nutrition, and juvenile delinquency. Her years at the iconic Hull House, which preceded her stewardship of the Children's Bureau, taught her valuable lessons in the importance of a focus not only on the child, but also that child's surrounding family and community.

The achievements of Julia Lathrop, her fellow social workers, and others at the Bureau who worked so tirelessly on behalf of children constituted a remarkable foundation and a legacy to grow upon. Then about sixty years ago, the Bureau joined the Department of Health and Human Services, reflecting society's changing perception of child welfare and an implicit realization and recognition that the problems facing vulnerable children stretch well beyond child labor.

And yet, for one hundred years, as the Bureau's mission evolved from one of pure advocacy to one of partnership (with states, tribes, and communities) and leadership in the struggle for safety, permanency, and well-being of children, our relationship to social work—both its education and its practice communities-remained as fundamental as it was in 1912.

As this book demonstrates, the Bureau has repeatedly turned to the social work education community to help establish an evidence base in practice and policy with real world positive impact on children in the United States. Throughout our intertwined history, we have not always agreed on the path to success but never disagreed on the goal. For this we remain grateful, and we look forward to continuing our relationship with the social work practice and education community in the years ahead.

On behalf of the Department of Health and Human Services, Administration for Children and Families Commissioner Bryan Samuels, and Acting Associate Commissioner of the Children's Bureau Joe Bock, thank you for a productive century of education, training, technical assistance, research, and advocacy on behalf of the children of our country.

Kathleen Sebelius
Secretary of Health and Human Services
March 22, 2012

INTRODUCTION

Alice Lieberman

On behalf of all the contributors, we are very happy to be able to participate in the celebration of the Children's Bureau (CB) centennial in such a meaningful way. We have spent a considerable portion of our careers as researchers and educators in the field of child welfare, and a great deal of our work has been conducted through the generous auspices of the CB. But I was unaware of just how deep the roots of the relationship between social work education and the CB were. As Paul Stuart notes in Chapter 1, Julia Lathrop, the first chief of the CB, actually had a distinguished career in social work education as the director of the research department of what is now the School of Social Service Administration at the University of Chicago. And it is clear that she brought the values of the nascent profession with her as she attempted to inculcate the CB in the "whole child" philosophy, which emphasized all aspects of a child's life, including education, recreation, and home life, as well as child health (including child labor). Although the mission of the CB was, to a degree, overshadowed by the vast architecture of the welfare state, it is clear that over the course of those early years, Lathrop and others brought a new attention to the needs of children that is still felt today.

The effects of Lathrop's emphasis on the whole child reverberated within social work education, even as its identity in the CB waned. Throughout the past five or six decades in social work education, the notion of person-in-environment has remained a central tenet. Its contemporary roots and the language that has grown around it can be traced more directly to the work of biologist Ludwig von Bertalanffy (1950), recognized as the father of general systems theory. But before von Bertalanffy, there was Lathrop, insistent that the physical, psychological, social, and economic well-being of children could not be viewed as discrete categories, and that these interrelated systemic influences were within the purview of an agency whose mission was to ensure the right of every child to a childhood.

Barbara Levy Simon does an outstanding job in Chapter 2 of deconstructing the layers of this relationship and examining how research and evaluation—even at this very early stage in our growth as a profession—was called upon to impact such scourges as infant mortality and the special problems of families with children in need of special care. In addition, Simon notes the influence of the CB on the incorporation of fieldwork into the heart of social work education, crediting the CB's "excellence and skill in using volunteers in sustained, orchestrated, and supervised ways" (p. 32).

Kristine Nelson picks up our narrative with Chapter 3, following the implementation of the New Deal and the concomitant withdrawal of the whole child perspective. Although the impact of this withdrawal is still felt, the period she writes about (1935–1960) also saw significant progress. For example, the entry of the United States into World War II and its illumination of the importance of women laborers to this effort forced the CB to abandon its long-standing opposition to day care for children and instead seek to improve it. Concomitantly, even as the CB retreated further from its roots in the whole child perspective, the centrality of research and what we now call best practices in child welfare gained a stronger foothold. Funding for research about and services for high-risk children grew rapidly, but labor shortages persisted. As Nelson notes, the rising preeminence of the graduate degree in social work meant that even fewer social workers were available for these jobs.

By the 1960s the functions of child welfare work, spurred by the abandonment of the whole child perspective earlier, were effectively replaced by a public welfare technocracy. *Income maintenance*, as it was then known, gained ascendance, and the status of the work of public child welfare declined. Contemporaneously, the creation of the Academy of Certified

Social Workers by NASW in 1960, and the passage of the Community Mental Health Centers Act of 1963 reinforced the importance of diagnosis and treatment of mental health issues as central to graduate education in social work. The National Institute of Mental Health subsequently expanded its reach in research and training. These developments served to further marginalize fields of practice such as child welfare and medical social work supported by the CB. As Joel Blau notes in Chapter 4, there were some offsetting developments, most notably the increase in funding of Title IV-B of the Social Security Act, which reached its highest point during the last years of the Carter administration. However, the conditions that fostered the strains in the relationship between the CB and the social work education enterprise were further reinforced by the philosophies that took hold during the Reagan administration, which viewed child welfare (and all social welfare programs) through an entirely different prism.

In 1978 and 1995 Congress passed the Indian Child Welfare Act and the Multi-Ethnic Placement Act, respectively. Both had a significant impact on the way child welfare practice is taught in social work education classrooms and conducted in the field. In Chapter 5 Ruth McRoy looks at the political and social environment in the United States, beginning even before the advent of the CB, which ultimately led to these pieces of legislation. These laws codify the profession's most deeply held beliefs about the ideals of culturally competent social work practice, and McRoy notes the efforts of the CB to educate social workers for such practice.

During the years of education and advocacy that culminated in the passage of these laws, the downward spiral of public child welfare as a central concern of professional social work was either continuing or worsening. It took a decade following the end of the Reagan years, and very effective advocacy by a number of social work education groups, working in concert, to begin a reversal of this trend by procuring an increase in Section 426 funding, which was partially restored in 1997 and has been level ever since. Its entitlement cousin, the Title IV-E program, was established in 1980 to cover a wide variety of educational supports. Both are central to the capacity-building efforts of the states, although the complex formulations that govern the drawdown of federal funding under Title IV-E have caused some states to abandon social work education (long-term) training.

In Chapter 6 Joan Zlotnik takes note of the 2003 U.S. General Accounting Office report that detailed concerns related to the recruitment and
retention of child welfare workers in the public sector. The aforementioned
funding streams (Section 426 and Title IV-E), while not wholly adequate
to the task, have been marshaled to ameliorate this problem as well.

Bart Grossman and Sherrill Clark in Chapter 7 offer the pioneering
experience of the University of California, Berkeley's California Social
Work Education Consortium as an exemplar of how social work education
programs, working collaboratively, were able to leverage Section 426 and
Title IV-E funds to develop curricula and provide student support across
the state, all in an effort to reprofessionalize public child welfare.

Anita Barbee contributes to the story of our continuing relationship in
Chapter 8 on the evolution of the various training and resource centers,
now established around the country, as well as the Training and Technical
Assistance Network. These centers and the network, established as a
response to the mandate for increased accountability, began in the 1970s
and 1980s and very much mark the beginning of the close relationship
between social work education and the CB that we see today. As Barbee
notes, the vast majority of these specialized resource centers were housed in
schools of social work. Not surprisingly, following the passage of the Indian
Child Welfare Act in 1978, and as these centers became more substantively
integrated, the CB emphasized the development of child welfare knowledge as applied to tribal practice and accountability to the principles and
mandates of the Indian Child Welfare Act.

In Chapter 9 Miriam Landsman offers an excellent review of the extant
research to date on recruitment and retention and the state of practice in
countering these problems.

The final three chapters offer us some solid advice and prescriptions for
the future, all in areas where the continued common interests of the CB and
the social work education enterprise converge. In Chapter 10 Crystal Collins-
Camargo calls for a reinvigoration of the role of the CB as the developer of
clear, consistent lines of research inquiry that require the urgent attention of
scholars in the academy. One way to reinforce our common interests in this
area, she notes, would be to establish a network of researchers who contribute
to the identification of those urgent questions, lay out the path for finding

answers, and ensure that this emergent knowledge is synthesized and disseminated to those in the field as quickly as possible.

Alberta Ellett in Chapter 11 makes an eloquent plea for a consistent, shared vision between the CB and the practice/education community, one that takes into account what she notes will be a shift from the CB's triumvirate aims of safety, permanency, and well-being to a focus on well-being as the primary prevention of abuse moves to the foreground.

We end our book with Chapter 12 by Debora Ortega and Colleen Reed, who chart our way forward by bringing us back to our roots. The focus of their chapter is on the history and development of community partnerships and lessons learned as we move forward. They note that our national value of individualism, which has played a significant role in creating barriers to communities of color in particular and in the development of interventions that have been historically unhelpful in these communities, must be replaced with a spirit and value of reconciliation and collectivism. These latter values resonate deeply with the historic underpinnings of our profession, first lived out loud by Jane Addams and her Hull House colleagues, including Julia Lathrop.

We hope this book, which extols a century of common aims and points a way forward, represents a milestone in our collective effort to bring the best possible life to all children in this country.

REFERENCES

Mental Retardation Facilities and Community Mental Health Centers Construction Act of 1963. 42 U.S.C. 2689 et seq., 6000 et seq.

Von Bertalanffy, L. (1950). An outline of general system theory. *British Journal for the Philosophy of Science*, 1, 134–165.

A CHRONOLOGY OF EVENTS IN THE EVOLUTION OF THE RELATIONSHIP OF THE CHILDREN'S BUREAU AND PROFESSIONAL SOCIAL WORK EDUCATION

1912   Congress establishes the Children's Bureau (CB) as a unit of the Department of Labor. Julia Lathrop is its first chief (https://cb100.acf.hhs .gov/cb_eBrochure_CBChiefs). Advocacy activities and education about infant mortality and child labor become its first strong priorities. In her initial statements regarding the mission of the CB, Lathrop alludes to the importance of research: the CB's role, she states, is to "investigate and report . . . upon all matters pertaining to the welfare of children and child life . . . , and shall especially investigate the questions of infant mortality, the birth rate, orphanage, juvenile courts, desertion, dangerous occupations, accidents and diseases of children, employment, legislation affecting children in the several states and territories" (Children's Bureau Act of 1912). The term *investigate* in 1912 certainly implies a research function with dissemination to follow.

1912–20   The CB and the Chicago School of Civics and Philanthropy (now the University of Chicago School of Social Service Administration) establish a strong working relationship (Rodems, Shaefer, & Ybarra, 2011).

1921   Grace Abbott becomes the second chief of the CB (https://cb100.acf .hhs.gov/cb_eBrochure_CBChiefs) and remains in that position for 13 years, reinforcing and continuing the relationship between the Chicago school and the CB; many of the social research investigations conducted during her tenure were the work of faculty at the school.

1921–29   Enactment of the Sheppard-Towner Maternity and Infancy Protection Act, the culmination of the CB's campaign for maternal and child health legislation. Mother's pensions, juvenile courts, and child welfare programs were all supported by Sheppard-Towner. This act was a model for future grant-in-aid legislation and provided health and social service funding to states. The act was defunded in 1929 (Lemons, 1969).

1934   Katherine F. Lenroot becomes the third chief of the CB, remaining in that post until 1951, an actor in the expansion of the welfare state through the post–World War II period (https://cb100.acf.hhs.gov /cb_eBrochure_CBChiefs).

1935   The Social Security Act becomes law. Under the act, all financial assistance programs, including Aid to Dependent Children, fall under the purview of a three-person autonomous board, and not the CB, as its leaders Grace and Edith Abbott and Sophonisba Breckenridge had envisioned (Hanlan, 1966).

1938   Advocacy by the CB leads to the passage of the Fair Labor Standards Act, the first time that child labor is federally regulated. However, its provisions are so narrow, only a small minority of children are covered (Lindenmeyer, 1997).

1942 (ca.)–45   The CB consults on the evacuation and care of European children, including 5,000 British children placed in foster homes in the United States. The CB also assists 2,000 unaccompanied adolescents brought to the United States and 100,000 children under 14 from displaced persons camps in Germany. Work with displaced children continues until President Harry Truman enforces immigration quotas to prevent concentration camp survivors from entering the United States (http://www .socialwelfarehistory.com/organizations/childrens-bureau-part-ii-4/).

1946   The CB is transferred to the Federal Security Agency, thus removing it from direct presidential Cabinet-level supervision. At this point, the focus of the CB on the whole child ceases to exist, as its reach into all aspects of a child's life is curtailed (Lindenmeyer, 1997).

1951   Martha Eliot, a pediatrician and former president of the National Council of Social Work (1949–50), becomes the fourth director of the CB (https://cb100.acf.hhs.gov/cb_eBrochure_CBChiefs). Contemporaneously with her tenure, setting standards and providing training for a professional child welfare workforce became a priority. By the end of this decade, every state has a child welfare unit to assist families and provide substitute care and prevention and treatment interventions. Over half the child welfare workforce had 1 or more years of graduate education, and the rest were college graduates (CB, 1956). Her tenure as chief ends in 1956 (CDC, 1999).

1952   The Council on Social Work Education (CSWE) is formed. CSWE continued the work of the American Association of Schools of Social Work to establish consistent curriculum and accreditation standards for graduate programs throughout the country. The CB and CSWE reject undergraduate education as preparation for entry-level social work at this time.

1957   Katherine Oettinger becomes the fifth CB chief, leaving her position as dean of the Boston University School of Social Work to do so (https://cb100.acf.hhs.gov/cb_eBrochure_CBChiefs). She remains chief until 1968, at which time she becomes a deputy assistant in the Department of Health, Education, and Welfare. Following her tenure, a series of CB chiefs occupy the position for relatively short periods, ranging from 1 to 3 years.

1962   Title IV-B, Section 426 provisions are implemented. The Section 426 program was specifically created as a response to a perceived workforce shortage of graduate-level social workers who were interested in and prepared to work in public child welfare (Zlotnik, DePanfilis, Daining, & Lane, 2005). According to a U.S. Department of Health,

Education, and Welfare (USDHEW, 1959) study, it was estimated there was a need for 10,000 graduate-level social workers to work in child welfare, requiring an almost 50% increase between 1958 and 1970. This law was most recently amended by the passage of the Child and Family Services Improvement and Innovation Act in 2011.

1964   President Lyndon Johnson announces the War on Poverty, presenting new opportunities and funding streams for casework activities. The failure to eradicate poverty results in part in the retrenchment of the federal government. Subdivisions in the CB are reassigned to other agencies, and the size of the CB is reduced from over 400 employees to 20 by 1969. During this same period, the bifurcation of social work practitioners by degree (undergraduate vs. graduate) continues (Hutchinson, 2002, pp. 71–72).

1967   Title IV-B, Section 426 of the 1967 Social Security Act Amendments provided grants to prepare individuals to work in the child welfare field (Zlotnik et al., 2005). The grants were mostly channeled from the CB to social work education programs, which provided financial aid for graduate and undergraduate education, curriculum enhancement in child welfare for BSW and MSW students, and in-service grants for briefer training sessions of current child welfare personnel.

1978   Congress passed the Indian Child Welfare Act, an implicit acknowledgment of the need for culturally sensitive child welfare practices to be codified and taught in schools of social work and social welfare.

1980   Title IV-E Foster Care and Adoption Assistance Training Entitlement is created through the passage of the Adoption Assistance Act and Child Welfare Act of 1980. Funding moves from the CB to the states.

1985   National Child Welfare Resource Center funding is awarded to six grantees for 3 years. Each is tasked to focus on one discrete area of child welfare: foster care, adoption, family-based preventive services, youth services, child welfare program management and administration, and legal resources for child welfare. The purpose of the resource centers is "to develop, expand, strengthen, and improve the capacity of State and local, public, and private child welfare agencies throughout the country to utilize exemplary methods and resources to provide effective services to children and families" (Barbee, Chapter 8).

1994   Congress passes the Multiethnic Placement Act, whose purpose is to prevent discrimination in placement. Under this act, diligent recruitment efforts are redoubled.

2001   The first regional Quality Improvement Centers are established, followed by the establishment of National Quality Improvement Centers in 2006. Two of the national centers were located in schools of social work (see Chapter 8).

2008   CB funds five child welfare Implementation Centers to complement the existing Training and Technical Assistance Network to enhance state–tribal systems change efforts. Social work faculties strongly influence the development, evaluation, and operation of these centers, which support and facilitate more intensive and longer-term communication and networking across state–tribal child welfare systems to leverage existing knowledge and expertise and foster collaborative problem solving.

2008   The CB funds the National Child Welfare Workforce Institute, a logical outgrowth of the work conducted under the auspices of Title IV-E, Sec. 426, and other funding streams.

2012   The collaboration between the CB and the National Child Welfare Workforce Institute sets the stage for the future in program development, training, evaluation, and research. A CB brochure titled "A Legacy of Service . . . a Vision for Change" (2011) hints at its vision, priorities, and strategy: partnership with states, tribes, other federal agencies; a Training and Technical Assistance Network to support states, tribes, communities, and professionals; matching funding of child welfare services from a number of legislative sources; supporting innovative research and program development through discretionary grants; monitoring outcomes through

Child and Family Services Reviews, IV-E Foster Care Eligibility Reviews, and federal and state reporting systems; and sharing results including Adoption and Foster Care Analysis and Reporting System reports, Child Welfare outcomes reports, and its user manual series (CB, 2011).

REFERENCES

Adoption Assistance and Child Welfare Act of 1980. Codified as amended, 42 USCA § 670 et seq.

Bradbury, D. (n.d.). Part II: Four decades of action for children (1912–1952). Retrieved from Social Welfare History Project website: Child and Family Services Improvement and Innovation Act, 112th Congress, 2011-12 (S. 1542/H.R. 2883).

Centers for Disease Control and Prevention. (1999, October 1). Martha May Eliot, M.D. *Morbidity and Mortality Weekly Report, 48*(38), 851.

Children's Bureau Act of 1912. (Stat. L., 79).

Hanlan, A. (1966). From social reform to Social Security: The separation of ADC and child welfare. *Child Welfare, 45*(9), 493–500.

Hutchinson, J. R. (with Sudia, C. E.). (2002). *Failed child welfare policy: Family preservation and the orphaning of children.* New York, NY: University Press of America.

Indian Child Welfare Act of 1978 (ICWA). 25 U.S.C. §§ 1901–1963.

Lemons, J. S. (1969). The Sheppard-Towner Act: Progressivism in the 1920's. *Journal of American History, 55*(4), 776–786.

Lindenmeyer, K. (1997). *"A right to childhood": The U. S. Children's Bureau and child welfare, 1912–46.* Urbana, IL: University of Illinois Press.

Multiethnic Placement Act of 1994. 42 U.S.C. § 5115a(a)(1)(A)–(B).

Rodems, E., Shaefer, L., & Ybarra, M. (2011). The Children's Bureau and passage of the Sheppard-Towner Act of 1921: Early social work macro practice in action. *Families in Society: The Journal of Contemporary Social Services, 92*(4), 358–363.

Sheppard-Towner Maternity and Infancy Protection Act. 42 Stat. 224 (1921).

U.S. Department of Health, Education and Welfare. (1959). *Report of the advisory council on child welfare services.* Washington, DC: Author.

Zlotnik, J., DePanfilis, D., Daining, C., & Lane, M. (2005, June). *Factors influencing retention of child welfare staff: A systematic review of research.* Unpublished report, Institute for the Advancement of Social Work Research. Conducted in collaboration with the University of Maryland School of Social Work, Center for Families and Institute for Human Service Policy, Washington, DC.

THE EARLY YEARS
Research and Advocacy 1912–1938

Paul H. Stuart

ongress established the Children's Bureau (CB) as a unit of the Department of Labor in 1912. During its first 25 years, the CB became the nation's premier agency for children and families and was the central agency for social workers in the federal government. Because of the leadership of its first two chiefs, Julia Lathrop and Grace Abbott, the CB developed constituencies in the women's movement and in reform circles generally in the years between 1910 and 1930. A particularly strong bond developed between the CB and the school of social work in Chicago, known as the Chicago School of Civics and Philanthropy prior to its merger with the University of Chicago in 1920 when it became the School of Social Service Administration (SSA). During the 1930s the CB fostered the development of the American Public Welfare Association (APWA) and campaigned for the inclusion of programs for children in the Social Security Act of 1935 and for the prohibition of child labor in the Fair Labor Standards Act of 1938.

FORMATION OF THE CB

The initial impetus for a federal children's bureau came during the first decade of the 20th century, as progressive reformers surveyed the landscape of American society. Increasing inequality in income, urban unrest, and rural decline signaled new kinds of social problems in a rapidly industrial-izing and urbanizing economy. In addition, college-educated women sought meaningful opportunities to contribute to the solution of social problems as well as career opportunities in a society that offered few choices for women outside marriage and motherhood (Addams, 1893a, 1893b). Middle- and upper-class women participated in women's clubs, settlement houses, and new opportunities for volunteer service in child saving, friendly visiting with the poor, and social reform.

Initially, child welfare reformers attempted to achieve reforms at the local and state levels, exemplified by state campaigns for regulating child labor, requiring school attendance, and developing public child welfare serv-ices. These campaigns coalesced in the movement for the creation of chil-dren's codes. Creating children's codes involved surveying state statutes relating to children and families and "simplifying, standardizing, and coor-dinating . . . their provisions" (Clopper, 1921, p. 157) to provide greater pro-tection for children. But it soon became apparent that the problems of children were not localized; if a state prohibited child labor, employers could move to a state with more liberal laws. Many reformers believed that national minimum standards were needed (Wald, 1909).

Nurse and settlement house worker Lillian Wald suggested the idea of a children's bureau to Florence Kelley in 1903 (Bradbury, 1962, p. 1). In 1906, Kelley proposed a U. S. Commission for Children "to correlate, make available, and interpret the facts concerning the physical, mental and moral condition and prospects of the children of the United States, native and immigrant." She suggested several specific problems of children that such a commission could investigate, including "infant mortality, registration of births, orphanages, desertion, illegitimacy, [and] degeneracy" (Bradbury, 1962, pp. 1-2). Members of the National Child Labor Committee, a major advocacy group working for the prohibition of child labor, drafted a law to establish a federal children's bureau, which was introduced in Congress in 1906 (Leiby, 1978).

Although the CB bill had the endorsement of President Theodore Roosevelt, and the bill was introduced in every session of Congress begin-ning in 1906, progress was slow. Many associated the proposal for a chil-dren's bureau with the campaign to prohibit child labor. In addition, social welfare legislation had been a state, not federal, responsibility, and some critics raised constitutional issues (Leiby, 1978). In 1909, however, the White House Conference on Dependent Children recommended the creation of a federal children's bureau, and President William Howard Taft endorsed the proposal in 1910. In 1912 President Taft signed the bill establishing the CB as a unit of the Department of Labor (Bradbury, 1962; Stretch, 1970). Taft appointed Julia Lathrop, who had been endorsed by the National Child Labor Committee, as first chief of the CB (Lindenmeyer, 1997).

Since graduating from Vassar College in 1880, Lathrop had carved out an enviable position as a leader in the new women's reform movement. A former associate of Jane Addams at Chicago's Hull House, Lathrop had served as a volunteer county poor relief worker during the depression of 1893–1894, a member of the Illinois Board of Charities, and the first director of the research department of the Chicago School of Civics and Philanthropy, while also helping to found the Cook County Juvenile Court, the National Committee for Mental Hygiene, and the Immigrant's Protective League (Addams, 1935/2004). A formative figure in the Progressive Era, Lathrop was a key figure in establishing the CB as an indispensable agency in the field of maternal and child health (Parker & Carpenter, 1981).

A daughter of a founder of the Illinois Republican Party, Lathrop grew up in Rockford, Illinois, and attended Rockford Female Seminary, where she knew Jane Addams and Ellen Gates Starr, the founders of Hull House, before she entered Vassar College. In 1890 she moved into Hull House and became an active participant in the settlement's activities. In 1892 she was the first woman to be appointed to the Illinois Board of State Commissioners of Public Charities, one of the early state boards of charities. The Illinois board was established in 1869, 6 years after the first board had been founded in Massachusetts (Brock, 1984). Lathrop, like other child welfare reformers, found a model for federal involvement in child welfare in the agricultural programs of the federal government. Although the federal government was not involved in social welfare activities during the 19th century, as constitutional theory and practice left domestic matters to the states, it became involved in assistance to agriculture during the Civil War as new

Republican congressional majorities explored the possibilities of a more active national state. In 1862 Congress created the Department of Agriculture and passed the Morrill Act, which established the land grant college system, fulfilling campaign promises by the new Republican president, Abraham Lincoln, to provide federal support for the development of agriculture. Together with the Homestead Act and the Pacific Railroad Act, these constituted the "Western measures" of the first Civil War Congress (Bogue, 1969). During the postwar period, Congress expanded federal assistance to agriculture by establishing agricultural experiment stations in the states (Hatch Act of 1887) and providing direct funding to agricultural colleges (Morrill Act of 1890). The Adams Act of 1906 increased federal funding for agricultural experiment stations "to be applied only to paying the necessary expenses of conducting original researches or experiments bearing directly on the agricultural industry of the United States" (Adams Act, p. 63; see also Rosenberg, 1964). By the first decade of the 20th century, the federal government was heavily involved in agriculture, mostly through federal–state programs (Hamilton, 1990). The Smith-Lever Act of 1914 established the cooperative extension service, providing extension services to farmers throughout the nation (Ferleger, 2000).

Lillian Wald and other advocates for children wondered, "If the [federal] Government can have a department to take such an interest in the cotton crop, why can't it have a bureau to look after the nation's child crop?" (Ladd-Taylor, 1994, p. 76). Like the federal government's activities in agriculture, the CB conducted research and gathered statistics, providing much better information about children than had been available before. Also, like the Department of Agriculture, the CB emphasized providing the information not only to citizens but also to parents, child care professionals, and state policy makers.

Lathrop's (1916) address on the 50th anniversary celebration in 1915 of her alma mater, Vassar College, was titled "The Highest Education for Women." Men's colleges and universities had added professional schools devoted to a variety of topics, but one field was as yet unexplored. The "highest education for women," Lathrop said, defined "in the needs of our own time," was "training in original research applied to the life and interests of the family" (Lathrop, 1916, p. 2). To support her conclusion, Lathrop identified lacunae in what was known about the family. Little was known about births and deaths of children, the mental development of children, the structure of American families, or the effects of the employment of mothers on their children. Although data bearing on some of these issues had been gathered by the federal census, little use had been made of the data. Research was needed "to correlate and inspire the many scattered educational activities now existing, all of which are making more effective the work of the average household by placing at its service the inventions and appliances of modern science" (p. 6). Her revolutionary goal was "a new specialization to be signalized by the creation of centers of study and research in the service of family life" (p. 7).

In cooperation with its constituencies in local women's groups and reform and child welfare organizations, the CB pushed for new services for children and expanded regulation of child labor. During the 1920s the CB administered a federal grant-in-aid program that provided state maternal and child health services and promoted state public assistance programs for single mothers and other services for families. During the next decade, the CB was involved in developing the Social Security Act. In particular, CB officials shaped the Aid to Dependent Children program (Title IV of the Social Security Act) as well as the maternal and child health, crippled children's, and child welfare programs (Title V; Poole, 2006). By the 1930s the CB was even involved in the development of a new national organization, the APWA.

ORIGINS OF THE CHICAGO SCHOOL OF SOCIAL WORK

The first chief of the CB, Julia Lathrop, had a background in settlement houses, social work education, and national reform movements. A long-time resident of Hull House, Lathrop became involved in social work education in 1907, when the Russell Sage Foundation, a newly created philanthropic organization, announced grants to the four social work training programs then in existence: the Chicago Institute of Social Science, headed by Graham Taylor, a professor at the Chicago Theological Seminary who was the head resident of Chicago Commons, and nascent schools in New York, Boston, and St. Louis (Glenn, Brandt, & Andrews, 1947). Taylor asked Lathrop, who had taught occasional courses for the Institute of Social

Science, to join the faculty of the school as director of the research department. Renaming the institution the Chicago School of Civics and Philanthropy, Taylor incorporated the school in May 1908 to promote "through instruction, training, investigation and publication, the efficiency of civic, philanthropic and social work, and the improvement of living and working conditions" (Wade, 1964, p. 169). Lathrop recruited a University of Chicago PhD graduate and fellow Hull House resident, Sophonisba Breckinridge, to assist her in the research department (Glenn, 1911). In 1908 Lathrop, who had become interested in mental health as a result of her service on the Illinois Board of Charities, helped to organize the National Committee for Mental Hygiene.

In 1908 Breckinridge became dean of the school and director of the research department, now known as the Department of Social Investigation, , and Edith Abbott, another former Hull House resident who had worked with Sidney and Beatrice Webb at the London School of Economics, joined the faculty of the fledgling school. They collaborated on the first book to be published as a result of the Russell Sage grants, *The Delinquent Child and the Home* (Breckinridge & Abbott, 1912), which was followed by a second volume, *Truancy and Non-Attendance in the Chicago Schools* (Abbott & Breckinridge, 1917).

Breckinridge and Abbott come to Chicago to study at the University of Chicago. Breckinridge was from Kentucky and Abbott from Nebraska. Both earned PhD degrees from the University of Chicago, Breckinridge in political science and Abbott in economics, but had not been able to secure faculty positions in male-dominated universities. Their careers spanned the first half of the 20th century. They managed the 1920 merger of the Chicago School of Civics and Philanthropy with the University of Chicago. The school, now called the School of Social Service Administration (SSA), became one of the first university-affiliated schools of social work in the United States. Breckinridge retired in 1942 but remained active in social work education until her death in 1948. Edith Abbott was dean of SSA from 1924 to 1942 and remained on the faculty until her retirement in 1953. Breckinridge and Abbott shaped social work education at Chicago and throughout the nation. They forged an alliance with the CB that would benefit both organizations (Costin, 1983a; Lenroot, 1948).

When Lathrop left Chicago to become chief of the federal CB in 1912, Taylor made her a member of the Board of Trustees of the Chicago School of Civics and Philanthropy. From 1910 to 1920, Taylor, Breckinridge, and Abbott developed an educational and research program for the school that included fieldwork for all students and research training for students electing the social investigation concentration. From 1908 until the foundation ended the program in 1915, the Sage grants provided financial support for the school and enabled Abbott and Breckinridge to initiate a program of research in social investigation modeled on the Webbs' research work at the London School of Economics (Costin, 1983b; Wade, 1964).

THE EARLY PROGRAMS

Beginning in 1917 the CB commissioned the Chicago School of Civics and Philanthropy to conduct research that could not be done by CB staff. Although the income from the CB never matched that from the Russell Sage Foundation, it did provide badly needed support for the struggling school. Edith Abbott and Sophonisba Breckinridge also gained experience in managing federal research grants, something that was rare for social work education programs at the time. Several new positions were added as a result of CB contracts, and graduates of the Chicago school found positions in the CB, whose staff was growing in the late 1910s (Muncy, 1991). By 1920 Julia Lathrop could say that more CB staff members were from the Chicago school "than from any other school" (Muncy, 1991, p. 87). The Chicago school was becoming a partner in constructing the U.S. welfare state.

Child Labor

In 1917 Grace Abbott (1878–1939), Edith Abbott's sister, was appointed director of the Child Labor Division of the CB. Grace Abbott had followed her sister from Nebraska to Chicago, where she lived in Hull House and was active in social work with immigrants. As director of the CB's Child Labor Division, Grace Abbott had been hired to enforce the Keating-Owen Child Labor Act of 1916, which made it illegal to sell products produced with child labor in interstate commerce (Abbott, 1939; Felt, 1970). In her administration of this program, Abbott and other CB staff members worked with state commissioners of labor and factory inspectors (CB,

1921). However, the U.S. Supreme Court found the Keating-Owen act unconstitutional in *Hammer v. Dagenhart* (1918) in a 5–4 decision, with the majority arguing that although the commerce clause gave Congress the power to regulate the interstate commerce, the manufacture of goods is not in itself commerce and the goods produced by Dagenhart (cotton) were "in themselves harmless," unlike intoxicating liquors or dangerous drugs (*Hammer v. Dagenhart*, 1918, p. 272).

Following the *Hammer* decision, many child welfare leaders favored a constitutional amendment to prohibit child labor. Grace Abbott was able to persuade the War Labor Policies Board to adopt the Keating-Owen standards for war contractors. Successful in persuading the board to prohibit federal contractors from employing children, Abbott also persuaded president Woodrow Wilson to allot funds to the CB to enforce the ruling (Costin, 1983b). When Julia Lathrop retired as chief of the CB in 1921, President Warren G. Harding appointed Grace Abbott chief of the CB, a post she would hold for the next 13 years.

A permanent solution to the child labor problem would be difficult to achieve. In 1919 Congress imposed a tax on products produced with child labor, to be enforced by the Internal Revenue Service, but this measure was found unconstitutional by the Supreme Court in *Bailey v. Drexel Furniture Co.* (1922) on grounds similar to the court's decision in *Hammer*. The Supreme Court's decisions in *Hammer* and *Bailey* increased pressure for a constitutional amendment (Abbott, 1923). The CB cooperated with the American Federation of Labor and the National Child Labor Committee in the campaign for a constitutional amendment. Congress passed the amendment in 1924, but only 15 states had ratified the amendment by 1933 (Lindenmeyer, 1997).

Maternal and Child Health

As chief of the CB during the 1920s, Grace Abbott was in charge of implementing the Sheppard-Towner Act of 1921, which provided the first federal grants-in-aid to the states for health and social services. The grant-in-aid mechanism had been used earlier, notably for agricultural colleges, agricultural experiment stations, and agricultural extension programs, but since president Franklin Pierce's 1854 veto of the Ten-Million-Acre Bill, which would have provided land grants to the states to support mental hospitals, Congress had not enacted legislation providing federal aid to the states for health and social services (Manning, 1962). Hailed as a prototype for federal health legislation of the 1930s and after, the Sheppard-Towner Act was criticized by conservatives as an unconstitutional intrusion by the federal government into domestic matters. However, the act resulted in new programs for maternal and child health in 45 states and the territory of Hawaii before funding ended in 1929 (Schlesinger, 1967).

Research and Public Education

The CB also continued its research and education programs, providing information to Congress and the general public on the conditions of children and promoting child labor prohibition, mothers' pensions, and other social welfare legislation. With Grace Abbott's sister, Edith, as dean and Sophonisba Breckinridge as a faculty member of SSA, the relationship between the CB and SSA in the 1920s resembled the relationship between SSA and the Chicago School of Civics and Philanthropy in the 1910s. SSA students worked on research projects for the CB, the CB employed SSA graduates, and Grace Abbott kept her sister and others in Chicago informed of developments in Washington.

Enactment of the Sheppard-Towner Act in 1921 was the culmination of the CB's campaign for maternal and child health legislation (Lemons, 1969). Administering the act provided CB staff new linkages with state governments and would be a model for later grant-in-aid legislation. It was unpopular with conservative groups, many physicians, and the U.S. Public Health Service, whose officials had hoped to administer the program, and Congress allowed the program to die in 1929. Yet in the 7 years the program was in effect (1922–29), 18 states adopted birth and death registration, bringing the total to 45 states by the end of the decade. Prenatal and well-baby clinics, health conferences with parents, and an increase in general awareness resulted in a reduction in infant mortality during the 1920s (Almgren, Kemp, & Eisinger, 2000; Lindenmeyer, 1997).

During its first 20 years, the CB had administrative responsibility for the short-lived Keating-Owen Child Labor Act, in addition to managing grants-in-aid to the states to provide maternal and child health services under the Sheppard-Towner Act. Perhaps even more important were the other responsibilities of the CB implicit in its charge to "investigate and report . . . on all matters pertaining to the welfare of children" (Children's Bureau Act, 1912, p. 79). Early in her tenure as chief, Lathrop initiated a campaign for birth registration as a way to develop accurate data on infant mortality. The CB also engaged in a public education campaign designed to alert parents to healthy ways to raise children and in the Children's Year Campaign, which involved cooperation with women's organizations, schools, health programs, and agricultural extension workers (Rude, 1918). Some scholars have suggested that the CB's public education activities may have been even more effective in reducing infant mortality than the services provided under the Sheppard-Towner Act (Almgren, Kemp, & Eisinger, 2000).

The research and public education campaigns had multiple effects on the direct constituencies of the CB and on the public, particularly parents. Borrowing from the techniques of agricultural extension, CB employees organized or helped to organize events such as baby days and baby weeks, which called attention to infant and child health and provided parents with accessible information on infant and child care. The CB also engaged in an active publication program, publishing popular pamphlets on prenatal care, infant care, child care, and other topics. Thousands of copies of these publications were distributed to parents, child care workers, and the general public (Abbott, 1923). "Infant Care," in particular, became a standard source for parents. CB publications expressed "a major body of professional opinion in the [child care] field," as psychoanalyst Martha Wolfenstein (1951, p. 15) observed in her examination of changes in American attitudes about child development.

Child Welfare

As the point of contact for child welfare in the federal government, the CB was involved in child welfare reform activities in the states. As the culmination of its Year of the Child in 1919, the CB conducted a series of conferences on child welfare standards in cities across the United States, beginning with an International Conference on Child Welfare Standards in Washington (Deardorff, 1919). Those attending the conference heard from

European dignitaries as well as American experts and agreed on standards of child health and nutrition, the regulation of child labor and women's work, birth registration, education, and "the welfare of . . . defective, dependent, and delinquent children" ("News From the Field," 1919).

The CB articulated a comprehensive program of reform, never focusing on one goal to the exclusion of others. The CB's whole child philosophy emphasized education, work, recreation, and home life as well as health. In 1919, at the end of the CB's Children's Year and World War I, Lathrop summarized goals for children that would provide an agenda for the CB in the coming decade. CB research in the years before the war showed a negative relationship existed between family income and infant mortality. Therefore, a program for "public protection of maternity and infancy" (Lathrop, 1919, p. 7) had a high priority. Legislation for grants-in-aid to the states for maternal and child health services had been developed in 1917 by the CB staff, reformers, and U.S. representative Jeanette Rankin, the first woman and the first social worker to serve in Congress (Lindenmeyer, 1997).

But what about those children who survived the first year of life? Lathrop (1919) asked. High rates of illiteracy, gaps in state school attendance laws, and a high rate of child labor suggested that states should regulate child labor and require children to attend school. Higher family living standards, in addition, would benefit all children by lessening "problems of social wreckage" (Lathrop, 1919, p. 8). Finally, implementing the standards adopted at the International Conference on Child Welfare Standards would provide protections and services to children and their families.

CB staff members encouraged state governments to develop state children's codes, which usually involved tightening child labor regulations and school attendance laws, creating mothers' pension programs and juvenile courts, and often establishing state child welfare commissions and county child welfare programs. In 1916, for example, CB staff member Evelyn Beldin visited Alabama at the request of the Alabama Federation of Women's Clubs. In speeches across the state, she promoted the development of a state child welfare program. The Alabama legislature established a state Department of Child Welfare in 1919, and department leaders stayed in touch with CB leaders throughout the 1920s (Burson, 2001). The most industrialized state in the South in the early 20th century, Alabama was a regional leader in the effort to prohibit child labor, although reformers emphasized occupations dominated by White children. Agricultural work and domestic service, occupations dominated by African American children, were neglected in child labor reform efforts (Sallee, 2004). Montgomery Episcopal priest Edgar Gardner Murphy was a founder of the National Child Labor Committee, and Alabama was one of the first six states in the nation to create county child welfare boards.

Mothers' Pensions

CB publications on child labor provided material for reformers and publications on child welfare services, mothers' pensions, and juvenile courts; other children's issues provided state-level reformers with ideas, arguments, and basic information. Heavily involved in the campaign for mothers' pensions, which 40 states had adopted by 1920, CB personnel fielded correspondence with prospective applicants, state and local officials, and reformers. Abbott and Breckinridge (1921) conducted the first study of mothers' pension administration under contract with the CB. But efforts to secure uniform administration of state mothers' pension laws were met with frustration. In the early 1920s, the CB collaborated with local-level social workers to organize a Committee on Public Aid to Dependent Children, organizing its allies in an effort to standardize the administration of state mothers' pension programs (Machtinger, 1999).

JUVENILE DELINQUENCY

Similarly, the CB sponsored studies of the juvenile courts and in 1921 helped to convene a meeting with the National Probation Association to develop standards for juvenile courts. The "fundamental standards" underlying the recommendations were articulated by the CB (1923) as follows:

1 that the court dealing with children should be clothed with broad jurisdiction, embracing all classes of cases in which a child is in need of the protection of the state, whether the legal action is in the name of the child or of an adult who fails in his obligations toward the child;

2 that the court should have a scientific understanding of each child;

3   that treatment should be adapted to individual needs; and

4   that there should be a presumption in favor of keeping the child in his own home and his own community, except when adequate investigation shows this not to be in the best interest of the child. (p. vi)

In addition, Katherine Lenroot (1925), assistant chief of the CB, argued that juvenile courts should be integrated into the community's child welfare service system.

FOUNDING OF THE APWA

Mothers' pensions, juvenile courts, child welfare programs, and the maternal and child health programs supported by the Sheppard-Towner Act were manifestations of a general shift toward public welfare services during the 1920s (Kelso, 1923). The increasing importance of public welfare was signaled by the creation of the American Association of Public Welfare Officials in 1930. A group of state public welfare administrators discussed creating a national organization at the 1929 National Conference of Social Work. At the 1930 conference, about 40 state administrators met with Katherine Lenroot of the CB, Sophinisba Breckinridge of SSA, and Louis Brownlow, a city planner who would soon be director of the University of Chicago's Public Administration Clearing House (PACH). Brownlow promised support for the new organization from the Spelman Fund, a Rockefeller philanthropy led by Beardsley Ruml. Ruml, who would soon be dean of the Division of Social Sciences at the University of Chicago, had been director of the Laura Spelman Rockefeller Memorial, another Rockefeller philanthropy that had supported SSA during the 1920s (Brownlow, 1958; Domhoff, 1978).

Assisted by the CB, the Spelman Fund, and the Rockefeller Foundation, the American Association of Public Welfare Officials initially opened its office in Washington, near the CB and the President's Emergency Committee for Employment, a Hoover administration Depression-era agency, but another of Brownlow's projects resulted in the relocation of the new organization to Chicago. The PACH had been designed as a center that would house the headquarters of major national public administration organizations together in one location. Organizers believed such an arrangement would facilitate dialogue and permit concerted action on important issues. In the winter of 1930–31, Spelman Fund administrators decided to finance the creation of PACH to provide a location for national public administration associations and to coordinate activities of the organizations housed there. Some had suggested Washington as the headquarters for PACH, but Brownlow (1958) "strongly opposed Washington [because] . . . the overshadowing presence of the federal government would almost compel the staff to think federally" (p. 254).

Chicago was selected as the location of PACH. The APWA, as the American Association of Public Welfare Officials was then known, moved into the PACH offices at 850 East 58th Street in Hyde Park, two blocks west of Cobb Hall on the University of Chicago campus where SSA was located. With Edith and Grace Abbott's assistance, funding was secured for APWA's move to Chicago and its ongoing operations. The organization's leaders were eager to secure funding for the group so that it could influence the development of public welfare programs (Halbert, 1931). A major objective of the APWA leaders' and of the Abbotts and Breckinridge was to involve the federal government in providing relief to the states, a move that many in Congress supported but President Hoover opposed. A compromise was reached whereby the Reconstruction Finance Corporation (RFC) provided loans to the states against future federal highway allocations to support relief for the unemployed (Olson, 1972). Since the federal funds were loans, not grants, the administration refused to regulate how the states spent the money, resulting in "a tremendous variety of state practice" (MacDonald, 1941, p. 22). In November 1932 officials of APWA, PACH, and SSA organized a national conference on welfare standards that "set the keynote" for the future development of the Federal Emergency Relief Administration (FERA) in the Roosevelt administration (MacDonald, 1941, p. 23). The conferees, who included representatives of the CB, agreed that all levels of government—federal, state, and local—were responsible for providing relief to the unemployed and laid out principles to guide the new Roosevelt administration, which took office in March 1933. Given the widespread suspicion of government among social workers, the conferees affirmed "the ability of government to administer relief and welfare as effectively as other types of organizations . . . [and] the absolute desirability of administering public funds through public agencies . . . [given] the provision of reasonable sums for administration . . . [and] employing qualified personnel . . . [under] state supervision and direction" (MacDonald, 1941, p. 23).

According to Brownlow (1958), "The result of this conference was the adoption of a set of principles . . . which has determined the federal, state, and local administration of public welfare . . . since that time" (p. 274). The resolutions placed the major responsibility for relief with governments— local, state, and federal—and called for the creation of public welfare agencies at each level of government. Relief programs should be administered as well by capable staff members prepared to do so by their education and experience. Finally, "public funds should be administered only by regularly established public agencies" (p. 274). The resolutions foreshadowed the administrative rules that would be adopted by Harry Hopkins's FERA the next year, in particular the controversial Rule No. 1 that provided that "public funds [were] to be administered by public agencies" (Colcord, 1934, p. 111), ending the practice of contracting with private agencies that had been widespread in the early 1930s. "Thus, all unnoticed and unnoted," Brownlow wrote in 1958, "began in the United States of America the then dreaded but now embraced 'Welfare State'" (p. 274).

A benefit of APWA's Hyde Park location was its closeness to the University of Chicago campus and to SSA. Edith Abbott and Sophonisba Breckinridge worked with the fledgling organization. The official history of APWA describes the Abbott sisters and Katherine Lenroot as "friends indeed" and notes that the CB "played the mother role from the start" providing "good counsel and strong backing" (MacDonald, 1941, pp. 12–13) and loaning a staff member, Marietta Stevenson, to act as the organization's first staff member. Grace Abbott served as the chair of the APWA Committee on Developing and Protecting Professional Standards (MacDonald, 1941).

During the last year of the Hoover administration and the first years of the New Deal, APWA advised states on the new emergency relief programs states set up to take advantage of federal loans and grants available from RFC and FERA. APWA staff members assisted state officials in setting up unemployment relief agencies. Especially in states that had not previously had extensive public relief programs, this was an important contribution. In

Mississippi, for example, the first director of the state's RFC-funded emergency relief program was Aubrey W. Williams, a field representative of the APWA, who had been sent to the state to assist in setting up a relief program (Venturini, 2003).

SHAPING THE SOCIAL SECURITY ACT

Grace Abbott resigned as chief of the CB in 1934 and returned to Chicago, where she became a professor at SSA and editor of the *Social Service Review*, the professional journal published by SSA. She maintained her connection with the CB and federal policy, corresponding with her successor, Katherine Lenroot, and traveling to Washington "periodically to offer advice, attend meetings, and testify before congressional committees" (Poole, 2006, p. 142). A major concern was the provisions of the Social Security bill that was being written in the fall of 1934 by the president's Committee on Economic Security. Abbott wanted provisions for maternal and child health, federal assistance for mothers' pensions, and a strong role for the CB in the new programs. Motivated in part, perhaps, by the CB's cooperation with the International Society for Crippled Children, a nonprofit advocacy and research organization, Abbott later added a program for crippled children to the list (Hitchcock, 2009).

In some respects Grace Abbott and her former colleagues at the CB were successful in their efforts to influence the development of the Social Security Act during the autumn of 1934. The act included social and health service programs that provided grants-in-aid to the states for maternal and child health programs, a crippled children's program, and child welfare programs, also administered by the states. The CB was put in charge of these programs, as Abbott had hoped. The act also created Title IV, a federal grant-in-aid program called Aid to Dependent Children (ADC), which enabled states to continue their mothers' pension programs with federal assistance. However, the act provided that ADC would be administered by the new Social Security Board, not the CB as Abbott had urged.

The CB had been given responsibility for ADC in early drafts of the bill. However, the major focus of the bill was on the old age insurance and assistance programs and on unemployment insurance. Congress placed all financial assistance programs under a three-person autonomous Social Security

Board. The CB, still located in the Department of Labor, administered only the social and health programs for children created by the Social Security Act (Hanlan, 1966). Even though CB officials had campaigned for mothers' pensions through the 1920s, and Grace Abbott and Katherine Lenroot had drafted the plan for ADC, administrative responsibility was given to the all-male Social Security Board, which was primarily focused on programs for retired workers and the unemployed.

In spite of this disappointment, Grace Abbott campaigned for the Social Security Act during the winter of 1934–35; her lobbying was credited with its passage (Costin, 1983b; Poole, 2006). Although they were not happy with all the provisions of the act, Grace Abbott and her sister, Edith, "were realists who believed that it was better to accomplish as much as possible in 'the here and now' and then attempt to build on that new base" (Costin, 1983b, p. 226).

The programs of FERA and the Social Security Act "brought a marked expansion in public relief and social services across the country and placed new demands on social work education" (Costin, 1983b, p. 227). During the 1930s, SSA became a leader in educating social workers for the new public agency social work. More important, much of the structure of the transformed social work profession was the result of the educational work of Edith Abbott and Sophonisba Breckinridge and the lobbying of Grace Abbott. Social work education was now an ally and a shaper of the welfare state, something that few had envisioned before 1929.

The Social Security Act established programs of maternal and child health services, crippled children's services, and child welfare services, all administered by the CB, which went well beyond the Sheppard-Towner Act program that Congress had allowed to die in 1929. In addition, some observers suggested that the ADC program would not have been included in the Social Security Act without the advocacy of the CB. Thus, the decision to have the Social Security Board rather than the CB administer the program came as a bitter blow (Hanlan, 1966),

The partial success of the CB in influencing the content and passage of the Social Security Act left the prohibition of child labor as the remaining major unresolved child welfare issue. The Child Labor Amendment, approved by Congress in 1924, had bogged down and the prospects for ratification seemed dim. Abbott had successfully lobbied to have the National

Recovery Administration (NRA) codes prohibit the employment of children under 16 in all occupations covered by the codes, and the codes prohibited the employment of children under 18 in dangerous occupations. After the Supreme Court found the National Industrial Recovery Act and the NRA codes unconstitutional in 1935, pressure increased for federal legislation similar to the Keating-Owen Act of 1917. Although the CB pressed for a child labor law, the Roosevelt administration wanted child labor regulation included in a comprehensive labor standards act, and the CB supported its adoption. Congress passed the Fair Labor Standards Act in 1938. It "virtually replicated the NRA codes," but "applied only to establishments producing goods shipped across state lines," covering only about 6% of child workers in the CB's estimation (Lindenmeyer, 1997, pp. 197–198).

THE AMERICAN WELFARE STATE

In 1943 at the height of World War II, SSA presented a series of lectures, published the next year as *Social Service in Wartime*, sponsored and published by the Charles R. Walgreen Foundation for the Study of American Institutions. The lectures included Dean Helen Wright's (1944) assessment, "Social Services at the Outbreak of the War," followed by lectures that assessed the war's impact on public assistance, social work with children, the American Red Cross, travelers' aid services, food programs, and federated fund-raising. Dean emeritus Edith Abbott, by now a senior stateswoman of social work, concluded the series with a lecture titled "Social Work After the War" (Abbott, 1944). Abbott's lecture was intended to provide a blueprint for postwar social welfare policy.

Abbott (1944) began by modifying the topic of her lecture; she would "deal with some of the basic services without which all our case work will always be 'too little and too late'" (p. 169). She predicted that *social welfare*, not *social work*, would be the term used after the war, reflecting changes in the social services since the 1920s: an expansion of public responsibility for social welfare reflected in the growth of public child welfare programs, the establishment of the CB and the Sheppard-Towner Act, and the expansion of public welfare during the Great Depression. By 1940, according to a CB survey of welfare services, "public funds furnished 91 per cent of all the welfare expenditures" in 34 urban areas. In addition, in some cities, "more than half of the private-agency expenditures came from public funds" (Abbott, 1944, pp. 172–173). Private agencies, responsible for a small percentage of welfare work, now had the responsibility to support the public social services by showing "by their own superior work . . . that adequate public funds should be available for similar work" (p. 174). Truly, the CB had produced a new era in social welfare.

The CB, together with the settlement houses and Chicago social work education, was an active promoter of the welfare state between the world wars. In many ways, the CB succeeded in creating a uniquely American welfare state, one that fit the federal political system and provided a variety of income and service programs to children and their families. It did so by building coalitions with a variety of constituencies that shared interests in the welfare of children, sometimes, as with the Committee on Public Aid to Dependent Children and the APWA, even helping to create those constituencies. But success may have undone the achievements of the reformers. The new welfare state created in 1935 was much larger than the CB and had interests that were at once broader and narrower than the whole child. In the words of Lindenmeyer (1997), a historian of the CB, the Social Security Board, which was given the responsibility for administering ADC, "was more interested in old age insurance than children's aid." In the push for social security legislation, the CB "had won the battle but lost the war," as it had failed to convince policy makers of the value of its whole child strategy (p. 195).

REFERENCES

Abbott, E. (1944). Social work after the war. In H. R. Wright (Ed.), *Social service in wartime* (pp. 169–196). Chicago, IL: University of Chicago Press.

Abbott, E., & Breckenridge, S. P. (1917). *Truancy and non-attendance in the Chicago schools.* Chicago, IL: University of Chicago Press.

Abbott, E., & Breckenridge, S. P. (1921). *The administration of the Aid-to-Mothers Law in Illinois* (Children's Bureau Publication No. 82). Washington, DC: U.S. Government Printing Office.

Abbott, G. (1923). Ten years' work for children. *North American Review, 218*(813), 189–200.

Abbott, G. (1939). Federal regulation of child labor, 1906–38. *Social Service Review, 13*(3), 409–430.

Adams Act, ch. 951, 34 Stat. 63 (1906).

Addams, J. (1893a). The subjective necessity for social settlements. In Henry C. Adams (Ed.), *Philanthropy and social progress* (pp. 1–26). New York, NY: Thomas Y. Crowell.

Addams, J. (1893b). The objective value of a social settlement. In Henry C. Adams (Ed.), *Philanthropy and social progress* (pp. 27–56) . New York, NY: Thomas Y. Crowell.

Addams, J. (2004). *My friend, Julia Lathrop.* Urbana: University of Illinois Press. (Original work published 1935).

Almgren, G., Kemp, S. P., & Eisinger, A. (2000). The legacy of Hull House and the Children's Bureau in the American mortality transition. *Social Service Review, 74*(1), 1–27.

Bailey v. Drexel Furniture Co., 259 U.S. 20 (1922).

Bogue, A. G. (1969). Senators, sectionalism, and the "Western" measures of the Republican Party. In David M. Ellis (Ed.), *The frontier in American development: Essays in honor of Paul Wallace Gates* (pp. 20–46). Ithaca, NY: Cornell University Press.

Bradbury, D. (1962). *Five decades of action for children: A history of the Children's Bureau.* Washington, DC: U.S. Government Printing Office.

Breckenridge, S. P., & Abbott, E. (1912). *The delinquent child and the home.* New York, NY: Russell Sage Foundation.

Brock, W. R. (1984). *Investigation and responsibility: Public responsibility in the United States, 1865–1900.* Cambridge, England: Cambridge University Press.

Brownlow, L. (1958). *A passion for anonymity.* Chicago, IL: University of Chicago Press.

Burson, H. I. (2001). *Alabama's mother's pension statute: Identification and analysis of institutional determinants.* Unpublished doctoral dissertation, University of Alabama, Tuscaloosa.

Children's Bureau. (1921). *Administration of the first federal child-labor law* (Children's Bureau Publication No. 78). Washington, DC: U.S. Government Printing Office.

Children's Bureau. (1923). *Juvenile-court standards* (Children's Bureau Publication No. 121). Washington, DC: U.S. Government Printing Office.

Children's Bureau Act, ch. 73, 37 Stat., 79 (1912).

Clopper, E. N. (1921). The development of the Children's Code. *Annals of the American Academy of Political and Social Science, 98,* 154–159.

Colcord, J. C. (1934). Report of the committee on current relief program. *Proceedings of the National Conference of Social Work, 61,* 111–129.

Costin, L. B. (1983a). Edith Abbott and the Chicago influence on social work education. *Social Service Review, 57*(1), 94–111.

Costin, L. B. (1983b). *Two sisters for social justice: A biography of Grace and Edith Abbott.* Urbana: University of Illinois Press.

Deardorff, N. R. (1919). For the children of two continents: An account of the International Conference on Child Welfare Standards. *The Survey, 42*(7), 269–274.

Department of Agriculture Organic Act. 12 Stat. 387 (1862).

Domhoff, G. W. (1978). *Who really rules? New Haven and community power reexamined.* New Brunswick, NJ: Transaction Books.

Fair Labor Standards Act, P. L. 75-78. 52 Stat. 1069 (1938).

Felt, J. P. (1970). The child labor provisions of the Fair Labor Standards Act. *Labor History, 11*(4), 467–481.

Ferleger, L. (2000). Arming American agriculture for the twentieth century: How the USDA's top managers promoted agricultural development. *Agricultural History, 74*(2), 211–226.

Glenn, J. M. (1911). *Some important results of our appropriations to the schools of philanthropy for the bureaus of social research, November 27, 1911* (Series 3, Box 29, Folder 220, Russell Sage Foundation Records). Tarrytown, NY: Rockefeller Archives Center.

Glenn, J. M., Brandt, L., & Andrews, F. E. (1946). *The Russell Sage Foundation, 1907–1946* (Vols. 1–2). New York, NY: Russell Sage Foundation.

Halbert, L. A. (1931). A review and forecast of the work of the American Association of Public Welfare Officials. *Social Service Review, 5*(1), 353–366.

Hamilton, D. E. (1990). Building the associative state: The Department of Agriculture and American state building. *Agricultural History, 64*(2), 207–218.

Hammer v. Dagenhart, 247 U.S. 251 (1918).

Hanlan, A. (1966). From social reform to Social Security: The separation of ADC and child welfare. *Child Welfare, 45*(9), 493–500.

Hatch Act, ch. 314, 24 Stat., 440 (1887).

Hitchcock, L. I. (2009). *The creation of federal services for crippled children, 1890–1941.* (Unpublished doctoral dissertation). University of Alabama, Tuscaloosa.

Homestead Act, ch. lxxv, 12 Stat. 392 (1862).

Keating-Owen Child Labor Act. P. L. 64-249. 39 Stat. 675 (1916).

Kelley, F. (1905). *Some ethical gains through legislation.* New York, NY: Macmillan.

Kelso, R. W. (1923). The transition from charities and correction to public welfare. *Annals of the American Academy of Political and Social Science, 105*, 21–25.

Ladd-Taylor, M. (1994). *Mother-work: Women, child welfare, and the state, 1890–1930.* Urbana: University of Illinois Press.

Lathrop, J. C. (1916). The highest education for women. *Journal of Home Economics, 8*(1), 1–8.

Lathrop, J. C. (1919). Child welfare standards as a test of democracy. *Proceedings of the National Conference of Social Work, 46,* 5–9.

Leiby, J. (1978). *A history of social welfare and social work in the United States.* New York, NY: Columbia University Press.

Lemons, J. S. (1969). The Sheppard-Towner Act: Progressivism in the 1920s. *Journal of American History, 55*(4), 776–786.

Lenroot, K. (1925). The place of the juvenile court in a community program for child welfare. *The Annals of the American Academy of Political and Social Science, 121,* 60–69.

Lenroot, K. F. (1948). Friend of children and of the Children's Bureau. *Social Service Review, 22*(4), 427–430.

Lindenmeyer, K. (1997). *"A right to childhood": The U. S. Children's Bureau and child welfare, 1912–46.* Urbana: University of Illinois Press.

MacDonald, A. (1941). *APWA, our autobiography.* Chicago, IL: American Public Welfare Association.

Machtinger, B. (1999). The U.S. Children's Bureau and mothers' pensions administration, 1912–1930. *Social Service Review, 73*(1), 105–118.

Manning, S. W. (1962). The tragedy of the ten million acre act. *Social Service Review, 36*(1), 44–50.

Morrill Act, ch. cxxx, 12 Stat., 503 (1862).

Morrill Act, ch. 841, 26 Stat., 417 (1890).

Muncy, R. (1991). *Creating a female dominion in American reform, 1890–1935.* New York, NY: Oxford University Press.

News From the Field: Child Welfare Standards. (1919). *Journal of Home Economics, 11*(8), 373.

Olson, J. S. (1972). Gifford Pinchot and the politics of hunger, 1932–33. *Pennsylvania Magazine of History and Biography, 96*(4), 508–520.

Pacific Railroad Act, ch. cxx, 12 Stat. 489 (1862).

Parker, J. K., & Carpenter, E. M. (1981). Julia Lathrop and the Children's Bureau: The emergence of an institution. *Social Service Review, 55*(1), 60–77.

Poole, M. (2006). *The segregated origins of Social Security: African Americans and the welfare state.* Chapel Hill: University of North Carolina Press.

Rosenberg, C. E. (1964). The Adams Act: Politics and the cause of scientific research. *Agricultural History, 38*(1), 3–12.

Rude, A. E. (1919). The Children's Year campaign. *American Journal of Public Health, 9*(5), 346–351.

Sallee, S. (2004). *The whiteness of child labor reform in the New South.* Athens: University Press of Georgia.

Schlesinger, E. R. (1967). The Sheppard-Towner era: A prototype case study in federal-state relationships. *American Journal of Public Health, 57*(6), 1034–1040.

Sheppard-Towner Act, 42 Stat. 224 (1921).

Smith-Lever Act, ch. 79, 38 Stat., 372 (1914).

Social Security Act, P. L. 74-271, 49 Stat. 620 (1935).

Stretch, J. J. (1970). The rights of children emerge: Historical notes on the first White House Conference on Children. *Child Welfare, 49*(7), 365–372.

Venturini, V. J. (2003). *Factors contributing to the creation of a public welfare department in Mississippi during the 1930s* (Unpublished doctoral dissertation).University of Alabama, Tuscaloosa.

Wade, L. C. (1964). *Graham Taylor: Pioneer for social justice.* Chicago: University of Chicago Press.

Wald, L. (1909). The Federal Children's Bureau: A symposium. *Annals of the American Academy of Political and Social Science, 33*(Suppl., 2), 23–28.

Wolfenstein, M. (1951). The emergence of fun morality. *Journal of Social Issues, 17*(1), 15–25.

Wright, H. R. (1944). Social services at the outbreak of the war. In H. R. Wright (Ed.), *Social service in wartime* (pp. 1-22). Chicago: University of Chicago Press.

2

THE CHILDREN'S BUREAU AS EXEMPLAR FOR SOCIAL WORK EDUCATION IN THE UNITED STATES

Barbara Levy Simon

The Children's Bureau (CB) was a dominant influence in shaping social work education in the United States. Established in 1912, the CB was coeval with the founding of Progressive-Era social work and early social work schools in the Northeast, Midwest, and Southeast, such as New York (Columbia University), Chicago (University of Chicago), Boston (Simmons College), Philadelphia (Bryn Mawr College), Richmond (Virginia Commonwealth University), and Cleveland (Case Western Reserve University). Some of the key givens of contemporary social work were borrowed from the CB and its progenitor, the settlement house movement. For example, the *person-and-environment* philosophy of practice (called by some authors *person-in-environment*) that has informed social work curricula and courses for decades was on full display at the CB from 1912 on, though those precise terms, of course, did not come into being until the late 1970s.

PERSON AND ENVIRONMENT

One of the hallmarks of social work theory and practice in the United States has been the insistence that social workers concomitantly assist clients in overcoming the pressing challenges they encounter as members or former members of families, schools, workplaces, religious organizations, and communities, while also targeting, in collaboration with clients, unjust elements in social, economic, and physical environments. Ecological, ecosystems, and strengths approaches within social work are examples of social work perspectives that define the profession as context sensitive and context attentive, one that seeks to examine and undermine the environmental impediments to clients' full membership in society and active exercise of human rights (Germain & Gitterman, 1980; Hartman, 1979; Meyer, 1983; National Association of Social Workers, 2008; Reynolds, 1934, 1951; Saleebey, 1992; Weick, 1983).

The architects of these approaches consciously stood on the shoulders of social work predecessors who had viewed clients (also known as neighbors, residents, citizens, patients, consumers, constituents, or members) as human beings who were actors and active in complex situations, relationships, networks, and systems. For example, founders of settlement houses, like Jane Addams, Graham Taylor, Florence Kelley, Reverend Reverdy Ransom, Robert Woods, and Lillian Wald, had prefigured the perspective of person-in/and-environment in their work and in their organizational, political, and—for many—spiritual commitments. Florence Kelley and Lillian Wald, two powerhouses of settlement life, had first introduced the idea of the CB to President Theodore Roosevelt in 1903, nine years before the concept was realized through legislative action (Smuts, 2006). Wald, Kelley, and Addams had lobbied the U.S. Congress and two presidents before the CB was approved, using their wide networks of influence in Progressive-Era organizations, clubs, and federal government offices to ensure that the first CB director was a settlement house veteran: Julia Lathrop (Lindenmeyer, 1997). Wald and Kelley did so to ensure that pivotal values and strategies of the Progressive Era's settlement house movement would steer the CB in its beginning decades (Parker & Martin, 1981). On learning of her nomination to be the first head of the new CB, Julia Lathrop, a woman who had lived for a quarter of a century at Hull House in Chicago, expressed her gratitude and loyalty to Lillian Wald, founder of the Henry Street Settlement on the Lower East Side of New York City: "Your message was the first. None could be kinder. . . . If Senate confirms, I fly to consult you. . . . I will try best to make good" (Parker & Martin, 1981, p. 62).

Under Lathrop's leadership between 1912 and 1921, and subsequently Grace Abbott's between 1921 and 1934, the CB proved to be a pioneering public agency whose policy and program designers assumed that improving children's health and welfare hinged upon enhancing the well-being of low-income, immigrant, Black, and rural families and communities. For the staff of the CB, work on behalf of children required changing societal factors that endangered them, such as child labor and the shortage of prenatal, maternal, and infant and toddler care in many parts of the rural United States.

In her first annual report as the original chief of the CB, Julia Lathrop recommended in 1914 that the agency prepare a summary of all state labor laws on child labor and then study the degree of rigor, comprehensiveness, and continuity of the enforcement of these regulations (CB, 1914). The CB took on this job and produced frequent reports on child labor, one of which was a huge document that encapsulated in 1915 child labor laws in every state (Sumner & Merritt, 1915). While establishing through research a baseline of data about child labor laws, the CB was able to point out major regional variations in child labor rates, laws, and enforcement. In early January, 1914, Lathrop and the CB staff combined their existing state lobbying work with a new initiative to get a federal child labor bill proposed and passed by both houses of the U.S. Congress (Lindenmeyer, 1997). The CB and its allies were quickly successful with the passage in 1916 of the Keating-Owen Act, a federal statute that prohibited the sale in interstate commerce of goods manufactured by children (Keating-Owen Child Labor Act of 1916, 1916). Unfortunately, the law was ruled unconstitutional in 1918 by the U.S. Supreme Court in *Hammer v. Dagenhart*. The Court's 5–4 majority argued that child labor was "purely a local matter to which the federal authority [does] not extend" (Lindenmeyer, 1997, p. 124).

Nonetheless, the CB kept up the fight against child labor. The agency helped write a child labor amendment to the U.S. Constitution in 1922, which did not pass. A decade later, in the early days of the New Deal, the CB made certain that child labor codes were part of the National Industrial Recovery Act of 1933, which was declared unconstitutional by the Supreme Court in 1935. The CB staff continued to gather data across 48 states about child labor, its scope, and consequences. Its staff joined other New Dealers in making sure that regulations concerning various forms of agrarian, suburban, and urban child labor were made part of the Fair Labor Standards Act of 1938.

Another pivotal example of the CB's early promotion of the welfare and health of children in a manner that social workers later would think of as a person-and-environment approach was its effort to diminish the number of deaths of pregnant women, fetuses, and infants in rural counties throughout the United States. The CB leadership consulted closely with representative Jeannette Rankin from Montana before she became the first member of Congress to introduce a bill designed to allocate federal monies to match state funding for countywide maternal and child health clinics, education for midwives, and visiting nurse programs to reduce levels of infant and maternal mortality. A long-time suffragist and settlement house alumna, Rankin was also a national legislator who knew rural circumstances firsthand, given that she had been born and raised outside Missoula, Montana (Lopach & Luckowski, 2005). Rankin's bill eventually morphed into the Sheppard-Towner Maternity and Infancy Protection Act (Sheppard-Towner Act), which received the necessary votes and signature of President Warren Harding in 1921. Rankin helped Lathrop and her staff view low-income, country women's contextual daily imperatives with the same intensive attentiveness to the conditions and causes of urban women's and children's poverty that CB staffers had invested. Rankin and Lathrop approached the nation's death rates of newborns and infants with deep respect for the localized nature of the search for health care for women living in poverty and the political necessity of involving federal dollars, state administrators and funds, and county visiting nurses and midwives. In sum, they attempted to reduce rural children's and mothers' deaths in pregnancy, childbirth, and infancy through inserting environment health practitioners in clinics that were geographically and financially accessible.

The CB copied the administrative and fiscal design for Sheppard-Towner from the U.S. Department of Agriculture's example of granting federal matching funds to states as agricultural aid to fund statewide webs of county-level experts who consulted directly with farmers seeking advice. In Sheppard-Towner, the CB embraced and capitalized on the layered political scaffolding of federalism that the Department of Agriculture had found to be politically, educationally, and agriculturally effective in establishing its system of county agrarian agents. Remarkably, the CB leaders and their many allies in Congress and the world of women's reform organizations were able to surmount bitter opposition from the American Medical Association to Sheppard-Towner, which was administered by the CB and which funneled federal funds to state-run and state-funded well-baby clinics. These clinics were lodged in rural county locations and staffed by public health nurses. The person-and-environment approach of the CB served rural pregnant women and mothers and their infants in their rural environs while honoring the political context of federalism's tiered divisions of responsibility and authority. In Julia Lathrop's words, the CB sought to "stimulate rather than usurp" (Smuts, 2006, p. 85) responsible actions on behalf of the nation's children of volunteer organizations, cities, counties, and states.

SOCIAL SCIENCE AS A BASIS FOR ACTION

Another approach the CB modeled for social work education was that of deploying social science methods to reduce social and economic injustice. In the words of Lathrop, soon after the CB was established, it "will become the nation's greatest aid in making effective the constantly richer terms in which the sense of justice toward all children is expressed. [Justice for children must be] based on truth secured through scientific inquiry" (Smuts, 2006, p. 71).

Pursuing knowledge for knowledge's sake was never a CB aim. Social work education reflected the same understanding that social science is an indispensable prelude to action rather than an end in itself. Indeed, Lathrop helped design social work research education in Chicago just a few years before she took charge of the CB and its research agenda and methodology.

Lathrop took up the reins of the CB after having created, alongside Sophonisba Breckinridge and Edith Abbott, the research department in 1907 of the Chicago School of Civics and Philanthropy. She lectured at the school and served as a member of its board of trustees until it later became the School of Social Service Administration of the University of Chicago in 1920. While heading the CB, Lathrop frequently hired graduates of the school, and in 1917 she signed a contract with the Chicago School of Civics and Philanthropy to conduct social surveys and other forms of research for the CB (Smuts, 2006, p. 84). The Chicago School of Civics and Philanthropy was an incubator of applied social science methods, which

Lathrop then brought to life at the federal level in the only social welfare unit in the federal government prior to the New Deal. The CB returned the favor by issuing federal contracts for some of its research to the Chicago School of Civics and Philanthropy.

From the start of the CB, statistical studies, social survey methods, program evaluation, document analysis, in-depth research interviews, and the use of focus groups were important social science tools that its staff relied on. The CB carried forward the dedication of settlement house leaders during the Progressive period to employing the still new social sciences of sociology, demography, anthropology, political science, and economics in pursuing its mission of improving children's welfare and health. Researching the economic and social situations children lived and worked in, the CB's executive director insisted, was "the basic safeguard which the government of the United States seeks to throw about its children" (Smuts, 2006, p. 86). For Lathrop, as for key settlement house and early social work education leaders, it was an article of Progressivism's faith that accurate data when clearly presented would galvanize the public and its elected representatives and administrators to redress the wrongs against children and their families stemming from poverty, impure water sources, harsh working conditions, and inadequate housing. "All we can do to save our faces with posterity," Lathrop noted, "is to go on experimentally in the slowly increasing knowledge of our day, doing what the caveman did—trying to improve things" (Smuts, 2006, p. 87).

In exploring the extent and causes of infant mortality, for example, the CB began its efforts in Johnstown, Pennsylvania, and then moved on to seven other industrial cities. Female agents of the CB conducted a house-to-house canvass in each of the cities, making sure to interview each family with an infant who had been born during a designated period. CB canvassers took down a history of each baby's development and sicknesses and gave particular attention in their recordings to the home environment's hygiene, degree of sanitation, condition of the apartment or house, mother's employment, and household income. This intensive and extensive set of investigations grounded in family interviews enabled the CB to identify pivotal factors in infant survival and death. In a brilliant rhetorical and graphic move, the CB generated from its data collection an "infant thermometer" (Smuts, 2006, p. 87) that demonstrated the inverse relationship between a father's income and infant mortality. Lathrop and her successor, Grace Abbott, used data from CB family interviews and the U.S. Census to hammer home the message that poverty caused infant death, illness, and a range of other severe developmental problems.

Social work schools embedded in their curricula three major lessons from the Lathrop-Abbott investigations of infant mortality: (a) the salience of rigorous social survey methodology in applied social science, (b) the causal relationship between infant death and household income, and (c) the importance of teaching social work students about local, state, and federal policies that hinder or help the well-being of children and families (Dunlap, 1993). Social science research methods, the welfare of children and families, and social welfare policy became core foci of social work education from that day to the present.

THE SALIENCE OF COALITIONS AND VOLUNTEER LABOR

Another legacy from the CB that helped shape the character of social work education in the United States was the efficacy, indeed, the necessity, of mobilizing squads and coalitions of allies, most of them volunteers, to document and improve families' and children's welfare. Unpaid individual and organizational partners joined CB campaigns in attempting to end infant and maternal mortality and to support families during wartimes. Most allies of the CB went unpaid because the CB budget was meager in relation to its mission. The original federal allocation to the CB in 1912 was a total of $25,640. Subsequently, during Lathrop's administration, the CB's annual appropriation ranged from $250,000 to $350,000 in an era in which the Department of Agriculture was allocated about 20 times that amount (Lindenmeyer, 1997).

What functions did volunteers perform to help the CB? To begin with, the CB would never have come into existence without a large coalition of volunteer supporters pressing for its creation. The General Federation of Women's Clubs (GFWC), the National Conference of Charities and Correction, the National Congress of Mothers, the Women's Christian Temperance Union, and confederations of settlement houses, educators, physicians, public health nurses, and other Progressive-Era reform organizations, like the National Child Labor Committee and the National

Consumers League, mobilized to create a vocal popular demand for the CB (Lindenmeyer, 1997). The activism of these organizations and individual members continued in support of the CB long after its founding. They wrote and circulated petitions, visited and lobbied state and federal elected officials, conducted door-to-door family interviews, wrote innumerable letters to newspapers and governmental decision makers, raised funds to amplify particular CB projects, and helped distribute the many CB publications written expressly for the public and parents. When the effort to pass the Sheppard-Towner Act was launched in 1919, many of these groups and individuals responded again with letters to newspaper editors, written communications, and visits to congressional delegates (Lindenmeyer, 1997).

Social work educators took careful note of the CB's success in organizing volunteers as political allies, research assistants, and public educators. Field placements, formally supervised volunteer internships, became a staple for every student of social work education by the end of the second decade of the 20th century. To be sure, fieldwork education within social work came about for at least three reasons. Certainly one influence was the popularity of philosophical and pedagogical pragmatists like John Dewey during the 1890s and early decades of the 20th century. Dewey's laboratory schools for children at the University of Chicago and Teachers College of Columbia University in New York City, along with his highly influential books and articles about the importance of children's classroom activity—learning by actual problem solving—also had a profound impact on the nature of social work education (Goldstein, 2001; Martin, 2002). Second, the volunteer college students, male and female, who chose to live in settlement houses and become immersed in settlement house activities for a summer, semester, or longer, during the Progressive period in major cities constituted an unintended pilot test for what soon became social work field education. Additionally, the CB's excellence and skill in using volunteers in sustained, orchestrated, and supervised ways was another impetus for social work schools in the United States to incorporate fieldwork into the heart of their educational project.

CHILDREN IN NEED OF SPECIAL CARE

During its first 20 years, the CB completed 49 studies about the social conditions of children "in need of special care—the dependent, the delinquent, and the mentally or physically handicapped" (Lindenmeyer, 1997, p. 139). In particular, the CB was referring to destitute, homeless, and abandoned children. Additionally, children in need of special care included those who relied on public economic support and who lacked guardians or prenatal care. Also, children who were begging or receiving charity were a focus of the CB. Similarly, for the CB, children in need of special care came from houses of prostitution or homes where they were subjected to neglect, cruelty, or parental criminal depravity, such as sustained substance abuse (Lindenmeyer, 1997). These varied categories of children who were at a high risk of being victimized or ignored or imprisoned constituted high priorities in the research efforts, policy recommendations, and educational outreach of the CB under the leadership of Lathrop from 1912 to 1921, Abbott from 1921 to 1934, and Katharine Lenroot from 1934 to 1951.

Schools of social work directly followed the lead of the CB in relation to the topic and population of children and adolescents whose own families, for one reason or another, were unable to take care of them. The very language that the CB chose to refer to children and youths who were dependent, delinquent, or living with physical, mental, and developmental disabilities— "children in need of special care"—was embedded in the curricula of schools in New York (Columbia) and Chicago (University of Chicago) within a year after the CB's founding in 1912 (Bernstein, 1942). Indeed, 100 years later, contemporary terminology in the 21st century in the fields of social work, child development, and early childhood education in the United States, "children with special needs," hews closely to the CB's original formulation.

The juvenile court movement, for example, is one that the CB and schools of social work labored to extend and expand. Lathrop's years as a young adult in Chicago's social reform efforts before going to the CB clearly had a great influence on the priorities she and her staff emphasized at the CB. Similarly, early faculties of schools of social work were drawn frequently from the ranks of Progressive-Era social welfare movements, such as the campaign to separate children from adults in court proceedings and in residential facilities. Children and youths required care, education, and guidance rather than punishment in the eyes of people who were advocating in the 1890s and the first two decades of the 20th century for the formation of juvenile and domestic relations courts that were completely distinct from civil and criminal courts that addressed adults. According to Lindenmeyer (1997), whose invaluable and meticulous book on the CB sheds much light on the links between early Progressive-Era social welfare initiatives and the choices made by the first three chiefs of the CB, Julia Lathrop had been central to creating a state reformatory for delinquent girls in Illinois in 1893 (Lindenmeyer, 1997, p. 141). She had also had firsthand experience in accompanying children and adolescents to the nation's first full-service juvenile court in Cook County, Illinois (Chicago's county), which had been established in 1899 (Bullard, 2006; Lindenmeyer, 1997; Schultz, 2004).

Parallel to the CB's advocacy of juvenile courts was the willingness of administrators and faculty members at Columbia's School of Social Work in New York and the Chicago School of Social Service Administration to institutionalize field placements in juvenile courts, domestic relations courts, and offices of juvenile probation (Bernstein, 1942). In addition, the CB and schools of social work were fully engaged in the Progressive project of preventing urban juvenile delinquency. To that end, CB leaders and social work school faculty members and administrators joined settlement house leaders and members of the Charity Organization Societies in becoming spokespersons for the movements to build urban playgrounds and community centers with recreational facilities and staff specially trained to lead sports, arts, crafts, dance, and dramatic activities with children and youths. They advocated for public swimming pools, public baths, vacation schools, and summer camps accessible to children and adolescents of all income levels. Urban and rural parks with supervisory staff and paths for walking, riding bicycles, and riding horses were other items of keen interest to CB staff and social work educators (Buenker & Kantowicz, 1988; Lubove, 1967).

Regarding children with disabilities, most of the CB's efforts focused on documenting the types and levels of need for state-sponsored schools and residential facilities. The CB also promoted the spread of undergraduate and graduate programs in public universities for educating professionals in several domains—teaching, early childhood education, medicine, nursing, public health, and social work—to work with children with physical and developmental disabilities.

ADVOCACY, PUBLIC EDUCATION, AND PUBLIC RELATIONS

One area of immense impact that the CB had on the curriculum and emphases of schools of social work concerned the skill set required in effective advocacy, education of the public, and public relations. A small public bureau with the gargantuan mission of improving the overall well-being of children in the United States, the CB staff learned quickly how to disseminate and trumpet their research findings to parents; newspapers editors; academics; federal, state, and county governments; the general public; and members of targeted professions, such as the clergy, social workers, physicians, midwives, public health specialists, educators, and nurses. It became obvious quickly to CB staff that their effectiveness in spreading the word about their research findings and points of view hinged upon reaching each of these audiences with highly particularized rhetoric and imagery (Straughan, 2007).

Communication strategies of the CB, designed to raise public awareness about children and youths in need of special attention and concerning infant and maternal mortality, took many forms. For example, CB staff members devoted much energy to producing annual reports that were, on the one hand, clear and readable, and on the other hand, carefully footnoted for those who wanted to track further the sources of the report's information. Educational pamphlets devised at several reading levels and degrees of density for differentiated audiences became a primary means of getting the word out about the CB's research findings and recommended actions. Targeting young mothers, for example, on topics of nutrition and health care during pregnancy, depended upon previous CB staff research on levels of education and literacy among women between the ages of 16 and 25 in each region of the country (Straughan, 2007).

Setting up exhibits in town halls and public schools that displayed visual and textual information about preventing infant and maternal deaths was an important and frequent activity of the CB that its staff had learned from observing the well-publicized campaign against the spread of tuberculosis carried on by the National Association for the Study and Prevention of Tuberculosis (1908) and the state associations. CB staff directly copied anti-tuberculosis campaigners' tactics, such as handing out to the public items that would be reminiscent of the exhibit's theme. The CB, for example, distributed free paper aprons designed for nursing mothers during the late 1930s (Lenroot, 1965).

After issuing press releases, giving speeches in small towns as well as in cities of every size was standard operating procedure for leaders and members of the public educational wing of the CB. Since travel for CB staff throughout the years between 1912 and 1950 was mostly on trains, except in the most rural communities where cars and wagons were relied upon, bulk amounts of educational pamphlets were usually sent ahead of time by train before scheduled speaking engagements. Katharine Lenroot, the CB's third executive head, remembered that she often spoke for less than a minute at each stop on a suburban or intercity train line on her way to or from scheduled speeches. She took pride in her 45-second communications with a megaphone on train platforms while the train was unloading and loading passengers (Lenroot, 1909–1974).

Special events were another communication strategy of the CB. Julia Lathrop knew that one of the CB's most reliable allies, the GFWC, had organizations in every state and more than two million members. She therefore asked GFWC to help the CB design and implement National Baby Week in March 1916. Baby Week, which became an annual affair, involved two key aspects: (a) a CB exhibit in a county town and (b) a child hygiene expert who examined well children and gave advice to parents about assisting in their child's normal development. The CB staff assiduously avoided framing any of their public activities as health screenings of sick or developmentally delayed children because they feared from 1912 on being incorporated into the U.S. Public Health Service (PHS). At the time of each annual reappropriation process, some members of Congress and the PHS recommended that the CB be taken out of the Department of Commerce and Labor, its original home, and shifted into PHS. Mindful of its social mission that included health concerns but extended far beyond them, the CB fought to stay within the Department of Commerce and Labor. Baby Weeks soon became popular and well advertised. In October 1916, for example, communities in the United States held 2,083 Baby Weeks. Two years later, President Woodrow Wilson declared 1918 "Children's Year" (Straughan, 2007).

Social work school faculties and administrators assigned students to help the CB and the GFWC staff Baby Weeks from 1916 on (Perkins, [ca. 1895–

1965]). They also inserted into course requirements oral reports, which required social work students to develop public speaking skills. The Columbia and Chicago schools of social work introduced course assignments into required social work practice courses that asked students to develop educational pamphlets and reports that could be easily read by the general public (Bernstein, 1942). Poster sessions at professional conferences, a contemporary mode of exhibiting social work knowledge and action recommendations in two- or three-dimensional formats, resemble in form the exhibits that the National Association for the Study and Prevention of Tuberculosis and the CB made famous.

CONCLUSION

Administrators and faculty members at early schools of social work in the United States followed the CB's example in teaching students to contextualize clients within complex and layered environments and to view the contexts themselves as subjects of social work. Like the CB, social work schools between 1912 and 1950 saw research as a springboard to action, rather than a separate academic project. Following the example of the CB, administrators of schools of social work founded in the Progressive period understood students to be supervised volunteers whose learning required immersion in practice in institutionalized and supervised field placements in public and nonprofit agency settings. Schools of social work also considered the CB's attentiveness to children and youths who were in need of special care to be one focus worthy of anchoring their own curricula. Finally, social work educators admired the creative communication strategies of the CB with the public and key stakeholders and have placed course content that addresses advocacy tactics and strategies, public speaking, and poster sessions in their curricula and professional conferences.

REFERENCES

Bernstein, S. (1942). *New York school of social work, 1898–1941.* New York: New York Institute of Social Welfare Research, Community Service Society of New York.

Buenker, J. D., & Kantowicz, E. R. (Eds.). (1988). *Historical dictionary of the Progressive Era, 1890–1920.* New York, NY: Greenwood Press.

Bullard, K. S. (2005). *Saving the children: Discourses of race, nation, and citizenship in America.* Proquest dissertation and theses, University of Illinois at Urbana-Champaign, 3198935, Section 2.

Chicago School of Civics and Philanthropy. (1909–1920). *Bulletin of Chicago, the school.* Chicago, IL: Chicago School of Civics and Philanthropy.

Child in the city: A series of papers presented at the conferences held during the Chicago child welfare exhibit. (1912). Chicago, IL: Department of Social Investigation, Chicago School of Civics and Philanthropy.

Children's Bureau. (1914). *First annual report of the chief.* Washington, D.C.: Children's Bureau.

Dunlap, K. M. (1993). A history of research in social work education, 1915–1991. *Journal of Social Work Education, 29*(3), 293–301.

Fair Labor Standards Act. (1938). Fair Labor Standards Act - FLSA - 29 U.S. Code Chapter 8.

Germain, C. B., & Gitterman, A. (1980). *The life model of social work practice.* New York, NY: Columbia University Press.

Goldstein, H. (2001). *Experiential learning: A foundation for social work education and practice.* Alexandria, VA: Council on Social Work Education.

Hammer v. Dagenhart, 247 U.S. 251 (1918).

Hartman, A., (1979). *Finding families: An ecological approach to family assessment in adoption.* Beverly Hills, CA: Sage.

Keating-Owen Child Labor Act of 1916. (1916). An act to prevent interstate commerce in the products of child labor, and for other purposes, September 1, 1916; Enrolled Acts and Resolutions of Congress, 1789–; General Records of the United States Government; Record Group 11; National Archives.

Lenroot, K. F. (1809–1974). *K. F. Lenroot Papers, 1909–1974* (Box 139, Folder 12.2). Rare Book Room, Butler Library, Columbia University, New York, NY.

Lenroot, K. F. (1965). *Reminiscences of Katharine Frederica Lenroot: Oral history.* New York, NY: Columbia University.

Lindenmeyer, K. (1997). *"A right to childhood": The U.S. Children's Bureau and child welfare, 1912–1946.* Urbana: University of Illinois Press.

Lopach, J. J., & Luckowski, J. A. (2005). *Jeannette Rankin: A political woman.* Boulder, CO: University of Colorado Press.

Lubove, R. (1967). *Urban community: Housing and planning in the Progressive Era.* Englewood Cliffs, N.J.: Prentice Hall.

Martin, J. (2002). *Education of John Dewey: A biography.* New York, NY: Columbia University Press.

Meyer, C. H. (Ed.). (1983). *Clinical social work in the eco-systems perspective.* New York, NY: Columbia University Press.

National Association for the Study and Prevention of Tuberculosis. (1908). *Campaign against tuberculosis in the United States and Canada.* New York, NY: Charities Publication Committee.

National Association of Social Workers. (2008). *Code of ethics.* Retrieved from http://www.socialworkers.org/pubs/code/code.asp

National Industrial Recovery Act. (1933). An Act to encourage national industrial recovery, to foster fair competition, and to provide for the construction of certain useful public works, and for other purposes, June 16, 1933; Enrolled Acts and Resolutions of Congress, 1789-1996; General Records of the United States Government; Record Group 11, National Archives.

Parker, J. K., & Martin, E. M. (1981). Julia Lathrop and the Children's Bureau: The emergence of an institution. *Social Service Review, 55*(1), 60–77.

Perkins, F. [ca. 1895–1965]. *Frances Perkins papers* (Box 102, Folder 3). Rare Book Room, Butler Library, Columbia University, New York, NY.

Reynolds, B. C. (1934). Between client and community: A study in responsibility in social case work. *Smith College Studies in Social Work, 5*(1), 5-18.

Reynolds, B. C. (1951). *Social work and social living: Explorations in philosophy and practice.* New York, NY: Citadel Press.

Saleebey, D. (Ed.). (1992). *Strengths perspective in social work practice.* New York, NY: Longman.

Schultz, A. (2004). My friend, Julia Lathrop. *Journal of Illinois History, 7*(3), 238–239.

Sheppard-Towner Maternity and Infancy Protection Act. (1921). Sheppard-Towner Maternity and Infancy Protection Act - 42 Stat. 224 (1921).

Smuts, A. B. (2006). *Science in service of children, 1893–1935.* New Haven, CT: Yale University Press.

Straughan, D. M. (2007). Women's work: Public relations efforts of the U.S. Children's Bureau to reduce infant and maternal mortality, 1912–1921. In D. M. Straughan (Ed.), *Women's use of public relations for Progressive-ear reform: Rousing the nation* (pp. 65–86). Lewiston, NY: Edwin Mellen Press.

Sumner, H. L., & Merritt, E. E. (1915). Child labor legislation in the United States, Children's Bureau. In H. L. Sumner & E. E. Hanks (Eds.), *Administration of child-labor laws: Part I, Employment-Certificate System.* Hartford, Connecticut: Children's Bureau.

Weick, A. (1983). Issues in overturning a medical model of social work practice. *Social Work, 28*(6), 467–471.

3

RETREAT FROM THE WHOLE CHILD PERSPECTIVE, 1935–1960

Kristine Nelson

erhaps the greatest victory of the Children's Bureau (CB) resulted in the beginning of its dismantling. As noted in previous chapters of this book, passage of the Aid to Dependent Children (Title IV, later renamed Aid to Families of Dependent Children), child welfare, and maternal and child health (Title V) provisions of the Social Security Act stemmed from earlier CB programs and vigorous advocacy by the CB and its allies. The CB was granted oversight of the child and maternal health, child welfare, and crippled children's provisions of the Social Security Act. However, administration of public assistance was delegated to the Social Security Board in the Department of Labor despite lobbying efforts to have the CB maintain its historic role in fostering mothers' pensions, the public assistance programs for single mothers. This was also a departure from the original purpose of the CB to "consider *as a whole* the conditions, problems, and welfare of childhood" (CB, 1937, p. 1, emphasis added). "The power to maintain a decent family living standard," seen by the first CB chief, Julia Lathrop, as "the primary essential of child welfare" (p. 15), was removed from the purview of the CB by the Social Security Act.

IMPLEMENTING TITLE V OF THE SOCIAL SECURITY ACT

The CB staff was confident that the Social Security Act had addressed most of the needs they had been advocating for by providing the "foundations for services which should bring nearer the ideal of health and security for every child" (CB, 1937, p. 46). During the prewar period, the third chief of the CB, child welfare specialist Katherine F. Lenroot, took on the enormous task of helping states develop infrastructure to implement Title V of the Social Security Act. Maternal and Child Health (Part 1) included grants-in-aid to states ($3.8 million), development of standards of care, and consultation, information, and technical assistance to public health agencies, voluntary organizations, and private citizens (CB, 1937, 1956). Crippled Children's Services (Part 2; $2.85 million) was organized in a similar fashion, emphasizing services, care, and facilities in rural areas. Both divisions were headed by physicians with advisory committees and consultants that included physicians, public health nurses, nutritionists, and, in the case of crippled children, medical social workers (CB, 1937).

The Child Welfare Division of the Children's Bureau, which administered Part 3, granted $1.5 million in aid to states "for the protection and care of homeless, dependent, and neglected children and children in danger of becoming delinquent" (CB, 1937, p. 9). Headed by a social worker, the division worked with state public welfare departments to disperse funds for district, county, and local child welfare services with a special emphasis on rural areas (CB, 1937). Funds were made available for training, staff, and services but not for direct foster care payments. The CB emphasized specialized professional services for children without fathers to avoid association with public relief (Leighninger, 1987). Forty-five states were receiving child welfare grants-in-aid by 1938 (Bradbury, 1962).

The CB also continued its earlier interest in delinquency with research into the causes and treatment of juvenile delinquency, the publication of annual statistics from juvenile courts, and bulletins for parents. These efforts were amplified by an upward trend in juvenile delinquency that peaked in 1945. Enforcement of laws and standards regarding child labor also continued to be the responsibility of the CB (Bradbury, 1962).

Unlike the more medically oriented advisory committees, the General Advisory Committee to the Children's Bureau on Maternal and Child-

Welfare Services comprised a broad array of social service organizations, leaders, and luminaries, including Grace Abbott from the University of Chicago School of Social Service Administration (SSA); C. C. Carstens, executive director of the Child Welfare League of America; and Homer Folks, secretary of the State Charities Aid Association of New York. Executives of the National Urban League, the American Public Welfare Association, Catholic Charities, and the Family Welfare Association of America also sat on this committee. The Advisory Committee on Community Child-Welfare Services and the Advisory Committee on the Registration of Social Statistics also included many representatives of social service agencies and social work programs, including Sophonisba Breckinridge and Edith and Grace Abbott from the SSA and Henry Lurie, executive director of the Bureau of Jewish Social Research (CB, 1937, pp. 49–53).

By 1937 the CB had 230 permanent and temporary employees including physicians, public health nurses, nutritionists, social workers, industrial economists, statisticians, lawyers, editors, and administrative and editorial staff, who were assisted by five regional offices that provided consultation to states and agencies from physicians, public health nurses, and social workers. The CB also collaborated extensively with other federal agencies including the U.S. Census Bureau, the Bureau of Indian Affairs, the Department of Justice, the National Recovery Administration, Public Health, Vocational Rehabilitation, the Bureau of Public Assistance, and the Works Progress Administration (CB, 1937). Partners outside the federal government included the Russell Sage Foundation, the American Public Health Association, and the American Public Welfare Association. Research studies continued in collaboration with state and local departments of public health and public assistance, and with universities, especially the SSA (CB, 1937).

The Bureau of Public Assistance (BPA) developed parallel to the programs administered by the CB. Social worker Jane Hoey, who was appointed to head the BPA in December 1935 and administer the Aid to Dependent Children program, advocated for graduate training in social work for directors and undergraduate education for public assistance workers. However, national and local political leaders saw existing state and local systems that administered public assistance and general relief as important patronage appointments and opposed merit and professional appointments. In addition, the numbers of workers needed overwhelmed the capacity of professional social work education despite the development of a social administration curriculum at the University of Chicago SSA and federal support for one term of training for relief workers in state universities (Leighninger, 1987).

THE CB IN WARTIME

While the onset of World War II solved the economic problems of the Great Depression, it also drained funding from other federal programs. For example, all research that did not directly support the war effort was discontinued, and these research dollars never returned to the CB (Bradbury, 1962). The CB built innovative programs to meet the needs of children, families, and mothers in wartime and to ensure prenatal care, safe births, and infant care for the wives of lower-ranking servicemen. The Emergency Maternal and Infant Care program started in 1941 when pregnant army wives at Fort Lewis were denied hospital care because they were not county residents. This program served to decrease infant and maternal mortality and to boost the morale of GIs concerned about the well-being of their pregnant wives (Eliot, 1972; see also Lindenmeyer, 1997). The program provided prenatal, hospital, and postnatal care to 1.5 million families until its termination in 1949. According to Bradbury, it was the "most extensive single public medical care program ever undertaken in this country" (p. 68).

In addition to child and maternal health programs for military wives, the CB reversed its opposition to day care for working mothers and developed standards, technical assistance, licensing, and effectiveness evaluations for government-sponsored and private day care. In 1941 the CB cosponsored a Conference on Day Care of Children of Working Mothers, stating that "in this period when work of women is needed as an essential part of the defense program it is more than ever a public responsibility to provide appropriate care of children while mothers are at work" (Bradbury, 1962, p. 60). The conference affirmed the need for Lanham Act funding for community facilities, but the CB still advocated that mothers with children under the age of 6 stay at home. Consultants worked with state and local public welfare providers to set up day care facilities, in-service training, and educational leave for teachers. By their peak in 1945, federally supported nurseries and day care centers served 1.6 million children out of an estimated 4.5 million in need (Bradbury, 1962; Lindenmeyer, 1997). Federal support for day care ended in 1946 with the termination of the war.

In 1942 Harper & Brothers published *The Family in a World at War,* a collaboration of the Child Study Association and the Children's Bureau. The CB's contribution drew on the experience of bombings and evacuations in England and stressed parents' responsibility for the psychological well-being of their children. Despite massive relocations to wartime boomtowns, deployment of fathers overseas, and mothers in industrial employment, the book did not address psychological stressors in depth.

During and after the war the CB was deeply involved in consultation on the evacuation and care of European children including 5,000 British children placed in foster homes in the United States. The CB also assisted 2,000 unaccompanied adolescents brought to the United States and 100,000 children under 14 from displaced persons camps in Germany. At the end of 1945 President Truman enforced immigration quotas to prevent concentration camp survivors from entering the United States. After the war the CB continued providing assistance to war-devastated areas and trained World Health Organization fellows in health specialties relating to mothers and children (Bradbury, 1962; see also Lindenmeyer, 1997).

In 1946 the CB, with the rest of the Social Security Administration, was transferred to the Federal Security Agency to increase functional efficiency in the federal government. The CB left behind its role in monitoring child labor and was removed from direct cabinet-level supervision, further eroding its responsibility for the whole child (CB, 1956). It retained four permanent programs, including child welfare, crippled children's services, child and maternal health, and research into the problems of child life. This reorganization reduced the CB's influence in the federal government and weakened ties with its traditional constituencies, women's organizations, and child advocacy groups. "The 1946 bureaucratic reshuffle ended the life of the Children's Bureau as a largely self-governing federal enclave for children's interests" (Lindenmeyer, 1997, p. 252), and its focus on the whole child.

POSTWAR EXPANSION

After the end of the war, the country experienced an economic and a baby boom. New understandings of child development and the mental health needs of children, plus the demand for information from millions of new mothers, continued the tradition of providing materials and education directly to consumers. The midcentury White House Conference on Children and Youth focused on the emotional development of healthy personalities in children and featured presentations by Erik Erickson and Kenneth B. Clark, whose work on the effects of prejudice and discrimination was cited in the U.S. Supreme Court's 1954 decision to end segregation in public schools (Eliot, 1972). Its primary report, *A Healthy Personality for Your Child*, sold 500,000 copies by 1961 (Bradbury, 1962). By the end of the 1950s the CB was serving as a clearinghouse for research on child life and producing countless bulletins for middle-class parents and professionals (CB, 1956). One popular manual, for instance, was *A Healthy Personality for Your Child* (Hymes, 1950).

In 1951 Dr. Martha M. Eliot became the fourth CB chief. A pediatrician, she had participated in drafting the child and maternal health provisions of the Social Security Act and directed the CB Division of Child and Maternal Health. As a result of a review of the research functions of the CB, the original focus on the whole child became further restricted, and research was directed toward children whose health and welfare were threatened. As outlined in *A Research Program for the Children's Bureau* (Witmer, 1953), in addition to carrying out its own studies, the CB was to formulate questions, establish methods, and provide assistance to external researchers. In 1953 analyses of costs and the effectiveness of child placement, institutional care, psychotherapy, school health, and juvenile delinquency services were completed (Bradbury, 1962; Schwartz & Wolins, 1958).

Medical and statistical advances also led to a new focus on premature infants and new ways to reduce childhood disability. By 1953 over half of neonatal deaths were found to be associated with prematurity (Bradbury, 1962). One case example of progress in treating premature infants featured an intervention team that included a pediatrician, nurse, medical social worker, nutritionist, and an administrative specialist (CB, 1956, p. 15). The particular role of the social worker was to provide casework services to deal with emotional and social problems during the pregnancy and after delivery. The development of the Salk polio vaccine, drugs for rheumatic fever and epilepsy, and hearing aids and other prostheses also held great promise in reducing and treating childhood disabilities (Bradbury, 1962; CB, 1956).

Although crippled children's grants-in-aid continued to provide essential services for a small number of children (about 260,000 a year suffering from orthopedic problems, cerebral palsy, polio, rheumatic fever, heart problems, and epilepsy) and training for health workers and medical social workers, the maternal and child health funds had much greater impact, affecting an estimated 5% of pregnant women and preschool children through prenatal clinics, public health nurses, well child clinics, school health programs, and training for professional workers (Bradbury, 1962; CB, 1956).

Setting standards and providing training for a professional child welfare workforce were also priorities during this period. The expectation was that child welfare workers would have at least 1 year of graduate education in social work and preferably 2 years. Workers were trained to treat emotional damage in children and family problems and to employ "aggressive casework" (CB, 1956, p. 10) with hard-to-reach families to prevent chronic problems. By the end of the 1950s every state had a child welfare unit to help families resolve social and emotional troubles, provide substitute care, and support prevention and treatment activities in the community (CB, 1956). Training for child welfare workers peaked in 1952 with 500 trainees in 47 states. At that time 53% of child welfare staff had one or more years of graduate education in social work, and the rest were college graduates (Bradbury, 1962).

In addition, state staff worked to improve foster and institutional care and increase homemaker services, day care for working mothers, parent–child counseling, and guidance services for unmarried mothers, as well as to support adoption, residential treatment, and shelters. Approximately 40% of child welfare clients were served in their own or relatives' homes, 40% in foster family homes, and 20% in institutions. Despite a dramatic increase in funding in 1951, more trained workers and a richer variety of services were deemed necessary to reach "all children with social and emotional problems" (CB, 1956, p. 35). In fact, the number of professionally trained staff was not keeping up with the 151% increase in foster care or the introduction in 1952 of in-home services to families on public welfare by the CB and the BPA. This led, as had the earlier rapid expansion of public assistance staff in the 1930s, to increased use of untrained staff and in-service training (Bradbury, 1962).

Although child welfare authorizations gradually increased from $1.5 million in 1936 to $10 million in 1956, child welfare lagged behind maternal and child health (increasing $3.8 million to $16.5 million during the same period) and services for crippled children ($2.85 million to $15 million). Starting at 10 cents per capita for maternal and child health in 1937, the amount rose gradually to 17 cents in 1955. Similarly, crippled children expenditures increased from 8 cents to 15 cents per child, and child welfare expenditures went from 3 cents to 10 cents (CB, 1956). Although overall much more was spent on child welfare services than on maternal and child health ($52 million) and crippled children ($40 million), only $39 million of the $135 million came directly from the CB. The rest was from state and local funds for foster care. Grants-in-aid funded social services for maltreated, illegitimate, and abandoned children; services to improve parent–child relationships and child behavior; and social work positions in social agencies, schools, recreation districts, youth organizations, juvenile courts, and health organizations (CB, 1956).

During the 1950s the CB was especially concerned with providing specialized services to the children of migrant farmworkers, children with mental retardation, children in unprotected adoptions, and the increasing number of juvenile delinquents. Standards were developed for the treatment of juvenile delinquents in the courts, training schools, and by the police, and for adoption and services for maltreated and emotionally disturbed children in their own homes (CB, 1956). In 1960 a joint report on juvenile delinquency by the CB and the National Institute of Mental Health recommended that the federal government take the lead in increasing research, field and pilot studies, and demonstration projects and incorporate social and behavioral science into training for psychiatrists, psychologists, and social scientists (Bradbury, 1962).

In this period the CB expanded to a staff of 250, half with professional training and many with social work education in casework, medical social work, group work, community organization, and delinquency. Forty-eight states had medical social workers in their child welfare agencies along with 200 nurses and nutritionists (CB, 1956).

SOCIAL CHANGES AFFECTING CHILDREN AND FAMILIES

While the CB continued programming for special populations during the 1950s, changes were afoot that would cause radical refocusing of the federal government's human services efforts in the 1960s. The mechanization of agriculture in the South and the pull of war-industry jobs led to a great migration of African Americans to eastern, midwestern, and western cities where they faced discrimination and residential segregation (Bradbury, 1962). The addition of mothers to what was now called Aid to Families With Dependent Children in 1950 coincided with the arrival of poor rural Black families in the cities, which after the end of wartime employment were increasingly headed by single women. Punitive enforcement of man-in-the-house rules meant that only by leaving could Black men secure public assistance for their families (Trattner, 1999). Although in 1958 most single-parent families were headed by widows, those with absent fathers were rapidly catching up, resulting in steep growth in Aid to Families with Dependent Children to 2 million families (Interdepartmental Committee on Children and Youth, 1960).

In addition to changes in public assistance, the end of segregation in education contributed to White flight to the suburbs that grew three times faster than the general population and six times faster than the central cities (Interdepartmental Committee on Children and Youth, 1960). While the CB recognized the lack of services for Black families and provided statistics that were used in the Supreme Court's 1954 desegregation decision (*Brown v. Board of Education*), the separation of public assistance from child welfare and child welfare's mandated focus on rural areas left the CB ill prepared to address these changes despite its inclusion in the newly formed Department of Health, Education, and Welfare in 1953.

In 1957 Katherine B. Oettinger, an expert on mentally retarded children, became the fifth CB chief. The CB participated in an Interdepartmental Committee on Children and Youth (1960) that produced an overview titled *Children in a Changing World*. Three major reports to Congress on child welfare services, juvenile delinquency, and children in migrant families recommended increased attention, funding, research, and training in these areas. The 1958 Social Security Amendments eliminated the requirement to prioritize rural areas, increased funding, and created a new funding formula based on state per capita income and child population (Green Book, 2012). Cumulatively, these changes resulted in a 74% increase in professional child welfare positions over the succeeding decade.

The 1960 Golden Anniversary White House Conference on Children and Youth attracted 14,000 participants, including 1,400 youths and 500 foreign attendees (Bradbury, 1962). These events marked the transition to a new era for the CB as the programs of the Kennedy administration began to take shape, and the United States officially became a "welfare state" (Trattner, 1999, p. 294) with 10.6% of the Gross National Product going to the needy.

THE RISE AND FALL OF SOCIAL ACTION IN SOCIAL WORK

Parallel changes were taking place in social work education beginning with the passage of the Social Security Act. At first, the American Association of Social Work (AASW) debated New Deal policies and strongly advocated for a permanent comprehensive system of public welfare "to insure . . . against the common hazards of our economic and social life" (Leighninger, 1987, p. 52). However, social workers in the federal government, including Federal Emergency Relief Administration head Harry Hopkins, supported Roosevelt's more limited emergency measures. Even former CB chief Grace Abbott advocated a nonpartisan approach to preserve political support for the CB (Leighninger, 1987).

By 1937 the AASW had given up lobbying for a national system of public welfare. Social work education leader Porter Lee declared the primary responsibility of social work education was to develop scientifically based methods of social casework and administration, not to advocate for social causes. "Agency and political pressures, and an image of 'true' professionals as non-partisan and objective, encouraged social workers to choose the expert role over that of political activist" (Leighninger, 1987, p. 68).

The rank-and-file movement in social work that had grown in conjunction with labor unions in the 1930s was also winding down. After garnering the support of thousands of public assistance workers in the 1930s with their rejection of professionalism and their alignment with unions and the working class, the rank-and-file movement decried the New Deal as too little too late. But Communist Party–affiliated leaders switched to the United Front perspective promoted by the Soviet Union after Hitler invaded Russia and supported Roosevelt's war effort, which included wage controls, restrictions on the right to strike, and other antilabor measures. With its position basically identical to that of the AASW, the rank-and-file movement dissolved (Austin, 1986; Hunter, 1999; Leighninger, 1989).

THE DEVELOPMENT OF SOCIAL WORK CURRICULA

During this period, the American Association of Schools of Social Work (AASSW) continued its efforts to define core curricula and establish accreditation standards. Although initially recognizing 1-year graduate programs, by 1939 accreditation was limited to 2-year graduate programs with university affiliations (Austin, 1986). Policy- and research-focused programs were far outnumbered by those that regarded social casework as "genuine social work" (Leighninger, 1987, p. 56). While the curriculum of SSA supported the CB's need to build efficient and effective state, county, and local administrative structures to implement the Social Security Act, social casework instruction was aimed at private, not public, agencies. By 1940 half of the schools of social work had public welfare faculty, and almost all had at least one course on public administration, but casework diagnosis and treatment remained at the core of the curriculum (Leighninger, 1987).

Undergraduate Social Work Education

Although graduate education leaned heavily toward social casework and specialized interventions, public and land grant universities developed programs to prepare undergraduates for work in the public sector. By the early 1940s there were 34 undergraduate programs, mostly in sociology departments in midwestern, southern, and western public universities oriented toward public service (Austin, 1986; Leighninger, 1987). However, the AASW and AASSW regarded undergraduate education as insufficient for a nascent profession that aspired to the status of law and medicine. This led to an almost insurmountable divide between the professional organizations and undergraduate programs. One midwestern university president characterized the AASSW as "an autocratic organization dominated by the thinking of two or three [urban, private] schools [concerned with] maintaining its own position at the expense of the needs of the field" (Austin, 1986; Leighninger, 1987, p. 131). Indeed, only 18 states had accredited graduate schools of social work at the time that produced only 10% of the number of workers needed in public service agencies alone (Leighninger, 1987).

Specializations

Specializations continued to flourish in graduate schools of social work. The earliest social work specialization to form its own organization was the American Association of Medical Social Work in 1918. Based in large city hospitals, medical social workers investigated the social conditions of patients and used casework methods to help them cope with their illnesses. Medical social workers were an important part of the maternal and child health teams formed by the CB and received stipends for training. Fourteen schools of social work had medical social work specializations in 1940 (Leighninger, 1987).

A second organization, the American Association of Psychiatric Social Workers, emerged from the AAMSW but grew in the 1940s and 1950s with the need for wartime psychiatric counselors to replace deployed psychiatrists, an increased emphasis on counseling in private agencies, and the rise in child guidance clinics. Especially on the east coast, psychiatric social work became predominant with the passage of the National Mental Health Act in 1946 and the creation of the National Institutes of Mental Health in 1949. The institutes soon became the major source of grants for professional education and research in mental health, including, initially, grants to 28 graduate schools of social work (Austin, 1986). The number of psychiatric social workers grew 150% in the 1950s to over 5,000 compared to 3,430 medical social workers; however, only 65% had 2-year graduate degrees.

Although school social work was the second specialty to organize in 1919, its educational affiliations and the need to meet local standards of certification for practice prevented it from developing the more rigorous social work education standards of medical and psychiatric social work (Leighninger, 1987). However, rising concerns about juvenile delinquency supported an increase in programs specializing in group work. Fourteen schools by 1939 offered specialized curricula on group work, and in 1944 the AASSW included group work as one of eight basic curriculum areas (Austin, 1986). In 1946 the American Association of Group Workers, previously a multidisciplinary organization, became affiliated with social work, but its focus was shifting from youth work and recreation to treatment (Andrews, 2001; Leighninger, 1987).

PROFESSIONAL CONSOLIDATION

The 1950s saw the emergence of the Council on Social Work Education (1952) that continued the work of the AASSW to establish consistent curriculum and accreditation standards for graduate programs throughout the country. The basic eight curriculum areas identified by the AASSW in its 1944 accreditation manual were modified after a study funded by the Carnegie Foundation of social service manpower needs by Hollis and Taylor in 1951. They recommended a balanced approach to social policy and casework, inclusion of more content from the social sciences and research, and specialized accreditation for different fields of practice, including community organization. Although undergraduate education was still excluded from accreditation, Hollis and Taylor criticized "faculty preoccupation with social work education shaped to the needs of private . . . agencies" (Leighninger, 1987, p. 141), and recommended including social welfare personnel as social workers. This once more raised the specter of social work being associated with public relief, or "the dole," at a time when the increasing influence of McCarthyism and conservative politics were challenging and cutting back the programs of the New Deal.

In 1955 seven specialty professional social work organizations merged into the National Association of Social Workers (NASW; Austin, 1986). In addition to the associations discussed here, two others that had formed broad-based interdisciplinary organizations in the 1940s, community organization and research, also joined the new professional organization, which grew to 20,000 members. The NASW soon developed a code of ethics, began working for state certification and licensing for social workers, and chose to focus on study and evaluation of social policy issues rather than lobbying or social action (Leighninger, 1987).

The greater unification of the social work profession through these organizations led to growth in the number of social work programs from 49 schools granting 1,923 MSW degrees in 1951 to 56 schools with 2,087 graduates in 1960 (Leighninger, 1987). However, only 20% of the 105,000 social workers in the country had graduate degrees, and only 3% of those in public assistance work had an MSW. Even the proportion of child welfare workers with graduate degrees had dropped to 26% (Leighninger, 1987; Lindenmeyer, 1997).

In the late 1950s, however, social work education was still in search of a common method and a common curriculum. In 1956 specialized accreditation was discontinued, and standards prescribed a psychodynamic view of human development and therapeutic interviewing as the common core of social work education (Austin, 1986). The 1958 report of the NASW Task Force on the Definition of Social Work Practice and Boehm's Curriculum Study in 1959 laid the basis for a common foundation curriculum composed of three elements: social science theories including those of human growth and development, social welfare policy, and five practice methods: casework, group work, community organization, administration, and research (Austin, 1986). However, the growing influence of the National Institute of Mental Health in research and training, the establishment of community mental health centers in 1963, and the creation of the Academy of Certified Social Workers by NASW in 1960 solidified the emphasis in social work education on diagnosis and treatment of mental health issues and further marginalized fields of practice such as child welfare and medical social work supported by the CB.

In many ways the CB and those in social work education plotted a similar course after the passage of the Social Security Act, insisting on the need for 2 years of graduate education for the professional practice of social work, distancing themselves from social action and public assistance, and developing a psychodynamic approach to casework better suited to private than to public social service agencies. The rejection of undergraduate education as preparation for entry-level social work meant that 90% of social service workers had no professional training or representation. This left social workers ill prepared to carry out the social service mandates of the 1962 amendments to the Social Security Act or respond to the national concern about poverty in the United States stimulated by Michael Harrington's *The Other America* in 1962.

REFERENCES

Andrews, J. (2001). Group work's place in social work: A historical analysis. *Journal of Sociology and Social Welfare, 28*(4), 45–65.

Austin, D. M. (1986). *A history of social work education.* Austin, TX: School of Social Work, University of Texas.

Bradbury, D. E. (1962). *Five decades of action for children.* Washington, DC: U.S. Department of Health, Education, and Welfare.

Brown v. Board of Education, 347 U.S. 483 (1954).

Children's Bureau. (1937). *The Children's Bureau, yesterday, today, and tomorrow.* Washington, DC: US Government Printing Office.

Children's Bureau. (1956). *Your Children's Bureau: Its current program.* Washington, DC: U.S. Government Printing Office.

Eliot, M. M. (1972). Six decades of action for children. *Children Today, 1*(22), 2–6.

Gruenberg, S.M. (1942). The family—war or peace. In Gruenberg, S.M. (Ed.), *The family in a world at war.* New York, NY: Harper & Brothers, 1-20.

Harrington, M. (1962). *The other America.* New York, NY: Macmillan.

Hunter, R. W. (1999). *Voices of our past: The Rank and File Movement in social work, 1931–1950.* Unpublished doctoral dissertation, Ann Arbor, MI: University Microfilms, Inc.

Hymes, J. L. (1950). *A healthy personality for your child* (U.S. Children's Bureau Publication No. 337). Washington, DC: U.S. Government Printing Office.

Interdepartmental Committee on Children and Youth. (1960). *Children in a changing world: A book of charts.* Washington, DC: Golden Anniversary White House Conference on Children and Youth.

Leighninger, L. (1987). *Social work: Search for identity.* New York, NY: Greenwood Press.

Lindenmeyer, K. (1997). *"A right to childhood": The U.S. Children's Bureau and child welfare, 1912–46.* Urbana: University of Illinois Press.

Committee on Ways and Means, U.S. House of Representatives. (2012). *Green book.* Washington, DC: U.S. Government Printing Office.

National Mental Health Act of 1946, 42 USC § 232 (1946).

Schwartz, E. E., & Wolins, M. (1958). *Cost analysis in child welfare services: Adoption and foster home costs.* Washington, DC: Children's Bureau.

Social Security Act of 1935, § 49 Stat. 620, 627 (1935), now codified as §§301–1304 (1988).

Trattner, W. I. (1999). *From poor law to welfare state: A history of social welfare in America* (6th ed). New York, NY: Free Press.

Witmer, H. L. (1953). *A research program for the Children's Bureau.* Washington, DC: U.S. Children's Bureau.

4

FROM THE GREAT SOCIETY TO THE RETREAT OF THE WELFARE STATE

Joel Blau

The Children's Bureau (CB) is the longest-running policy agency in the executive branch. In its early years it was the primary funnel for national social welfare spending. Subsequently, as the federal government's leader in statistical research during the 1920s, it provided policy expertise to President Franklin D. Roosevelt's Committee on Economic Security for the second New Deal. All throughout its history, it has been the social work establishment's closest kin within the federal government—the source of advice on casework techniques and the model for the kind of agency that social workers would love to replicate in other policy areas, if they only had a free hand (Amenta, 1998; Gordon, 1994).

These functions are critically important. As one of the leading social welfare agencies in the federal bureaucracy, the well-being of the CB tracks closely the rise and fall of social welfare in the United States. Impelled by the social movements of the 1960s, social welfare in the United States peaked in the early 1970s, which—consistent with the principle of less eligibility and the notion that welfare should pay less than employment—was also the high point of the average American worker's wages. For a brief moment, amid the optimism of the 1960s, it seemed as if the U.S. would follow the trajectory of the European welfare states. But then the conservative counterattack on social welfare began, and the CB, along with U.S. social policy as a whole, regressed to its usual, more begrudging pattern.

The first great optimism about social welfare originated in the Kennedy administration. Seeking a novel method of addressing the issue of poverty in America, the administration willingly adopted the service approach advocated by 25 prominent social welfare figures including many college and university deans who made up the ad hoc Committee on Public Welfare. Inserted into the 1962 amendments to the Social Security Act, the deal promised something for both parties: The Kennedy administration benefited from the appearance of doing something about poverty without relying on cash assistance, and social work got a permanent funding stream through the committee (Stern & Axinn, 2012). Relishing their new-found cachet as policy advisers to the Kennedy administration, the leaders of the profession also got decisive evidence that social work had finally arrived.

The 1967 amendments further extended this pact by authorizing the purchase of services. But where the 1962 amendments increased reimbursement from 50% to 75% and granted eligibility to anyone who might be on public assistance within the next year, the 1967 amendments expanded eligibility to anyone who might be on public assistance within the next 5 years, opening up services to what was potentially a much larger population (Gilbert, 1981; Trattner, 1999). Services plainly constitute an essential component of any social policy repertoire. Yet by promising that casework could help to extricate people from poverty, these service amendments set the stage for a conservative counterattack. Henceforth, whenever there was talk of the Great Society's War on Poverty, conservatives would reply that there was a War on Poverty, and poverty had won (Murray, 1984; Reagan, 1988, p. 87). Amid globalization spurred by computer technology, the outsourcing of jobs, and much of the population's declining living standards, this argument would retain its resilience for the next 4 decades.

RETRENCHMENT AT THE CB

The CB in the 1970s follows this trajectory. During the 1960s when it focused on poor, marginalized families, the CB had teetered on the brink of a broader mandate. Collaborating actively with private child welfare organizations and the Child Welfare League of America, it provided expertise from well-respected professionals on foster care, protective services, and licensing. These policies were developed in consultation with academics, members of professional organizations, and service organization representatives. Although they never approached universalism, they did forge modern child welfare policy as we know it today (Hutchinson, 2002, p. 70).

At the same time, however, the CB was also subjected to a series of bureaucratic upheavals. In 1963 it was moved from the Social Security Administration, where it had been located since 1946, into the Welfare Administration division of the Department of Health, Education, and Welfare, which was itself renamed Department of Health and Human Services in 1980. In 1967 it was placed under the administration of the Social and Rehabilitation Service, where its subdivisions included Maternal and Child Health, Child Welfare Services, Family Services, Delinquency and Youth Services, a research division, and a department for publication and reports. Over the next couple of years, however, federal policy makers reassigned these divisions to other agencies. Maternal and child health migrated to the Public Health Service, Juvenile Delinquency was sent to the Department of Justice, and a new Office of Child Development was established to oversee the CB. As a consequence, between 1967 and 1969, the number of CB staff plummeted from 400 to 20. Altogether, these changes deprived the agency of its institutional capacity to oversee child welfare policy and triggered its programmatic decline (Hutchinson, 2002, pp. 71–72).

By trying to retrieve child welfare services from the Social and Rehabilitation Service and renew support for state child welfare administrations, Frank Ferro, CB associate chief and acting chief from 1970 to 1982, made a valiant effort to revitalize the CB. His efforts to draw on research that would identify new program models and disseminate them to the field culminated in the establishment of the National Center on Child Abuse and Neglect. This initiative led to a $1 million contract for the Child Welfare Resource Information Exchange (CWRIE), which paid developers to provide technical assistance to state and local agencies interested in adopting the best programs (O'Neill Murray, & Gesiriech, 2004).

Established outside the CB, CWRIE was part of the Child Abuse Prevention and Treatment of Act of 1974, which provided federal funding to the states for the establishment of a mandatory child abuse reporting system (O'Neill Murray, & Gesiriech, 2004). Its independence may partly explain why CWRIE's 5-year contract was not renewed: CB officials realized that the exchange had essentially commandeered many of their former tasks and was treading on their turf. Seeking to regain control over the dissemination of technical assistance, the CB then funded three national resource centers in each of ten regions of the country plus one Native American center, most of which were located in university-based schools of social work. Nevertheless, despite this effort, the CB itself soon shrank to just three national programs in adoption, foster care, and child abuse and neglect (Hutchinson, 2002, p. 79).

These bureaucratic struggles all occurred amid the continuing bifurcation of the social work profession into social workers with and those without MSWs. Beginning in the 1970s the wages of child welfare personnel stagnated (Pecora, Whittaker, Maluccio, & Barth, 2000). In an increasingly conservative environment where human service workers were devalued, it was easy to replace one worker with another with fewer credentials at lower pay. Nor were these staff necessarily social workers: In fact, by 1988 one study estimated that only 28% of the nation's child welfare workers had a social work degree (Lieberman, Horby, & Russell, 1988).

At the same time that the child welfare labor force detached from social work, or certainly from social work degrees, social work education turned to educating students to become psychotherapists in private practice. In contrast to the 1960s, when almost 10% of all students in graduate social work programs had majored in community organizing, between 1975 and 1985 these trends led to a 500% increase in the number of private practitioners (Austin, 1986; Specht & Courtney, 1994). The low pay and declining status of the public sector contributed to this trend, but other factors fed it too. One was certainly the influx of college-educated women who sought the autonomy in the workplace that a private practice offers. In their role as private psychotherapists, these women established what were essentially small businesses. Finance capital in the form of insurance companies and managed care began to squeeze these small businesses in the 1990s, but even as this squeeze intensified, few of these experienced social workers ever returned to child welfare (Hutchinson, 2002, pp. 20–21).

Training for child welfare did offset some of these trends. Title IV-B, Section 426 of the 1967 Social Security Act amendments provided grants to prepare individuals to work in the child welfare field (Social Security Act, 2012). The grants were mostly channeled to social work education programs, which provided financial aid for graduate and undergraduate education, curriculum enhancement in child welfare for BSW and MSW students, and in-service grants for briefer trainings of current child welfare personnel. Funding peaked at $8,150,000 under the Carter administration, but declined steadily in the next decade; by 1992 the inflation-adjusted funding level was a mere one quarter of what it had been only 14 years earlier (Zlotnik, 2003, p. 8).

By the late 1970s, then, the position of the CB had become increasingly precarious. Downsized in numbers, it struggled to cope in an environment that was withdrawing its support for the public sector, devaluing the skills of child welfare workers, and losing the expertise of the most credentialed social work staff. Although these trends would have undermined the CB under any circumstances, they were particularly enfeebling in the face of the political upheaval brought about by the Reagan administration's hostility to social welfare.

THE CONSERVATIVE TIDE

The conservative tide began in the Nixon administration. In his first term Nixon seemed to have an ambiguous attitude toward social welfare. Capitalizing on the widespread feeling that Great Society programs sidestepped White ethnics to aid poor African Americans, Nixon won the 1968 presidential election with political rhetoric that spoke to the silent majority. Under what was later termed the New Federalism, Nixon did return many social service programs to the states. Yet, Nixon liked to centralize power, and in social welfare, to centralize power means boosting federal social welfare spending and nationalizing state programs. It was Nixon as the American version of a Tory reformer who early in his administration came as close as we ever have in this country to a guaranteed, though admittedly quite modest, minimum income. Though this initiative got caught up in the crosscurrents of congressional politics, Nixon did succeed in raising the Social Security benefit by 20% and indexing it to inflation. In 1972 he also transformed the states' aged, blind, and disabled programs into the federalized Supplemental Security Income program. Finally, in the midst of the most serious postwar economic stagnation to date, he enacted the Comprehensive Employment Training Act of 1973, which employed 750,000 people and became the largest federal employment program since the New Deal (Blau, 2010, p. 283).

Yet the core conservative beliefs about social welfare were not to be long suppressed. In his 1973 testimony before the Senate Committee on Finance about regulations that the Department of Health, Education, and Welfare had proposed to govern social services, defense secretary Caspar Weinberger said the social service provisions of the Social Security Act "were intended to be of principal benefit to welfare recipients, not to some more general segment of the public" (Kamerman & Kahn, 1976, p. 44). Nixon may have briefly dabbled in a sketchy universalism, but henceforth for the rest of the century a residual approach infused most of social welfare policy.

This policy shift found a willing reception in the American electorate. In a country with another ideological tradition, a more centralized government, and a different political history, the prospect of a softening economy might have led to demands for an expanded social safety net. In the United States, however, as deindustrialization intensified and wages fell, the prospect of less social welfare and lower taxes seemed to present the only method of maintaining workers' standard of living. The residualism of American social welfare neatly dovetailed with this calculation. If residualism is deeply entrenched and social welfare only comes through categorical programs whose recipients are consistently typecast as poor people of color, then the White majority would differentiate itself from people on welfare by voting their aspirations. These aspirational politics offered them the opportunity to act not on their current economic interests but for the upwardly mobile people they could once again become. It is these dynamics that prompted a large segment of the American electorate to shift its allegiance from the working and middle-income bloc that energized the New Deal and the Great Society to a late-20th-century coalition in which social welfare was cut back, privatization and deregulation proliferated, and the market reigned (Blau, in press).

THE CHILDREN'S BUREAU IN THE REAGAN ADMINISTRATION

The conservative tide reached its first full crest in the Reagan administration. Although president Jimmy Carter was a moderate Democrat who accepted many of the premises about the need for social welfare cutbacks and cost control, the Democrat-controlled Congress, a fragmented civil rights movement, and the other remnants of the old New Deal coalition were still powerful enough to limit his policy initiatives. Conflict about the First White House Conference on the Family in 1980 signaled the trouble to come. The proliferation of single-parent families deviated from the model of a nuclear family, a deviation that had particular relevance for welfare recipients, since it has always been difficult for a two-parent family to obtain public assistance in the United States. To compound the divisiveness of that issue, gay and lesbian households for the first time were making claims that they too constituted families. These centrifugal forces engendered so much controversy about the White House conference that for a while it deterred any legislation in which the term *family* might have required a more precise definition (Hutchinson, 2002, p. 83).

When the Reagan administration took over the federal bureaucracy in 1981, the consequences for social welfare, and more specifically for family policy, were powerful and immediate. Title I V-E of the Social Security Act, introduced in 1980 in the Adoption Assistance and Child Welfare Act, had assumed that social work education would have an important role in preparing students for child welfare practice. Indeed, to implement this assumption, a 1980 Government Accountability Office report, *Increased Federal Effort Needed to Better Identify, Treat and Prevent Child Abuse and Neglect*, recommended more federal support and better standard setting. Although the Department of Health and Human Services was planning to refine staff qualifications for child welfare workers in the months before Reagan's ascension to the presidency, the Reagan administration quickly halted this effort. Instead, it decreased funding and sought to disconnect social work education and child welfare. These actions in turn led to staffing cuts, regulations that remained unwritten, an inability to provide technical assistance, and the failure to maximize use of Title I V-E funds or carry out monitoring visits. Primed to take action before the

Reagan administration, the CB soon found that it could not do so (Zlotnik, 2003, p. 15).

The Reagan administration also disabled the other portions of the Adoption Assistance and Child Welfare Act of 1980 that were intended to alleviate problems in the foster care system and to replace multiple foster placements with a pathway to permanency. Social workers were supposed to make reasonable efforts to prevent out-of-home placement and pursue reunification of the family. Before the 1980 presidential election, the CB tried to specify what would constitute reasonable efforts to keep or reunite children with their families, but when the Reagan administration took office, it withdrew the draft regulations. In addition, by placing limitations on travel funds, the administration compromised opportunities for joint planning between the federal government and the states. It also cancelled most of the CB's regular publications, and following the Grace report on cost control (The Grace Commission, 1984), determined that all training should be limited to "continuing federal assistance." (Hutchinson, 2002, pp. 80–81). This prohibition was devastating to the child welfare policy because it meant that henceforth all "technical assistance" (Hutchinson, 2002, pp. 80–81) not in accordance with the Office of Human Development Services assistant secretary's policy would be discontinued.

Dorcas Hardy, assistant secretary for the Office of Human Development Services, which housed the CB, was responsible for many of these changes. An MBA from Pepperdine University, Hardy typified the Reagan administration's view that from a business perspective social welfare spending encumbered the rest of the economy. Operating on this premise, she dismissed social work with families as mere social engineering. It was all part of the Reagan administration's efforts to naturalize the marketplace. From the minimum wage to tax policies that encourage job outflows, virtually every public policy affects families (Katz, 1989). In the Reagan administration, however, a marketplace that conservative social policy modified was natural, and only social work constituted social engineering.

Hardy's other policies flowed from the same ideological premises. When she closed the CB publications department, she reasoned that these publications were available commercially. Although it is true that the grantees could have published their reports, most of them had not budgeted for publication, so reports containing valuable information for those in the child welfare field went unpublished and unread. Hardy also replaced liberal reviewers with conservatives and tried to terminate all preexisting longitudinal studies. When the professional community successfully counterattacked to preserve the CB's long-term databases, Hardy responded by creating a cross-agency discretionary grant program that diversified the grantees beyond social work to include law, psychology, and public administration. To ensure the outcome she desired, she also personally approved each grant and each grant reviewer. Eventually, the personal favoritism and politicization of this granting process led to a 1983 report critical of her administration by the Intergovernmental Relations and Human Resources Subcommittee in the House of Representatives (Hutchinson, 2002, pp. 85–87).

Under the Reagan administration, the CB returned to some bedrock principles in American social welfare policy. Foremost among these themes is a neat division between the market and the nonmilitary portion of the public sector. This division evokes the mythic power of the free market. It assumes the government should refrain from involvement in the economy because its interventions jeopardize economic well-being and run counter to the antipathy to social welfare. The family, this view insists, is the basic unit of society: presumptively nuclear, unchanging, and immune to shifts in the economy. Though subsequent administrations rearticulated these views, they are worth examining here, because the Reagan administration gave expression to them in their purest form (O'Connor, 2001).

At the simplest level, three problems bedevil this perspective. For starters, despite repeated invocations of an idyllic past, there never was a time in the American economy when government was not actively involved. Whether it was New York State's financing of the Erie Canal, the U.S. government's distribution of land for railroad construction, the establishment of land grant colleges, or the critical importance of federal Civil War pensions, the melding of private and public is a long-standing feature of American economic development. Conservatives may object that its prominence has grown, but they are wrong to imply that it was never a crucial factor (Blau, in press).

The second related issue flows from the first: Every government intervention—even those that are not explicitly designated as social welfare—has social and economic consequences. The tax code, for example, subsidizes dependents; military spending employs soldiers but may also stress families by sending them overseas; and infrastructural investment on railroads and bridges can speed commutes and increase the amount of time workers are able to spend with their children. Although none of these policies would typically be characterized as social welfare, they all influence families' income and quality of life and, thereby, affect their ability to form, remain together, and raise healthy children (Blau, 2010).

Ultimately, then, for the CB as well as for all the other social welfare institutions, government intervention is by itself not the real issue. The Reagan administration always avoided framing the issue in this way, but whether it is tax credits to promote business investment or help for abused children, the government has and will continue to intervene. The mere fact of government intervention is not debatable. Instead, as always, the question is who will that intervention benefit (Baker, 2011)? For the most part, ever since the Reagan administration, a full inventory of government interventions suggests that its main beneficiaries have not been workers or the recipients of social welfare (Baker, 2007; Perelman, 2007; Wolff, 2010).

THE CB AFTER REAGAN

The Reagan administration bequeathed a set of policy controls to all the social agencies in federal government. For the CB, as well as the Department of Health and Human Services more generally, social welfare could never again aspire to the universal social policies that seemed just over the horizon in the 1960s. Henceforth, social welfare would be restricted to the poor, limited by budgetary constraints, and treated as an unfortunate burden. Inevitably, the reconstruction of the CB within this framework was patchy and partial, because while existing law allowed it to continue some of its statutorily approved activities, the fear that it might have to justify those activities was always close at hand.

This pattern is evident in the two main child welfare training programs, one that the federal government targeted to social work, and another that targeted states, which would then contract with universities to train staff. Funding for both remained uncertain. Sixty-eight programs in 29 states received Title IV-E grants for BSW and MSW education in 1996. But by

1998–99, only 48 of 282 social work schools were receiving these funds. Although 37 social work education programs did get Section 426 (discretionary grants) in 2000, the demand for cost neutrality capped the training budget: If training expenses rose, the expectation was that they would be offset by lower service costs (Pierce, 2003, pp. 21–32; Zlotnik, 2003, p. 16). It was difficult for the CB to regain its footing in these circumstances.

This pattern did not change significantly in the first decade of the 21st century. In fiscal year 2002, 49 states received an estimated $286 million in Title IV-E training reimbursements. Reimbursements ranged from an estimated low of about $10,000 in Alaska to a high of more than $79 million in California (U.S. House Committee on Ways and Means, 2003). Threats to the program included eliminating the funding entitlement or deploying a fixed sum that would place the costs of training in competition with the costs for services. At the same time, the National Association of Social Workers (NASW, 2004) noted several ways that Title IV-E could be improved to aid the states in creating a competent and stable child welfare workforce. Among these changes were the elimination of the requirements for cost allocation based on the percentage of the Title IV-E eligible case load, so that all children, not just those meeting the 1996 Aid to Families with Dependent Children income test, could benefit from better qualified staff, expansion of the eligibility for training content beyond out-of-home placement or adoption, adding private universities to the list of institutions eligible to receive Title IV-E monies, and applying the 75% reimbursement rate to all real costs of training, direct and indirect, including the costs of administering the program (NASW, 2004).

Of course, this more expansive conception of Title IV-E could never take root in such an austere social welfare environment. As a result, in its latest incarnation the CB is one of the two bureaus in the Administration on Children, Youth, and Families of the Department of Health and Human Services. Although its budget has now risen to almost $8 billion, and it still works with state and local agencies to develop programs that focus on preventing the abuse of children in troubled families (Administration for Children and Families, 2012), its mandate is cramped and residual, and its mission has now been fully reconciled with the traditions of U.S. social welfare.

CONCLUSION

In retrospect, programmatic, strategic, and ideological constraints all limited the development of the CB. Programmatically, Title IV-E's enabling legislation was vague and subject to a variety of different policy interpretations. It did not state the legislation's goals and objectives, and it did not specifically address the issue of social work education. This imprecision was probably not random. The legislation was unlikely to provide support for either child welfare workers or well-trained social workers, because given the denigration of social welfare, policy makers did not really believe that well-paid skilled workers were truly important.

The strategic issue is also a problem. Advocates for comprehensive social welfare policy have often practiced what Linda Gordon refers to as "strategic immorality" (Gordon, 1994, p. 29). Children are appealing; a focus on them not only circumvents the issue of legitimacy but is more likely to get help for the whole family. The CB embodies the best American version of this strategy. The problem is that amid the American antipathy to social welfare, even this strategy never really worked.

It never really worked because of a critical ideological factor. To conservatives inside and outside government, the family is the cheapest method of delivering social services. Though most social problems—health, housing, and economic well-being—manifest themselves in individual families, when they manifest themselves in many families, they are plainly social in their nature. Although this fact implies a broader social response, the cheapest method of addressing these problems is to devolve the responsibility to each family unit. That is what has been done for the past 40 years (Hacker, 2006). If the aid provided to families can be further restricted to just those families in the most desperate need, then the responsibilities of government for an interventionist social policy can be even more completely offloaded. On the way down from the heights it attained in the 1950s, the CB since the Reagan administration fits neatly into this pattern.

REFERENCES

Administration for Children and Families. (2012). *About the Children's Bureau.* Retrieved from http://www.acf.hhs.gov/sites/default/files/assets /FS_CB_0.pdf

Adoption Assistance and Child Welfare Act, 42 USC § 1305 (1980).

Amenta, E. (1998). *Bold relief: Institutional politics and the origins of modern American social policy.* Princeton, NJ: Princeton University Press.

Austin, D. M. (1986). *A history of social work education.* Austin, TX: University of Texas at Austin.

Baker, D. (2007). *The United States since 1980.* New York, NY: Cambridge University Press.

Baker, D. (2011). *The end of loser liberalism: Making markets progressive.* Washington, DC: Center for Economic and Policy Research.

Blau, J. (with Abramovitz, M.). (2010). *The dynamics of social welfare policy* (3rd ed.). New York, NY: Oxford University Press.

Blau, J. (In press). The political economy of U.S. social policy. In Reisch, M. (Ed.), *Social policy and social justice.* Thousand Oaks, CA: Sage.

Gilbert, N. (1981). The transformation of social services. In N. Gilbert & H. Specht (Eds.), *The emergence of social welfare and social work* (2nd ed., pp. 107–118). Itasca, IL: F. E. Peacock.

Gordon, L. (1994). *Pitied but not entitled: Single mothers and the history of welfare.* Cambridge, MA: Harvard University Press.

Government Accountability Office. (1980). *Increased federal effort needed to better identify, treat and prevent child abuse and neglect,* HRD-80-60. Washington, DC: Author.

The Grace Commission. (1984), *The private sector survey on cost control.* Retrieved from http://www.uhuh.com/taxstuff/gracecom.htm

Hacker, J. (2006). *The great risk shift.* New York, NY: Oxford University Press.

Hutchinson, J. R. (2002). *Failed child welfare policy: Family preservation and the orphaning of children.* New York, NY: University Press of America.

Kamerman, S., & Kahn, A. J. (1976). *Social services in the United States.* Philadelphia, PA: Temple University Press.

Katz, M. (1989). *The undeserving poor: From the War on Poverty to the war on welfare.* New York, NY: Pantheon.

Lieberman, A., Horby, H., & Russell, M. (1988). Educational backgrounds and work experiences of child welfare personnel. *Social Work, 33*(6), 485–489.

Murray, C. (1984). *Losing ground: American social policy 1950–1980.* New York, NY: Basic Books.

National Association of Social Workers. (2004). *Fact sheet: Title IV-E child welfare training program.* Retrieved from http://www.socialworkers.org/advocacy/updates/2003/081204a.asp

O'Connor, A. (2001). *Poverty knowledge: Social science, social policy, and the poor in twentieth century U.S. history*. Princeton, NJ: Princeton University Press.

O'Neill Murray, K., & Gesiriech, S. (2004). *A brief legislative history of the child welfare system*. Retrieved from http://www.pewtrusts.org/uploadedFiles/wwwpewtrustsorg/Reports/Foster_care_reform/LegislativeHistory2004.pdf

Pecora, P., Whittaker, J. K., Maluccio, A. N., & Barth, R. P. (2000). *The child welfare challenge: Policy, practice, and research*. Piscataway, NJ: Aldine Transaction.

Perelman, M. (2007). *The confiscation of American prosperity*. New York, NY: Palgrave Macmillan.

Pierce, L. (2003). Use of Title IV-E funding in BSW programs. In K. Briar-Lawson & J. Zlotnik (Eds.), *Charting the impacts of university child welfare collaboration* (pp. 21–33). Binghamton, NY: Haworth Press.

Reagan, R. W. (1988). *State of the Union Address, January 25, 1988* (Public papers of the presidents of the United States, 1988). Washington, DC: U.S. Government Printing Office.

Social Security Laws. (2012). Compilation of Social Security laws. Retrieved from http://www.ssa.gov/OP_Home/ssact/title04/0426.htm

Specht, H., & Courtney, M. E. (1994). *Unfaithful angels*. New York, NY: Free Press.

Stern, M. J., & Axinn, J. (2012). *Social welfare: A history of the American response to need* (8th ed.). New York, NY: Pearson Education.

Trattner, W. (1999). *From poor law to welfare state* (6th ed.). New York, NY: Free Press.

U.S. House Committee on Ways and Means. (2003). *Green book*. Washington, DC: U.S. Government Printing Office.

Wolff, R. D. (2010). *Capitalism hits the fan: The global economic meltdown and what to do about it*. New York, NY: Olive Branch Press.

Zlotnik, J. L. (2003). The use of Title IV-E training funds for social work education: An historical perspective. In K. Briar-Lawson, & J. L. Zlotnik (Eds.), *Charting the impacts of university child welfare collaboration* (pp. 5–20). Binghamton, NY: Haworth Press.

5

THE INDIAN CHILD WELFARE ACT AND THE MULTIETHNIC PLACEMENT ACT
Implications for Vulnerable Populations

Ruth G. McRoy

To better understand the significance of the passage and implementation of the Indian Child Welfare Act (ICWA) of 1978 and the Multiethnic Placement Act (MEPA) of 1994, it is important to consider the context in which these major pieces of legislation were passed. In the 1960s several factors, including growing racial conflicts, calls for social change, the Civil Rights Movement, and the subsequent passage of the 1964 Civil Rights Act, brought a resurgence of attention to the issues of poverty and racial inequality in the United States (McGowan, 2005). During this period, child welfare service delivery was primarily a combination of state and local responsibility, and federal "participation in child welfare services was minimal" (McGowan, 2005, p. 30). It was the Children's Bureau's (CB's) primary responsibility to set standards and directions for service delivery.

EVOLVING ADOPTION PRACTICES AND POLICIES

First founded in the 1920s, adoption agencies were established to assist White couples seeking healthy White infants primarily placed for adoption by unmarried mothers who were unable to raise their children (McRoy, 1989). These adoption agencies were primarily funded through the fees paid by these couples for services, and their mission was to place as many infants as possible. However, by the late 1960s and early 1970s many adoption agencies, which had traditionally operated to place White infants with childless White middle-income couples, found that they were beginning to experience a declining availability of healthy White infants because of the "widespread use of contraceptives, liberalized abortion laws, and increased social acceptance of unwed parenthood, which contributed to a significant decrease in the number of healthy White infants available for adoption" (McRoy & Zurcher, 1983, p. 6).

In the mid-1960s about 31.7% of children born to unmarried women were placed for adoption, while in the early 1990s only about 3% of White unmarried mothers placed their infants up for adoption. During this same period, the number of White couples seeking to adopt increased to about 2 million (McRoy, 1994). Billingsley and Giovannoni (1972) described public child welfare services in the 1960s as largely separate and unequal. Specifically, they noted that public agencies were serving a larger portion of White children compared to Black children and that Black children were more likely to receive foster care services over adoption services. Additionally, Black children remained in care longer than White children. Jeter (1963) reported:

> The largest groups of both Negro and American Indian children were in foster care, 49 percent of the Negro children served by public agencies and 53 percent of the American Indian children. In the voluntary agencies the proportions were even higher, 57 and 59 percent in foster care. (p. 132)

For many years non-kin adoptions were not considered an option for African American children. Historically, African American children were informally adopted by extended family, due to segregationist practices that excluded African Americans from services provided by private adoption agencies until the mid-1920s. With the advent of public social service offerings beginning in the 1930s, African American children entered the child welfare system, but were primarily offered foster care services rather than adoption services (McRoy, 2004a). Also, many workers tended to view African American families as "pathological" (Jackson-White, Dozier, Oliver, & Gardner, 1997, p. 246) and were not interested in adoption. Some

African Americans were deemed ineligible for adoptive parenthood because of being single or over the age of 40. African American parents were often designated as "hard to reach" and African American children were viewed as "hard to place" (Billingsley & Giovannoni, 1972, p. 151). Other factors that have been identified as possibly contributing to the overrepresentation of African American children in care are (a) racial discrimination in state child welfare systems, (b) marginal representation of people of color in positions of power in child welfare organizations, and (c) the lack of training of child welfare workers on service provision to families of color (Lakin & Whitfield, 1997; McRoy, Oglesby, & Grape, 1997).

This reduction in the availability of White healthy infants for adoption and the over-availability of older children, especially minority children needing adoption, were two factors that led to the development of transracial adoptions. White couples who did not meet the criteria for a White healthy infant were often considered by adoption agencies as potential adoptive parents for a child or children with *special needs*, a term often used to describe a Black child, bi- or multi-racial child, school-aged child, or one who had physical or emotional disabilities (McRoy & Zurcher, 1983).

Placing children across racial lines represented a real shift from traditional placement practices and policies. For example, in 1958 the Child Welfare League of America (CWLA, a privately supported organization of public and private agencies), which historically set the standards for adoption practices, "cautioned that children with the same racial characteristics as their adoptive parents can be more easily integrated into the community and family" (McRoy, 1989, p. 149). However, the changing profile of children available for adoption as a result of the decline in the number of White infants and the increase in the number of Black children in the child welfare system needing placement led to a change in this standard 10 years later. By 1968 the CWLA's standards stated that "in most communities there are families who have the capacity to adopt a child whose racial background is different from their own. Such families should be encouraged to consider such a child" (Child Welfare League of America, 1968, p. 34). This represented a complete reversal from its earlier position on transracial placements.

Other factors, such as the U.S. Civil Rights Movement and societal attempts to move away from segregation, led to greater societal acceptance of transracial adoptions. For example, in 1967, the Supreme Court ruled that state laws prohibiting interracial marriages should be struck from state constitutions. State statutes that had previously included race of parent as a criterion to consider in assessing the suitability of a family for a child were challenged in the mid-1970s, and many were declared unconstitutional, leaving transracial adoptions a viable option for the placement of African American children.

Many believed that transracial adoptions would be the answer to the growing number of African American children needing placement, as there were insufficient numbers of African American families seeking to adopt these children (Simon, Altstein, & Melli, 1994). According to the CWLA Research Center, during the first six months of 1972, "about 119 White families were approved for adoption per 100 White children needing adoptive placement in comparison to about 50 non-White-approved adoptive homes per 100 non-White children needing adoptive placement" (Smith, 1972, p. 586). Agencies responded by trying to develop new ways to find adoptive homes for African American children by moving away from policies and practices of racial matching and beginning to give incentives to White families that might consider adopting African American or racially mixed children.

Along with the decrease in the number of White infants available, increasingly stringent selection criteria for White families seeking to adopt healthy White infants emerged, resulting in many White parents fostering children in the child welfare system. As a result, many families became very attached to their foster children. Since African American children often remain in care longer than White children, the likelihood for parental attachment to develop in foster families is greater, and the likelihood of the foster parent's seeking to adopt the child if he or she becomes legally free is potentially greater as well. In fact, prior to consideration of MEPA, frequent media accounts appeared of an adoption worker trying to place an African American child or infant with an approved African American prospective adoptive family, and the child's White foster family requesting to adopt the same African American child whom they had been fostering. In such cases, often the children had come into care as infants or young children, and because of court delays, failed attempts at reunification, or kinship placement, final termination of parental rights may have been delayed. Because agencies often wait until termination of parental rights is certain or almost certain before seeking a prospective adoptive family, the foster family often becomes very attached to their foster child and seeks to adopt once the child becomes legally free. The question became whether attachment to a child's caregiver is more or less important than race matching in placement decision-making (McRoy, 1994).

After reports that between 1967 and 1972 over 10,000 Black children had been placed with White families (Costin, 1979), the National Association of Black Social Workers (1972) issued a strong position statement against transracial adoptions and called for Black children to be placed with Black families where they could "receive a total sense of themselves and develop a sound projection of their future" (p. 2). In 1973 the CWLA responded and reversed its initial support of transracial adoptions and noted that children in same-race placements could become more easily integrated into the family and community (McRoy, 1989). As a result of this debate, the movement toward more transracial adoptions declined by the mid-1970s, and several new African American adoption agencies and programs were established (e.g., Homes for Black Children, One Church, One Child, and Black Adoption Program and Services) to address the need for more culturally specific recruitment and retention of African American adoptive families and to increase the number of approved African American families seeking to adopt African American children (McRoy, 2011). Other organizations, such as the Black Administrators in Child Welfare, were formed in 1975 to begin to respond to the problem of the overrepresentation of African American children in child welfare.

In 1981 the North American Council on Adoptable Children (NACAC; Gilles & Kroll, 1991) took the position that the placement of children with a family of like ethnic background was desirable. They also, however, supported multiethnic adoption as a way to prevent unnecessary delays in placement (McRoy, 1989, p. 151; NACAC, 1981).

In 1988 NACAC once again emphasized the need for aggressive and culturally sensitive recruitment and retention programs (Gilles & Kroll, 1991). Moreover, in 1993, NACAC released the findings of a study of specialized minority adoption programs and found that minority placement agencies place 94% of their African American children inracially, whereas traditional agencies place about 51% of their children inracially (NACAC, 1993).

The debate over transracial versus inracial placements continued over the years as increasing concerns were raised over the growing disproportionate representation of African American and other minority children in care and their longer waits for permanency through adoption. Some noted that these delays to find a family of the same racial background served to deny opportunities to Black children (Bartholet, 1991) and that same-race placement practices and policies were in violation of the rights of families seeking to adopt transracially (McRoy, 1994, p. 62.). The National Association of Black Social Workers altered its position regarding transracial adoptions in 1994. Although still stating a preference for same-race adoptions, the organization acknowledged that in some situations transracial adoptions should be considered.

To increase adoptions from foster care, several other pieces of federal legislation were passed during this period, including the Child Abuse Prevention and Treatment and Adoption Reform Act of 1978, which established the Adoption Opportunities Program to facilitate the placement of children with special needs into adoptive homes. The Adoption Assistance and Child Welfare Act of 1980 required agencies to demonstrate "reasonable efforts" to preserve the birth family or reunify the child with the birth family, before considering adoption for children in care and terminating parental rights. In 1993 the Family Preservation and Support Services Program Act was passed to implement a continuum of services for families at risk. Despite these several pieces of major child welfare legislation, in 1994 growing numbers of children still remained in care, and 46% were African American (McRoy, 2004b, 2005).

MEPA

To address concerns that race-matching policies might be a barrier to the placement of African American children, in 1994 Congress passed the Multiethnic Placement Act, and the following year, the Department of Health and Human Services (DHHS) issued guidance for states and agencies to assist in the implementation of the law. In 1996, the law was amended through the Interethnic Placement Provisions (IEP), which contained the

Removal of Barriers to Interethnic Adoptions Provision. These laws prohibit states and other entities, which provide foster and adoption services and receive federal assistance, from basing the foster or adoptive placement of a child on the race, color, or national origin of the child or the adoptive or foster parent. These factors no longer play a role in denying or delaying placement of the child or denying any adult to be an adoptive or foster parent. Additionally, the IEP require states to actively recruit a diverse population of foster and adoptive parents to meet the needs of the children in the state in need of care in order to remain eligible for federal funding (Hollinger & American Bar Association Center on Children and the Law, 1998). The Children's Bureau continues to work with states to implement the requirements of MEPA and IEP. "The Bureau, the U.S. Department of Health and Human Services Office for Civil Rights have provided extensive guidance to States on the requirements of MEPA/IEP in the form of Information Memoranda, program instructions, technical assistance, and training" (Administration of Children and Families [ACF], 2008, p. 1).

In keeping with its mission the Children's Bureau aims "to provide for the safety, permanency and well being of children through leadership, support for necessary services, and productive partnerships with States, Tribes, and communities" (ACF, 2012). Over the years, the Children's Bureau has funded and awarded several grants for the purpose of increasing permanency for all youth in the child welfare system including AdoptUSKids, the National Center for the Recruitment and Retention of Foster and Adoptive Families at AdoptUSKids, the National Resource Center on Permanency and Family Connections, the National Resource Center on Adoption, and Diligent Recruitment Grants. Through the provision of training and technical assistance to states, territories, and tribes; photolisting children needing families and of families seeking to adopt; public advertising campaigns; as well as providing information and assistance in the development of specific diligent recruitment for kinship, foster, concurrent, and adoptive families, these federally funded programs seem to be having a positive effect on service delivery and outcomes for children. For example, since 2006 there has been a reduction in the number of all children in foster care awaiting adoption from 135,000 in to 104,000 in 2011 (DHHS, 2012). Through these grants and innovative programs, it is hoped the number of children in care awaiting adoption will continue to decrease.

Many still believe that MEPA was passed primarily to expand the access of White prospective parents to Black children for adoption rather than as a means to increase the likelihood of adoption for African American children by all types of parents, a controversy that remains today. Since the passage of MEPA/IEP, there have been some increases in the percentages of transracial adoptions from foster care (from 17.2% in 1996 to 20.1% in 2003; Evan B. Donaldson Adoption Institute, 2008). However, the overall adoption rates for African American children continue to remain lower than those of other ethnic groups Eighteen years after this controversial legislation, African American children today remain disproportionately represented among children in care and among those needing adoption.

ICWA

Sixteen years prior to the passage of MEPA, a completely different legislative policy direction was taken to address the placement needs of American Indian children in the United States. To understand the factors that led to the passage and implementation of ICWA in 1978, it is important to first review events that occurred during the two major eras preceding ICWA—the boarding school era and the Indian adoption era (George, 1997).

Beginning around the 1880s Indian culture was denigrated and was considered by many in the United States to be immoral and inferior. In the United States the "Indian problem" (George, 1997, p. 166) was thought to be solved by removing Native children from their families and tribes and placing them in government-run boarding schools where the children would essentially be educated and socialized to act as Caucasian (George, 1997, p. 166; Price, 1973). Until the mid-1930s, the Bureau of Indian Affairs appointed Indian agents who were generally White men sent to reservations to separate families and also educate them on what they would consider appropriate lifestyles (Price, 1973). Policies associated with American Indian populations changed in the mid-1930s when the Indian Reorganization Act was passed, calling for day schools to be established on reservations and allowing more tribal control on reservations (George, 1997).

Ongoing economic challenges and nonexistent child welfare service provisions on the reservations led to the continuing suffering of many Indian children and families. By the 1950s, after concerns were raised that Native children were returning to reservations to live a life of poverty and, potentially, neglect and abuse, the Bureau of Indian Affairs contracted with the CWLA to establish a clearinghouse to encourage interstate adoption of Native children with non-Native families (George, 1997). Transracial placements across state lines was justified because many believed that families in nonwestern states would be less prejudiced against Indians and that such placements would be in the best interest of the child. In this process almost 400 Native American children were placed by public and private agencies, as David Fanshel (1972) aptly refers to in the title of his book, *Far From the Reservation*.

Besides the ethnocentric belief that Indian children would be better off and have more opportunities with White families, a decrease in the pool of adoptable Caucasian babies led to the increase in transracial adoptions (Fanshel, 1972). According to Abourezk (1991), "in Minnesota, in the years 1971–72, nearly one in four Native American infants under the age of one year were placed for adoption and 90% of those adoptions were in non-Indian homes" (p. 16). Jones (n.d.), litigation director for Dakota Plains Legal Services, noted that before 1978 in certain states, 25% to 36% of Indian children were being placed in non-Indian homes. "Non-Indian judges and social workers—failing to appreciate traditional Indian child-rearing practices—perceived day-to-day life in the children's Indian homes as contrary to the children's best interests" (Jones, n.d., p. 1).

These alarming statistics led to congressional hearings, which documented that many of the child removals were inappropriate and unnecessary (Byler, 1977). Byler, executive director of the Association on American Indian Affairs, testified that the separation of children from their families is perhaps the most tragic and destructive aspect of American Indian life. Moreover, he and others attributed this family destruction to "culturally biased social workers and judges who used placement standards that discriminated against poor families without due process for either Indian children or their parents" (MacEachron, Gustavsson, Cross, & Lewis, 1996, p. 452). After more than 4 years of hearings, including "the bitter testimony of Tribal leaders and Native American parents" (George, 1997, p. 173), the debate led to the passage of ICWA in 1978, in which Congress stipulated the following:

> It is the policy of this Nation to protect the best interests of Indian children and to promote the stability and security of Indian tribes and families by the establishment of minimum Federal standards for the removal of Indian children from their families and the placement of such children in foster or adoptive homes which will reflect the unique values of Indian culture. (MacEachron et al., 1996, p. 452)

This act acknowledged Indian tribes as governmental entities, which have sovereign authority and jurisdiction in child welfare. Specifically, they have the "power to enact formal adoption procedures and to conduct adoption of children pursuant to custom or traditional law as part of tribal law, and formally certify through the legal process, adoptions made pursuant to tribal custom" (Cross & Fox, 2005, p. 423). According to ICWA:

> Termination of parental rights is more difficult than in mainstream families, and, when a child is removed from his or her parents, the placement preferences for adoption are as follows: 1) with a member of the child's extended family, 2) with other members of the child's tribe, or 3) with other Indian families. (Cross & Fox, 2005, p. 424)

Although only limited research has been conducted on the outcome of this legislation, data suggest that since the passage of ICWA, Indian tribes have "achieved substantial control over the foster care and adoptive placement of Indian children" (MacEachron et al., 1996, p. 458). In 1985, the Administration of Children, Youth and Families of the DHSS and the Bureau of Indian Affairs commissioned a study on the impact of ICWA. The findings suggested that although there was improved notification of Indian families and tribes about involuntary placements, disproportionately high numbers of Indian children were placed in foster care at a rate 3.6 times greater than that of the general population (Freundlich, 2000). To address this ongoing disproportionality, some suggest the need for more tribally and culturally based programs that include a continuum of services for Indian children and families (Freundlich, 2000; Kunesh, 1996).

Over the years the National Indian Child Welfare Association, a private, nonprofit organization that evolved from the Northwest Indian Child Welfare Institute, has facilitated the development of trained Indian child welfare workers and has continued to advocate for the development of community-based culturally appropriate services to American Indian children and families (see http://www.nicwa.org/history). Also, as a means of continued support to tribes, the CB established the National Child Resource Center for Tribes in October 2009, which is part of the CB's Child Welfare Training and Technical Assistance Network. It is designed to assist tribes in the enhancement of child welfare services and to promote safety, permanency, and well-being for American Indian/Alaska Native children (McRoy, 2011).

There are clear differences between the ideologies of MEPA and ICWA in making placement decisions. Under MEPA, even considering racial/ethnic factors may put an agency's federal funding at risk. Moreover, failure to comply with MEPA is considered a violation of Title VI of the Civil Rights Act of 1964. It is also important to note that MEPA "has no effect on the provisions of the Indian Child Welfare Act of 1978" (ACF, 2008, p. 2). As mentioned earlier, under ICWA placement, workers are required to take into consideration cultural differences and values. Under ICWA, child welfare workers aim to place a child within this culture or extended family. As we grapple to understand how these two pieces of legislation can exist side by side, we need to ask ourselves which practices can truly help us best meet the needs of children. Should we be able to take into account race, culture, and ethnicity in placement decision making for Indian children and not for African American children?"

IMPLICATIONS FOR SOCIAL WORK EDUCATION AND PRACTICE

The provisions of MEPA and ICWA are typically implemented by social workers in adoption programs who have the responsibility of recruiting and retaining prospective families for the children in care. According to the latest data from the CB, of the approximately 104,000 children in care waiting for adoption, 28% are African American and 2% are American Indian/Alaska

Native (DHHS, 2012). Both of these populations continue to be dispro-portionately represented in comparison to their representation in the U.S. population (13.1% and 1.2%; U.S. Census Bureau, 2011).

It is evident that much more needs to be done, not only to find perma-nence through adoption but also to successfully implement strategies to support and preserve birth families and prevent children from being removed from their homes and communities. Factors that may increase the likelihood of these children being removed, such as poverty, abuse, and neg-lect, should be addressed through the development of more federal poli-cies and programs. For example, the Family Preservation Act of 1992 and the Fostering Connections and Adoption Support Act of 2008 have served to provide additional services and support to vulnerable families.

It is critical that social workers who are charged with service delivery to diverse populations of children and families are knowledgeable and cultur-ally competent. Unfortunately, as Green (1982) observed, often social work-ers, while believing they are operating in the best interests of children, actually are often applying ethnocentrism when assessing Native American families, because they often did not have knowledge of the culture and ended up imposing their own values in child welfare decision making in the placement of Native American children.

Social work organizations, like the National Association of Social Workers (NASW) and the Council on Social Work Education (CSWE), over the years have been working to raise expectations for professionally trained social workers to better serve diverse populations. For example, the NASW (1997), the largest membership organization of social workers in the world, specifically recommended that efforts should be made to "main-tain a child's identity and his or her ethnic heritage" when placing children in foster care and adoption, "including adherence to the principles articu-lated in the Indian Child Welfare Act" (p. 138). NASW also recommended that prospective adoptive families representing each relevant ethnic group should be sought and made available to meet the needs of children in care.

The profession of social work has historically focused on serving vulner-able/disadvantaged populations, and the CSWE, formed in 1955, recognized the need for social work undergraduate and graduate schools accredited by CSWE to provide training on ethnic minority issues in practice and to address inequities. In the 1960s and early 1970s, CSWE focused on ways to "increase the number and effectiveness of minority faculty in social work programs" (Trolander, 1997, p. 116). In 1969, the Special Committee on Minority Groups (changed to the Commission on Minority Groups in 1970) was formed by CSWE to provide guidance on recruitment as well as curriculum development. Also, specialized task forces formed by CSWE for specific population groups (American Indians, Puerto Ricans, Chicanos, Asian Americans, and Whites) called for minority faculty and staff recruitment and specific courses in the curriculum that address issues of diversity (Trolander, 1997). For example, the Black Task Force called for the inclusion of content specific to African Americans and content on institutional racism to be included in social work curricula to better prepare future social workers for working with diverse populations (Eun-Kyoung & McRoy, 2008). Similarly, the Native American Task Force noted that critical content on Native Americans is needed in social work curricula, and there is a need for many more Native American faculty and students (Cross et al., 2007).

CSWE has continued over the years to emphasize a focus on integrating diversity issues into the social work curriculum. For example, in its Educational Policy and Accreditation Standards, CSWE (2001) identified 14 sources of oppression and specifically called for social work educators to prepare "social workers to practice without discrimination, with respect and with knowledge and skills related to clients' age, class, color, culture, disability, ethnicity, family structure, gender, marital status, national origin, race, religion, sex, and sexual orientation" (CSWE, 2001, p. 5). These standards are used to evaluate social work programs to assess their commitment to diversity and their ability to prepare social workers to recognize the extent to which "a culture's structures and values may oppress, marginalize, alienate, or create or enhance privilege and power" (CSWE, 2001, p. 5). To further promote the issue of diversity, in 2004 CSWE also established the Commission on Diversity and Social and Economic Justice to further the mission of addressing issues confronting social work educators today.

Within the social work profession we must continue to adhere to the implementation of the federal child placement laws, while also recognizing the factors that may have differentially affected vulnerable children and families, and advocate for culturally sensitive prevention, family preservation, recruitment, and retention programs. Since poverty is clearly a causal factor leading to disproportionate out-of-home placements for American Indian and African American children, ongoing advocacy for policies and practices to address these inequities is needed to improve outcomes for all children and families.

REFERENCES

Abourezk, J. (1991). Chair of the 1974 Congressional Committee hearings on Indian child welfare. In T. R. Johnson (Ed.), *The Indian Child Welfare Act: Indian homes for Indian children*. Los Angeles, CA: University of California, Los Angeles American Indian Studies Center.

Administration of Children and Families. (2008). Legislative background of the Multiethnic Placement Act. *Children's Bureau Express, 9*(6). Retrieved from https://cbexpress.acf.hhs.gov/index.cfm?event=website.viewArticles&issueid=96&sectionid=1&articleid=2112

Administration of Children and Families. (2012). *About the Children's Bureau.* Retrieved from http://www.acf.hhs.gov/programs/cb/aboutcb/about_cb.htm

Adoption Assistance and Child Welfare Act of 1980, 42 U.S.C. 42, sec. 620.

Bartholet, E. (1991). Where do Black children belong? The politics of race matching in adoption. *University of Pennsylvania Law Review, 139,* 1164–1256.

Billingsley, A., & Giovannoni, J. M. (1972). *Children of the storm: Black children and American child welfare*. New York, NY: Harcourt Brace Jovanovich.

Byler, W. (1977). The destruction of American Indian families. In S. Unger (Ed.), *The destruction of American Indian families* (pp. 1–11). New York, NY: Association on American Indian Affairs.

Child Abuse Prevention and Treatment and Adoption Reform Act of 1978, 42 U.S.C. 5111 et seq. (1978).

Child Welfare League of America. (1968). *Standards for adoption service*. New York, NY: Author.

Civil Rights Act, P.L. 88-352, 78 Stat. 241 (1964)

Costin, L. B. (1979). *Child welfare: Policies and practice*. New York: McGraw-Hill.

Council on Social Work Education. (2001). *Educational policy and accreditation standards*. Retrieved from http://www.cswe.org/File.aspx?id=14115

Cross, S. L., Brown, E. F., Day, P. A., Limb, G. E., Pellebon, D. A., Proctor, E. C., & Weaver, H. N. (2007). *Task force on Native Americans in social work education. Final report: Status of Native Americans in social work higher education*. Alexandria, VA: Council on Social Work Education.

Cross, T. L., & Fox, K. (2005). Customary adoption as a resource for American Indian and Alaska native children. In G. P. Mallon & P. M. Hess (Eds.), *Child welfare for the 21st century: A handbook of practices, policies, and programs* (pp. 423–431). New York, NY: Columbia University Press.

Eun-Kyoung, O. L., & McRoy, R. G. (2008). Multiculturalism. In T. Mizrahi & L. E. Davis (Eds.), *Encyclopedia of social work, 20th edition* (pp. 276–282). New York: NASW Press and Oxford University Press.

Evan B. Donaldson Adoption Institute. (2008). *Finding families for African American children: The role of race and law in adoption from foster care.* New York, NY: Author.

Family Preservation and Support Services Program Act, 107 Stat. 312 (1993)

Fanshel, D. (1972). *Far from the reservation.* Metuchen, NJ: Scarecrow Press.

Fostering Connections and Adoption Act 42 U.S.C. § 675(1)(G)(ii) (2008)

Freundlich, M. (2000). *Adoption and ethics: The role of race, culture, and national origin in adoption.* Washington, DC: Child Welfare League of America Press.

George, L. J. (1997). Why the need for the Indian Child Welfare Act? *Journal of Multicultural Social Work, 5*(3-4), 165–175.

Gilles, T., & Kroll, J. (1991). *Barriers to same race placement.* St. Paul, MN: North American Council on Adoptable Children.

Green, J. W. (1982). *Cultural awareness in the human services: A multi-cultural approach.* Englewood Cliffs, NJ: Prentice Hall.

Hollinger, J. H., & American Bar Association Center on Children and the Law. (1998). *A guide to the Multiethnic Placement Act of 1994 as amended by the Interethnic Adoption Provisions of 1996.* Washington, DC: American Bar Association.

Indian Child Welfare Act, 93 Stat. 3071 (1978).

Jackson-White, G., Dozier, C. D., Oliver, J. T., & Gardner, L. B. (1997). Why African American adoption agencies succeed: A new perspective on self-help. *Child Welfare, 76*(1), 239–254.

Jeter, H. R. (1963). *Children, problems, and services in child welfare programs* (Children's Bureau Publication No. 403-1963). Washington, DC: U.S. Department of Health, Education, and Welfare.

Jones, B. J. (n.d.). *The Indian Child Welfare Act: The need for a separate law.* Retrieved from http://www.americanbar.org/content/newsletter/publications/gp_solo _magazine_home/gp_solo_magazine_index/indianchildwelfareact.html

Kunesh, P. H. (1996). Transcending frontiers: Indian child welfare in the United States. *Boston College Third World Law Journal, 16,* 17–34.

Lakin, D. S., & Whitfield, L. (1997). Adoption recruitment: Meeting the needs of waiting children. In R. J. Avery (Ed.), *Adoption policy and special needs children* (pp. 107–126). Westport, CT: Auburn House.

MacEachron, A. E., Gustavsson, N. S., Cross, S., & Lewis, A. (1996). The effectiveness of the Indian Child Welfare Act of 1978. *Social Service Review, 70*(3), 451–463.

McGowan, B. G. (2005). Historical evolution of child welfare services. In G. P. Mallon & P. M. Hess (Eds.), *Child welfare for the 21st century: A handbook of practices, policies, and programs* (pp. 10–46). New York, NY: Columbia University Press.

McRoy, R. G. (1989). An organizational dilemma: The case of transracial adoptions. *Journal of Applied Behavioral Science, 25*(2), 145–160.

McRoy, R. G. (1994). Attachment and racial identity issues: Implications for child placement decision-making. *Journal of Multicultural Social Work, 3*(3), 59–74.

McRoy, R. G. (2004a). African American adoptions. In J. E. Everett, S. P. Chipungu, & B. R. Leashore (Eds.), *Child welfare revisited: An Africentric perspective* (pp. 256–274). New Piscataway, NJ: Rutgers University Press.

McRoy, R. G. (2004b). The color of child welfare. In K. E. Davis & T. Bent-Goodley (Eds.), *The color of social policy* (pp. 37–64). Alexandria, VA: Council on Social Work Education.

McRoy, R. G. (2005). Overrepresentation of children and youth of color in foster care. In G. P. Mallon & P. M. Hess (Eds.), *Child welfare for the 21st century: A handbook of practices, policies, and programs* (pp. 623–634). New York, NY: Columbia University Press.

McRoy, R. G. (2011). Selected resources for addressing African American adoption disproportionality. In D. K. Greene, K. Belanger, R. G. McRoy, & L. Bullard (Eds.), *Challenging racial disproportionality in child welfare: Research, policy, and practice* (pp. 331–340). Washington, DC: Child Welfare League of America.

McRoy, R. G., Oglesby, Z., & Grape, H. (1997). Achieving same-race adoptive placements for African American children: Culturally sensitive practice approaches. *Child Welfare, 76*(1), 85–104.

McRoy, R. G., & Zurcher, L. A. (1983). *Transracial and inracial adoptees: The adolescent years.* Springfield, IL: Charles C Thomas.

Multiethnic Placement Act, Pub. L. 103-382 (1994).

National Association of Black Social Workers. (1972, April). *Position statement on transracial adoptions.* Paper presented at the National Association of Black Social Workers Conference, Nashville, TN.

National Association of Social Workers. (1997). *Social work speaks: NASW policy statements* (4th ed.). Washington, DC: NASW Press.

North American Council on Adoptable Children. (1981). Position statement. Washington, DC: Author.

North American Council on Adoptable Children. (1993). *NACAC policy statement on race and adoption.* St. Paul, MN: Author.

Price, M. E. (1973). *Law and the American Indian: Readings, notes, and cases* (Contemporary Legal Education Series). New York: Bobbs-Merrill.

Simon, R. J., Altstein, H., & Melli, M. S. (1994). *The case for transracial adoption.* Washington, DC: American University Press.

Smith, M. J. (1972). Adoption in the first half of 1972. *Child Welfare, 51*(9), 585.

Trolander, J. A. (1997). Fighting racism and sexism: The Council on Social Work Education. *Social Service Review, 71*(1), 110–134.

U.S. Census Bureau. (2011). *State and county quick facts.* Retrieved from http://quickfacts.census.gov/qfd/states/00000.html

U. S. Department of Health and Human Services. (2012). *The AFCARS report: Preliminary FY 2011 estimates as of July 2012.* Retrieved from http://www.acf.hhs .gov/sites/default/files/cb/afcarsreport19.pdf

6

LAYING THE FOUNDATION FOR A STRONGER PARTNERSHIP UNDER TITLE IV-E

Joan Levy Zlotnik

From the Children's Bureau's (CB's) earliest days, its initiatives and the role of professional social workers have been closely intertwined. Not only have social workers directed and staffed the CB, but the CB has supported the education and training of social workers to pursue child welfare careers and worked closely with social workers across the United States to develop, study, implement, and evaluate the broad array of child welfare services, from community-based prevention to postadoption interventions (CB, 2012; U.S. Department of Health, Education and Welfare [DHEW], 1962).

Although the CB and the social work profession have a long history, this chapter will specifically focus on the efforts between the social work profession, including social work education, and the CB to educate social workers to prepare them for child welfare work and, most specifically, on the use of Social Security Act Title IV-E training funds. The commitment to social work was well articulated even in the 1930s by CB director Katherine Lenroot. In the report on the status of child welfare services under Title V of the Social Security Act, she noted that the following efforts were undertaken to ensure the necessary workforce:

> The States, therefore, were encouraged to include in their plans for child-welfare services one or more of the following procedures: 1. Granting

educational leave to qualified persons for attendance at recognized schools of social work. 2. Improving quality of service through providing more adequate supervision of workers. 3. Using specially staffed local units for orientation of new workers; for periods of intensive supervision of workers brought into the unit from other counties; and in some instances, for a limited number of students of schools of social work, usually those regarded as potential child-welfare workers in the particular State. (CB, 1939)

As described in the rest of the chapter, these efforts were further formalized after the 1959 report on the workforce needs in child welfare (DHEW, 1959).

The two most notable sources of CB funding currently used to support the education of social workers are

- Title I V-B Section 426 provisions, created in 1962 and most recently amended by the passage of the Child and Family Services Improvement and Innovation Act in 2011
- Title I V-E Foster Care and Adoption Assistance Training Entitlement, which was created through the passage of the Adoption Assistance and Child Welfare Act of 1980

TITLE IV-B SECTION 426 FUNDS

Title I V-B Section 426 authorized discretionary funds, appropriated annually, to be awarded by the CB through grants and cooperative agreements to specific institutions of higher education. Although the CB had always supported the use of some federal child welfare funds for training and social work education, the Section 426 program was specifically created in 1962 as a response to a perceived workforce shortage for graduate-level social workers who were interested in and prepared to work in public child welfare. According to a DHEW (1959) study, it was estimated there was a need for 10,000 graduate-level social workers to work in child welfare, requiring an almost 50% increase between 1958 and 1970.

Funded at $3.6 million in 1965, the Section 426 provision supported fieldwork opportunities, traineeships, and doctoral stipends in more than

30 states (DHEW, 1965). In the late 1970s, the CB supported regional training and technical assistance centers that included providing stipends to social work students (Zlotnik, 2002). In 1978 the Section 426 program reached a funding high of $8,150,000; however, in 1982 the program was cut to $3.8 million and remained at about that level through 1995. That was similar to the funding level in 1965 when the program began. In 1992 constant dollars this was a 75% reduction from the 1978 funding level, and a far greater reduction from its 1965 inception (U.S. General Accounting Office [GAO], 1993). In the 1980s the Section 426 program began to languish— the regional centers lost their funding, and grants were awarded for brief periods (17 months) with less attention and commitment to ensuring that professional social workers were specifically being educated to address the public child welfare agencies' workforce needs (Zlotnik, 2002).

As will be discussed in more detail, beginning in the late 1980s collaboration between national organizations and renewed advocacy with the CB brought attention to the importance of the Section 426 program to address public child welfare agencies' workforce needs, and efforts were made to strengthen the focus of the program and the strategic direction of its grants toward social work education. The 1990s saw the funding of 11 five-year interdisciplinary training grants and stronger partnerships between child welfare agencies and schools of social work, as well as closer ties between the CB and organizations of the social work profession (National Association of Social Workers [NASW], Council on Social Work Education [CSWE]). In addition, the congressional report language at the time of the initial passage of the Promoting Safe and Stable Families Program (initially created as the Family Preservation and Support Program as part of the Omnibus Reconciliation Act of 1993) required that the universities, especially schools of social work, work in partnership with these grants and that people who received a stipend would be required to work in the child welfare agency.

As a result of advocacy by the Action Network for Social Work Education and Research (a coalition of NASW, CSWE, the National Association of Deans and Directors of Schools of Social Work, the Association of Baccalaureate Social Work Program Directors, the Society for Social Work and Research, and the Group for the Advancement of

Doctoral Education), the Section 426 appropriation was increased to $7 million in 1997, where it remains to this day.

In response in part to a report from the GAO (2003) highlighting concerns related to the recruitment and retention of child welfare workers, the CB used some of its Section 426 funding to support eight 5-year recruitment and retention grants, each of which targeted critical issues in recruitment and retention of the child welfare workforce (Child Welfare Information Gateway, n.d.). To strategically use the $7 million appropriated for the Section 426 program, the CB, building on the strong outcomes of those eight recruitment and retention grants, announced a request for proposals in 2008 to create a national institute that would focus on workforce issues. The successful applicant, the University at Albany, created collaboration among the eight recruitment and retention grantees and the National Indian Child Welfare Association (NICWA). The National Child Welfare Workforce Institute (http://www.ncwwi.org) is now a collaboration among NICWA and nine universities (University at Albany, University of Denver, University of Southern Maine, University of North Carolina, University of Iowa, University of Michigan, Michigan State University, Portland State University, and Fordham University) and includes an array of training, knowledge exchange, and technical assistance strategies. This includes supporting traineeships involving 12 schools of social work, along with an online Leadership Academy for Supervisors and Leadership Academy for Middle Managers, and several other initiatives that address child welfare workforce concerns in the field. In 2008 the CB also funded five additional comprehensive workforce projects that included a traineeship component (see http://www.ncwwi.org/comprehensive.html for more information).

Although the Title IV-B Section 426 program continues to be an essential component of targeted workforce enhancement strategies, the reach of these funds is limited. The finite amount of the appropriation is no longer sufficient to support traineeships in 30 states as it did when it began in the 1960s. Although there have always been variations in how these funds are used, during the past 15 years, the CB has expanded the length of the grants to focus more on sustainable outcomes from this funding mechanism and has been much more directive and rigorous in how these funds are used and how the findings are disseminated.

A cohort of social work education programs regularly pursues the CB's grant announcements, causing stiff competition for the limited funds available. In addition, the reach of most of the funded initiatives supporting BSW and MSW education is local, statewide, and sometimes regional.

Because of the limitations of this appropriated pot of money and the opportunity that was identified in accessing Title IV-E entitlement funds to support BSW and MSW education, in the early 1990s states and social work education programs began to work more collaboratively to access these Title IV-E funds and to encourage sustainable university–child welfare agency partnerships.

TITLE IV-E ENTITLEMENT TRAINING FUNDING

Different from a discretionary grant program, Title IV-E is entitlement funding sent to states for services provided. Under the training entitlement, these funds can be accessed by colleges and universities to provide degree education through a contractual agreement with the state agency. Created by the Adoption Assistance and Child Welfare Act of 1980, Title IV-E provides federal support for foster care services for children who meet eligibility (based on the 1996 eligibility level) for the Assistance to Families with Dependent Children, now called Temporary Assistance to Needy Families) and adoption assistance for hard-to-place children.

One provision, Section 474A, specifically supports training by providing an enhanced federal match (Federal Financial Participation [FFP]) of 75% to states to train public child welfare staff or those preparing for employment in those agencies (GAO, 1993). Funds can be provided through state child welfare agencies to universities for curriculum development, classroom instruction, field instruction, or any combination of these that is directly related to the agency's program. Title IV-E provides funds to cover an array of educational supports, including faculty stipends or ongoing salaries for employees while receiving their degrees, leave costs, replacement staff for employees on educational leave, fieldwork instructors, evaluation of field units and curriculum, program coordinators, educational materials, books, supplies, tuition, travel, and stipends for students being recruited to work in public child welfare services (Zlotnik, 2002). The state must specify how it will use the training funds in its child and family services plan, which has to be approved by the

Department of Health and Human Services, and report specifics of its use in the quarterly Title IV-E expenditure report. Details of how these funds can be accessed can be found in the CB's *Child Welfare Policy Manual* (n.d.).

The legislation did note that the funds could be used for long-term training at educational institutions, and they could support those preparing to work for the state agency administering the Title IV-E plan (GAO, 1993, p. 3). It does not specifically state that funds can be used to educate social workers preparing for child welfare employment, although social work programs could receive such funds for this purpose (GAO, 1993).

Since the late 1980s a growing number of BSW and MSW programs, especially in public colleges and universities, have used Title IV-E funds to prepare students for child welfare careers, including efforts to enhance the social work education curricula, provide stipends and other supports to students, and cover the costs of field supervisors and field liaisons (Zlotnik, 2002).

Title IV-E training funding is of particular interest to social work education programs since it is a potential funding stream accessible in every state to support the preparation of social work students for child welfare careers. However, the findings of a national survey distributed in 1996 found that in 1989 only four states indicated they were accessing these funds for social work education; by 1996 the number had grown to 29 states (Zlotnik & Cornelius, 2000). According to a report from the Council on Social Work Education (CSWE, 2011), in 31 states 34.1% (147) of the administrators of 431 BSW programs who responded to the question use Title IV-E funding, and in 35 states and the District of Columbia, 50.3% (94) of the 187 MSW programs use funding from Title IV-E to prepare students to pursue careers in child welfare.

As it has turned out, the use of Title IV-E training funds to support BSW and MSW programs is extremely beneficial but often complex in implementation. Thus, these funds have not been used for social work education in every state; in the states that do access such funding, the size, scope, and consistency of BSW and MSW educational initiatives have varied (Social Work Policy Institute, 2012).

To best understand and appreciate why Title IV-E training funds to support BSW and MSW education are not accessed in every state requires an examination of the history of the use of Title IV-E funding in social work programs as well as an understanding of the policy and funding context and constraints that surround the Title IV-E entitlement overall, and IV-E training in particular.

USE OF THE TITLE IV-E TRAINING PROVISION

It is important to understand Title IV-E within the political context of its time. The legislation was passed and signed into law in the spring of 1980. However, the inauguration of Ronald Reagan in January 1981 brought major changes to the role of the federal government, curtailed federal technical assistance to states, and weakened the intent of the legislation by withdrawing the regulations drawn up by the Carter administration and replacing them with less-stringent regulations (Zlotnik, 1998). At the time of the law's passage, it was expected that there would be a major expansion in the federal role in foster care and adoption, and this would be coupled with a commitment to raise the quality and qualifications of staff working in public child welfare. The initial Notice of Proposed Rulemaking (NPRM), which was promulgated in December 1980, stated that "implementation requires a wide range of skills. . . . To ensure the availability of essential skills, staff training must be an important part of the State agency's management plan" (p. 86826) and "plans for staff recruitment and selection which will increase the number of professionally trained personnel so as to ensure that the task and responsibilities of child welfare workers required by the Act are handled with maximum competence" (p. 86844).

However, the NPRM was withdrawn, and the weakened final rules published in May 1983 gave little guidance to states regarding workforce issues. Funding for the Title IV-B Section 426 program and Title XX was also cut. At the time the Adoption Assistance and Child Welfare Act of 1980 was passed, one federal staff person surmised that Title IV-E training was probably intended to be used for staff training and that the other mechanisms through IV-B and XX would be used to support social work education (Zlotnik, 1998). In 1980 $13.5 million of Title XX funds were being used for educational leave (often in social work) and preparation for employment, and $31.4 million was being used for teaching grants to schools of social work and other schools (CSWE, 1980, p. 2). However, in 1980 a cap was put on Title XX training because of congressional concern that states were using federal dollars to supplant what they should have been using state dollars for (Zlotnik, 1998). Thus, the expectation of broad availability of Title IV-B Section 426 funds coupled with Title XX and Title IV-E funding to support the education and training of staff was never fully realized (Zlotnik, 1998).

In the early 1980s the national organizations—American Public Welfare Association (now the American Public Human Services Association [APHSA], NASW, CSWE, and the Child Welfare League of America (CWLA)—that had initially advocated for the legislation, as well as for federal support for the education of social workers to meet the needs of the growing number of child welfare and social service programs, focused on their own key priorities as funding for social programs was being dramatically cut and the CSWE began to experience its own fiscal crisis.

Thus, some of the collaborative work that had focused on the links between social work staff and enhanced service delivery faded away until a staffing crisis was declared later in the decade (Zlotnik, 1998, 2002). In the late 1980s the NASW launched an initiative to promote professional social work practice in public child welfare and embarked on renewed collaborations with the National Association of Public Child Welfare Administrators (NAPCWA, an affiliate of APHSA) and the CWLA (NASW Family Commission, 1989; Pecora, Briar, & Zlotnik, 1989; University of Southern Maine, 1987). This included hosting of several meetings that brought together agency directors, social work educators, and social work leaders to develop an agenda to address the burgeoning workforce crisis. It also included renewed efforts to collaborate among the national organizations mentioned previously and to increase conversations with CB staff about how to address agencies' workforce needs.

STRENGTHENING UNIVERSITY–AGENCY PARTNERSHIPS

Around the same time, from 1989 to 1990, administrators of several schools of social work began to discuss how they were using Title IV-E training funds to support social work students and to enhance the child welfare curricula in their schools. Realizing that the IV-E regulations mirrored earlier regulations of the Title IV-A foster care program, states and universities worked together to set up the financing (often using university overhead and faculty time as matching funds) and began to support students who were acquiring a BSW or MSW to pursue child welfare employment. In some instances, child welfare workers were provided the opportunity to return to school to earn an MSW degree.

Working with the NAPCWA, NASW hosted a colloquium in 1989 and also published *Addressing the Program and Personnel Crisis in Public Child Welfare* (Pecora et al., 1989). Social work educators, who had long been committed to child welfare, reengaged in their communities with their local agencies, and learning from the early adopters who used Title IV-E to support social work education began to develop child welfare training partnerships. NAPCWA invited representatives from NASW and CSWE to serve as organizational representatives on its executive committee, and sessions were planned that helped to foster university–agency IV-E partnerships and other strategies that would address agencies' workforce needs.

In 1991 the CB supported a cooperative agreement with Florida International University to support a range of efforts to foster agency–university partnerships, including development of the *Partnerships for Child Welfare* newsletter and hosting a major conference, the National Public Child Welfare Symposium, to promote partnerships (Briar, Hansen, & Harris, 1992). The efforts to access Title IV-E funds became a good example of what Everett Rogers (1995) talked about regarding innovation diffusion. Early adopters provided guidance to colleagues, serving as catalysts and consultants (Harris, 1996; Zlotnik, 1993, 1998, 2002). Charismatic leaders, including some deans of schools of social work and child welfare administrators, highlighted the value of these partnerships, and the Ford Foundation provided funding to CSWE to launch an initiative to promote university–agency human service partnerships (Harris, 1996; Zlotnik, 1993, 1997).

This effort to promote educational and training partnerships highlighted the importance of technical assistance and of using multiple avenues of communication. Not only was it important for interested faculty to engage with state and county public child welfare agencies, it was also important for deans and directors of social work education programs to engage with public child welfare administrators. CWLA hosted a 1992 meeting, and among other recommendations, encouraged deans and child welfare agencies to take each other to lunch (CWLA, 1992). In the same year, APHSA, in collaboration with the CSWE, hosted a meeting in San Diego that targeted bringing together agency administrators with their university partners. In addition, several experienced administrators and educators served as consultants, helping colleagues in other states set up the necessary contracts and program structures within the universities and within the state agencies to be able to access these funds to educate BSW and MSW students.

A briefing paper was developed on how the funds might be used to support social work education (Logan, 1991), and in March 1991 the *Federal Register* announcement by the CB for its Section 426 program encouraged grantees to form partnerships with their states to attempt to access IV-E funds.

The 1996 survey of all social work education programs found that by 1992, 24 programs were accessing these funds, and by 1996, 68 schools were accessing IV-E funds, with 91% of them beginning after 1991 (Zlotnik & Cornelius, 2000). There were large variations across the country, with at least one regional office making great efforts to help facilitate state–university partnerships, whereas several others provided little or no guidance (Zlotnik, 1998). According to Austin, Antonyappan, and Leighninger (1996), Title IV-E training would result in an expansive federal investment in social work education as had occurred with the briefly funded Section 707 of the 1967 Social Security Amendments to expand BSW education.

As noted earlier, the partnerships that began to develop in the states were also modeled at the national level. NASW, CSWE, NAPCWA, and CWLA began regular lunch meetings with the CB staff most responsible for workforce issues. This provided an opportunity to exchange ideas and resulted in the development of several workforce initiatives and conferences sponsored by the CB, as well as presentations on workforce issues and the use of Title IV-E funding at each organization's conferences. As new leaders joined the CB, this lunch group would set up a meeting to discuss the imperative of attending to workforce issues.

FACILITATORS OF AND BARRIERS TO PARTNERSHIPS

As these IV-E educational partnerships began to develop and mature, several different models occurred, often based on the history of relations between the universities and the child welfare agency, already existing child welfare capacity in a university, and other leadership and collaboration factors. Lawson and colleagues (2006) examined the facilitators of effective partnerships between universities and agencies to address public child welfare workforce issues, including

- unity of purpose,
- development of interdependent relationships,
- negotiation of specialized roles and responsibilities,
- shared power and authority,
- conflict resolution mechanisms,
- norms of reciprocity cemented by social trust,
- barrier-busting strategies, and
- embedded evaluations and continuous improvement.

In examining how universities and agencies can work together to enhance child welfare outcomes, these facilitators need to be juxtaposed to the barriers that may need to be eliminated in order to have successful partnerships. Barriers might include

- differing organizational values,
- differing philosophies,
- differing reward systems,
- differing priorities,
- lack of institutional commitment for the long term,
- differing time frames—the needs of agencies are often specific and immediate and the focus of academia is broader and not created to address a specific problem or concern,
- concerns about the complexity of public child welfare practice— faculty members may be hesitant to promote students' interest in pursuing child welfare careers because of the complexity and organizational environments of public child welfare practice and agency settings,
- inconsistencies in the recognition of and role for professional social work in public child welfare—child welfare agencies frequently do

not require an MSW or BSW degree for employment or advancement, providing limited incentive for social work graduates to seek jobs in those settings,

- absence of a funding stream that can preclude development of a long-range strategy since funding decisions are made in year-to-year contracts, and

- substantial time and resources required by both partners to establish and maintain collaborations at the leader level and among the staff and faculty involved. (Zlotnik, 2010 p. 335)

As these training partnerships develop, the university and agency players as well as other collaborators, such as foundations or NASW state chapters, need to keep the facilitators and barriers in mind as they effectively move the partnerships forward.

MODELS OF IV-E PARTNERSHIPS

During the past two decades, each IV-E partnership has been created with variations in structure and purpose. Some initiatives support only the education of BSWs for child welfare careers, some support only the education of MSWs, and some do both. In some states the target population is the people who are already working in child welfare, providing them an opportunity to return to school to acquire a social work degree, usually an MSW. In some states Title IV-E training supports a combination of employees returning to school as well as the preparation of new students for child welfare careers; in some states the target is solely encouraging social work students to pursue child welfare careers. In several jurisdictions, the university (or a consortium of universities) provides degree education and the public child welfare agency's preservice and in-service training for staff.

Of particular note are the states that have developed large-scale coordinated consortia bringing together several schools, developing coordinated curricula and evaluation mechanisms, and having one university take the lead administrative role with responsibility for coordinating with the state and overseeing other curricula development, policy, and evaluation efforts. Programs in California, Pennsylvania, and Kentucky are a few examples of this type of structure.

THE FLUIDITY OF TITLE IV-E PARTNERSHIP

As states and universities worked together to develop these partnerships, with the goals of increasing the number of people with BSW and MSW degrees in child welfare agencies, they were also faced with a number of issues that have led to changes in the size and scope of the partnerships. This has occurred because of changes in agency leadership. For example, a newly appointed child welfare commissioner or human services secretary may not see the value of these partnerships with the university or may not prioritize workforce issues and the interest in bringing more MSW and BSW workers into the agency. In addition, since the Title IV-E funding is tied to 1996 rates of children eligible for Aid to Families with Dependent Children, and there have been no rate adjustments during the past 16 years, states have less money available to them (CWLA, 2012; NAPCWA, 2010); thus, even with the 75% match, the funding mechanism has become less viable to support IV-E training efforts. In these times of tight state budgets, states that were providing some of the federal matching funds to the IV-E partnership may reprioritize how they wish to use their funds and not see this investment in social work education as a priority. In addition, states vary in the extent to which they hire and require staff to have social work degrees. As the state of Illinois sought to acquire recognition by the Council on Accreditation, it provided the opportunity for its child welfare supervisors to return to school to acquire an MSW degree (McDonald & McCarthy, 1999). Although two federal grants and some foundation initiatives addressed recruitment and retention issues, Michigan also eliminated its IV-E educational partnership in the first decade of this century. However, faced with workforce challenges, the state reported in 2009 it was seeking to reinstate it (personal communication, Carol Siemon, 2009).

In addition, as will be better understood from the next section on IV-E policy and its lack of clarity, some IV-E partnerships have decreased in size and scope or been terminated because of determinations by the federal regional office that the scope of the program may not meet federal policy guidelines or that the costs of the program were not allocated appropriately. *Funding Permanency Services: A Guide to Leveraging Federal, State, and Local Dollars* (Schmid, Freundlich, & Greenblatt, 2010) provides useful guidance for accessing and using Title IV-E training funds.

POLICIES GOVERNING TITLE IV-E TRAINING:
TWO DECADES OF AWAITING CLARIFICATION

As states and universities began to explore accessing Title IV-E training funds to support social work education, the number of steps to follow was based on vague policy guidance. Thus, different states and universities interpreted the policies differently. Because of this confusion, U.S. Senator Daniel Inouye requested a 1993 GAO report, which noted that "HHS [Department of Health and Human Services] and some states disagree on whether the federal government should help pay costs for training that benefits all children in foster care or costs for training that benefits only children in the IV-E foster care program" (GAO, 1993, p. 1). The GAO goes on to note that the dispute exists because Title IV-E policy does not discuss cost allocation and leaves room for multiple interpretations, further suggesting that Congress may want to clarify this issue; however, that has never occurred.

According to Section 8.1H8 of the CB's *Child Welfare Policy Manual*, and reiterated in *Funding Permanency Services* (Schmid et al., 2010), the costs for training must be allocated across all benefiting programs (CB, n.d; Schmid et al., 2010). But even as late as 2011 this was not the case in how all Title IV-E training partnerships were structured.

Although there has yet to be a legislative fix to the lack of clear policy guidance on IV-E training, in 1996 the Clinton administration attempted to clarify the problems universities and states were facing. On August 21, 1996, the *Federal Register* reported that the CB was seeking a "Request for Public Comments Concerning the Implementation and Management of Child Welfare Training for Which Federal Financial Participation Is Available Under Title IV-E of the Social Security Act." More than 160 comments were received from social work education programs, state and county child welfare agencies, students, and service recipients. CSWE (1996) analyzed the comments, noting that the benefits of using Title IV-E include (a) providing an opportunity for the career enhancement of workers who can return to school to obtain and MSW, (b) reenergizing staff by providing opportunities for new learning and enhancing skills, (c) educating a pool of workers who are ready to take on child welfare work, (d) supporting collaboration between the university (or a consortium of universities) and the public child welfare agency, (e) improving skills and knowledge of workers, (f) providing the opportunity for the agency to develop new services, (g) providing supports for agency service delivery by providing some additional workforce through field placements, and (h) providing new workers that supervisors say are able to hit the ground running more quickly than new hires.

The issues of concern that were identified related to IV-E degree education partnerships included

- variations in regional office interpretations, creating confusion in some instances where something approved by the regional office was later disallowed in an audit;
- inability to use private university matching funds;
- confusing interpretations of policy since they are based on outdated IV-A regulations, policy memos, audits, and departmental appeals board rulings; and
- interpretations appear to restrict the use of the program rather than supporting quality training for staff serving children and families (CSWE, 1996).

Although CB administrators asked for this input, for whatever reasons no revised policy guidance emerged from this request; thus, another 16 years have gone by, and the lack of clarity has continued. Many of the recommendations suggested in 1996 are still relevant, including the following:

- The 75% FFP should not need to be cost-allocated between Title IV-E eligible and non-Title IV-E eligible cases, since the same skills are required whether you serve one Title IV-E case or 20.
- The 75% FFP should apply to all real costs of training, including the costs of the administration of the training program.
- Title IV-E training funds should cover the costs of training based on the Adoption Assistance and Child Welfare Act and subsequent legislation supporting permanence, safety, and well-being, and not just be related to out-of-home placement.
- Because the policy is unclear, states and their university partnerships should be held harmless of interpretation discrepancies regarding Title IV-E training FFP.

- States should be encouraged to develop long-term training plans so agreements between the child welfare agency and the states do not need to be renegotiated annually (CSWE, 1996).

THE RECENT PAST AND A LOOK TO THE FUTURE

A 2003 GAO report titled *HHS Could Play a Greater Role in Helping Child Welfare Agencies Recruit and Retain Staff* indicated that university–agency Title IV-E training partnerships are promising practices for addressing the staffing crisis in child welfare, in part by improving recruitment and retention. Since 2003 Title IV-E educational partnerships have flourished in some states, been launched in some states, and been terminated or decreased in size in others. The results of the federally required Child and Family Services Review reinforced attention to workforce issues. For more than a decade Alberta Ellett, of the University of Georgia, has chaired the Child Welfare Symposium at the CSWE Annual Program Meeting, including convening a preconference exchange of university and agency representatives that is attended by about 150 people annually, mostly those involved in IV-E partnerships. In 2002 the National Association of Deans and Directors and NAPCWA convened for a national dialogue at the University of Minnesota to reinforce the criticality of addressing workforce issues to improve child welfare outcomes (Ferguson, 2002). In 2005 the CB once again convened a national conference, the Child Welfare Workforce Development and Workplace Enhancement Institute: Knowledge Development and Application, that brought together state representatives with their university partners to (a) highlight productive/action-planning strategies for recruiting and retaining a stable and skilled workforce, (b) share best practices, (c) develop innovative solutions to common challenges, and (d) build a shared knowledge base (CB, 2006). The presenters and participants included the eight recruitment and retention grantees and successful Title IV-E partnerships.

Following the launch of the Human Services Workforce Initiative by the Annie E. Casey Foundation, the Institute for the Advancement of Social Work Research and the University of Maryland (with funding from the Casey Foundation) carried out a systematic review of research on retention of child welfare workers. This review found that Title IV-E educational partnerships increased success in retaining staff and that these partnerships contributed to our knowledge base of child welfare workforce issues because of the requirement to evaluate the use of the IV-E funds (Zlotnik et al., 2005).

In addition, at the national level, the Children's Defense Fund and Children's Rights (2007), a national child welfare workforce policy working group, recognized that a competent, committed staff is the backbone of enhancing the delivery of child welfare services. The working group developed a set of legislative recommendations as well as some that could be implemented by the executive branch, which included being able to expand the use and scope of Title IV-E training and other recommendations related to data collection and workforce demonstration grants.

The National Child Welfare Workforce Institute that began in 2008 has helped facilitate communication among Title IV-E partners across states on program issues, created webinars to exchange ideas, and helped support the annual meeting Alberta Ellett had regularly convened at the CSWE Annual Program Meeting.

In the tight economic environment between 2009 and 2011 several universities reported that after many years their state had eliminated, reduced, or suspended their IV-E partnership program. This occurred just at the time when provisions in the Child Abuse Prevention and Treatment Reauthorization Act of 2010 and the Safe and Stable Families Program of the Social Security Act (reauthorized in the Child and Family Services Improvement and Innovation Act) brought renewed attention to addressing workforce concerns, and Bryan Samuels, commissioner of the Administration on Children, Youth and Families, had spoken extensively about the absence of the desired skills and competencies for child welfare workers. However, there is no clear funding source to ensure that the workforce has the suggested clinical competencies, a focus not currently directly supported by Title IV-E. In addition, national organizations have been working to develop new child welfare financing proposals that might broaden the Title IV-E entitlement to cover all children in need of services, not just foster care and adoption (NAPCWA, 2010).

In December 2011, because of concerns that some schools and states were no longer working to support BSW and MSW degree acquisition when states were trying to enhance the competency of the staff, the NASW Social Work Policy Institute launched an online survey to better understand the current status of Title IV-E educational partnerships. The online survey asked administrators of BSW and MSW programs that currently have or in the past 3 years have had a Title IV-E partnership to respond to questions related to program structure, benefits, and challenges. Results from the respondents indicated the following:

- One half of the IV-E programs offer BSW and MSW degrees, less than 20% are BSW only, and about 30% are MSW only.
- About two thirds of the educational partnerships have been operating for more than 15 years, and less than 5% have only been operating for less than five years.
- During the past 3 years about 70% of the Title IV-E educational partnership programs have remained the same or decreased, including five programs that have been terminated during this time. About 30% of the programs have grown during this period. For schools whose programs changed over the past 3 years, more than 50% of respondents indicated that it was because of funding, and about one third indicated it was because of policy interpretations. (Social Work Policy Institute, 2012).

For the past 20 years, the Title IV-E entitlement has served as a critical source of funding to support BSW and MSW education. Although the regulations have never been clear, and different states and universities have implemented the use of Title IV-E training funds in different ways, the percentage of social workers in child welfare has probably increased because of this funding source. Data from the 1970s and 1980s (Russell, 1987) suggested that less than 30% of child welfare staff had social work degrees. In 2008 the analysis of data from the National Study of Child and Adolescent Well-being found that number to be a little less than 40% (Barth, Lloyd, Christ, Chapman, & Dickinson, 2008). Perhaps equally important to the increase in the number of professional social workers in child welfare is the fact that there are new or renewed partnerships between child welfare agencies and social work education programs, helping to support research and training efforts as well (Institute for the Advancement of Social Work Research, 2008). Perhaps Austin and his colleagues (1996) were correct in forecasting the importance of Title IV-E in strengthening the federal investment in social work education.

To keep this moving forward will require nurturing the partnerships, ensuring that curricula are relevant to contemporary child welfare practice needs, ensuring that the organizational culture and climate of child welfare agencies are places that the best and the brightest social workers aspire to work, and keeping advocacy collaborations moving forward at the national and state levels to ensure that the linkages between a highly qualified workforce and improved outcomes for children and families are understood.

Regarding specific recommendations for the future, sustaining these education and training partnerships and continuing the professionalization of the child welfare workforce will require

- federal financing policies that continue to support mechanisms that will provide consistent and sustainable funding sources and educational and training strategies to ensure that the child welfare workforce has the necessary practice competencies to promote the health, safety and well-being of children, across the full array of child welfare programs, which should include support for specific policies that promote the acquisition of social work skills for the child welfare workforce;
- rigorous, multisite evaluation of Title IV-E educational partnerships to better ascertain their impact on social work education, staff recruitment and retention, and child welfare outcomes; and
- leadership and collaboration among national social work organizations, national provider organizations, child welfare advocates, and the CB to ensure there are continual strategies to educate and support the workforce.

A lot has been accomplished since the potential opportunity found in the enhanced FFP in Title IV-E of 75% to use for short- and long-term training was identified and promoted in the late 1980s. NASW, CSWE, CWLA, NAPCWA, and others must continue to ensure that policymakers and the public understand the importance of these workforce investments, not only for the recruitment and retention of child welfare workers, but also for the well-being of the children and families who come in contact with the child welfare system each day.

REFERENCES

Adoption Assistance and Child Welfare Act, 4 Stat. 500 (1980).

Austin, M. J., Antonyappan, J. M., & Leighninger, L. (1996). Federal support for social work education: Section 707 of the 1967 Social Security Amendments. *Social Service Review, 70*(1) 83–97.

Barth, R. P., Lloyd, E. C., Christ, S. L., Chapman, M., & Dickinson, N. S. (2008). Child welfare worker characteristics and job satisfaction: A national study. *Social Work, 53*(3), 199–209.

Briar, K., Hansen, V., & Harris. N. (Eds.). (1992). *New partnerships: Proceedings from the National Public Child Welfare Symposium.* Miami: Florida International University.

Child Abuse Prevention and Treatment Reauthorization Act, 124 Stat. 3459, (2010).

Child and Family Services Improvement and Innovation Act, 125 Stat. 369 (2011).

Children's Bureau. (1939). *Child-welfare services under the Social Security Act Title V, Part 3: Development of program 1936–1938* (Bureau Publication 257). Retrieved from http://www.mchlibrary.info/history/chbu/20688.pdf

Children's Bureau. (2006). *Child Welfare Workforce Development and Workplace Enhancement Institute: Knowledge development and application: Meeting report.* Washington, DC: Author. Retrieved from http://www.childwelfare.gov/pubs/wf_institute/intro.cfm

Children's Bureau. (2012). *The story of the Children's Bureau.* Retrieved from https://cb100.acf.hhs.gov/cb_ebrochure

Children's Bureau. (n.d.). *Child welfare policy manual.* Retrieved from http://www .acf.hhs.gov/cwpm/programs/cb/laws_policies/laws/cwpm/index.jsp

Children's Defense Fund and Children's Rights. (2007). *Promoting child welfare workforce improvements through federal policy changes.* Houston, TX: Cornerstones for Kids. Retrieved from http://www.childrensdefense.org/child-research-data -publications/data/promoting-child-welfare-workforce-improvements.pdf

Child Welfare Information Gateway. (n.d.). *Synthesis: Developing models of effective child welfare staff recruitment and retention training.* Retrieved from

http://www.childwelfare.gov/management/funding/funding_sources/synthe
sis/randrt.pdf

Child Welfare League of America. (1992). *Building partnerships: Schools and agencies advancing child welfare practice*. Washington, DC: Author.

Child Welfare League of America. (2012). *2012 legislative agenda for children & families*. Washington, DC: Author.

Council on Social Work Education. (1980, February 14). *Washington Alert* (80-800-04).

Council on Social Work Education. (1996). *Social work education programs and state child welfare agencies comment on Title IV-E regulations: An analysis of comments*. Alexandria, VA: Author.

Council on Social Work Education. (2011). *2010 statistics on social work education in the United States*. Retrieved from http://www.cswe.org/File.aspx?id=52269

Family Preservation and Support Provisions, 107 Stat. 312 (1993).

Ferguson, S. M. (Ed.). (2002). *Proceedings from professional education to advance child welfare practice: An invitational working conference*. St. Paul: MN: University of Minnesota School of Social Work.

General Accounting Office. (1993). *Federal policy on Title IV-E share of training costs*. Retrieved from http://www.gao.gov/assets/220/218667.pdf

Harris, N. (1996). *Social work education and public human services partnerships: A technical assistance document*. Alexandria, VA: Council on Social Work Education.

Lawson, H., McCarthy, M., Briar-Lawson, K., Miraglia, P., Strolin, J., & Caringi, J. (2006). A complex partnership to optimize and stabilize the public child welfare workforce. *Professional Development: The International Journal of Continuing Social Work Education, 9*(2), 122–139.

Logan, J. (1991). *Federal funding for child welfare training programs. P.L. 96-272, Adoption Assistance and Child Welfare Act of 1980: Briefing paper*. N. Miami Beach, FL: Jean S. Logan Management Group.

McDonald, J., & McCarthy, B. (1999). Effective partnership models between the state agencies, community, the university and community service providers. In *1999 Child Welfare Training Symposium. Changing paradigms of child welfare practice: Responding to opportunities and challenges* (pp. 43–72). Washington, DC: U.S. Children's Bureau.

National Association of Public Child Welfare Administrators. (2010). *Child welfare finance reform policy proposal*. Retrieved from http://www.napcwa.org/home/docs/NAPCWAFinancingProposal.pdf

NASW Family Commission. (1989). *The staffing crisis in child welfare: Report from a colloquium.* Silver Spring, MD: Author.

Notice of Proposed Rulemaking. (31 December 1980). *Federal Register, 45,* 86817-50.

Pecora, P., Briar, K., & Zlotnik, J. (1989). *Addressing the program and personnel crisis in child welfare: A social work response.* Silver Spring, MD: National Association of Social Workers.

Request for public comments concerning the implementation and management of child welfare training for which Federal Financial Participation is available under Title IV-E of the Social Security Act. (1996). *Federal Register, 61,* p. 43250.

Rogers, E. M. (1995). *Diffusion of innovations* (4th ed.). New York, NY: The Free Press.

Russell, M. (1987). *1987 national study of public child welfare requirements.* Portland, ME: University of Southern Maine, National Child Welfare Resource Center for Management and Administration.

Schmid, D., Freundlich, M., & Greenblatt, S. (2010). *Funding permanency services: A guide to leveraging federal, state, and local dollars.* Retrieved from http://www.aecf .org/KnowledgeCenter/Publications.aspx?pubguid={F818604B-BF1E- 4DA3-9A5B-513E9EE3011D}

Social Work Policy Institute. (2012). *Educating social workers for child welfare practice: The status of using Title IV-E funding to support BSW and MSW education.* Policy brief. Retrieved from http://www.socialworkpolicy.org /news/new-policy-brief-highlights-use-of-title-iv-e-funding-to-support -social-work-students.html

Temporary Assistance to Needy Families, Personal Responsibility and Work Opportunity Reconciliation Act of 1996, 110 Stat. 2105. (1996).

Title XX of the Social Security Act, Social Services Block Grant, Omnibus Budget Reconciliation Act, 95 Stat. 483 (1981).

University of Southern Maine. (1987). *Professional social work practice in public child welfare: An agenda for action.* Portland, ME: Author.

U.S. Department of Health, Education and Welfare. (1959). *Report of the advisory council on child welfare services.* Washington, DC: Author.

U.S. Department of Health, Education and Welfare. (1962). *Five decades of action for children: A history of the Children's Bureau.* Washington, DC: Children's Bureau.

U.S. Department of Health, Education and Welfare. (1965). *Closing the gap in social work manpower.* Washington, DC: Author.

U.S. General Accounting Office. (1993). *Foster care: Federal policy on Title IV-E share of training costs* (GAO/HRD 94-7). Washington, DC: Author.

U. S. General Accounting Office. (2003). *HHS could play a greater role in helping child welfare agencies recruit and retain staff* (GAO-03-357). Washington, DC: Author. Retrieved from http://www.gao.gov/new.items/d03357.pdf

Zlotnik, J. L. (1993). *Social work education and public human services: Developing partnerships.* Alexandria, VA: Council on Social Work Education.

Zlotnik, J. L. (1997). *Preparing the workforce for family-centered practice: Social work education and public human services partnerships.* Alexandria, VA: Council on Social Work Education.

Zlotnik, J. L. (1998). *An historical analysis of the implementation of federal policy: A case study of accessing Title IV-E funds to support social work education* (Unpublished doctoral dissertation). University of Maryland, Baltimore.

Zlotnik, J. L. (2002). Preparing social workers for child welfare practice: Lessons from an historical review of the literature. *Journal of Health & Social Policy, 15*(3/4), 5–21.

Zlotnik, J. L. (2010). Fostering university agency partnerships. In M. Testa & J. Poertner (Eds.) *Fostering accountability* (pp. 328–356). New York, NY: Oxford University Press.

Zlotnik, J. L., & Cornelius, L. (2000). Preparing social work students for child welfare careers: The use of Title I V-E training funds in social work education. *Journal of Baccalaureate Social Work, 5*(2), 1–14.

Zlotnik, J. L., DePanfilis, D., Lane, M. M., Daining, C., Summers, L., & Wechsler, J. (2005). *Factors influencing retention of child welfare staff: A systematic review of research.* Washington, DC: Institute for the Advancement of Social Work Research. Retrieved from http://www.socialworkpolicy.org/wp-content/uploads/2007/06/4-CW-SRRFinalFullReport.pdf

7

THE CHILDREN'S BUREAU'S INFLUENCE ON THE SOCIAL WORK CURRICULUM
One State's Experience

Bart Grossman and Sherrill Clark

t would not be an exaggeration to say that the staff of the Children's Bureau (CB) supported a process in the early 1990s that significantly altered the focus of social work education in the United States. From the 1970s through the 1980s, the most popular curriculum track in schools of social work was mental health. The efforts of the CB staff and their support of funding for child welfare training moved child and family social work to a much more central position in many, if not most, schools.

A key element in instituting this change was a modification in the funding formula of Title IV-E of the Social Security Act under the Adoption Assistance and Child Welfare Act of 1980, which increased the rate of matching funds to the states for certain aspects of child welfare social work training. Joan Levy Zlotnik, who was staff director of the Commission on Families of the National Association of Social Workers at the time the law was passed, played a significant role in making social work faculty aware of the funding possibilities. Katherine Briar-Lawson had been a child welfare administrator in Washington State and in the early 1990s was a faculty member at Florida International University. Briar-Lawson led the creation of one of the first state partnerships for child welfare social work training. She worked with the CB and found a cadre of staff who were eager to reach out to the schools of social work. Working with Children's Bureau project officer Jake Terpstra, she orchestrated a pivotal event: the National Public Child Welfare Training Symposium in 1991 (Briar, Hansen, & Harris, 1992). This event and the funding change it featured revolutionized child welfare training in social work education.

In California, Harry Specht, dean of the School of Social Welfare at the University of California, Berkeley, had shared the vision of the New Deal social workers. For him, social work was the central profession staffing the public social services poor families and children depended on. In the book *Unfaithful Angels: How Social Work Has Abandoned its Mission* (Specht & Courtney, 1994), Specht complained that social work was migrating from a concern for the poor to a focus on counseling the "worried well." Working with Ed Nathan, director of the Zellerbach Family Foundation in San Francisco, he had already brought together the regional leadership in child welfare and was looking for funding for a statewide stipend program for social work students who would make a career commitment to child welfare services.

SOCIAL WORK AND PUBLIC SOCIAL SERVICES: OVERCOMING THE OBSTACLES

To understand the background of this effort, and the obstacles the CB sought to overcome, it is important to acknowledge that social work's commitment to public services had always been tenuous. The profession began in the late 19th century in the Charity Organization Societies (Leiby, 1978). One aspect of these private philanthropies was the friendly visitor program. Friendly visitors were protosocial workers concerned with the moral uplift of the poor. In the early decades of the 20th century, these volunteers evolved into professional social workers and sought a scientific base for their work (Leiby, 1978; Trattner, 1999).

For a fairly short period, the search was in the macro social sciences, economics and sociology, and the goals of the emerging profession related to large-scale social change. But service agencies needed theory that could inform the booming business of direct practice. In the 1930s many social work leaders embraced a radical theory emerging in Europe called *psychoanalysis*. It seemed to offer concepts and tools that would help social workers understand and motivate individual clients. Unfortunately, it lacked all but the most general ideas about the effects of the social context. Its focus was on individual mental disorders, and so it drew the attention of social workers to psychology and mental health concerns (Leighninger, 1987; Trattner, 1999).

The commitment of social work to private nonprofit settings and to the individual as the locus for change thwarted the dreams of the New Deal social work pioneers who believed theirs would become the lead profession for the public agencies of the emerging welfare state. MSW social workers were never represented in large numbers in these public settings (see Chapter 4).

The Social Security Act, Public Welfare Amendments (1962) and the Social Services Amendments (1974) could have marked a change. With these acts, the government began to assume responsibility for the personal social services. This change did provide money for social work training and new employment opportunities. But the social work currents of the 1960s ran in two directions, and the public agencies got caught in the riptide (see Chapter 4). The 1960s saw an explosion of new individual and group treatment technologies. Although these approaches were critical of psychoanalytic and psychodynamic orthodoxy, most of them were equally lacking in an environmental perspective. These humanistic models tended to address clients looking for personal meaning in life, not for dealing with basic survival issues; so these approaches lent themselves to private, not public, agency practice (Trattner, 1999). On the other hand, the civil rights and other liberation movements pulled a significant part of the profession back to its roots in social change. For many in this group, social work in public agencies was a tool for repression, a way of regulating the poor (Piven & Cloward, 1971), certainly not for ending poverty.

Of course, there was truth in the charge, but the old saw about the baby and the bathwater was never more apt. The public agencies endured years of battering. Social work educators tended to lead the march, and social work students in public agency placements often acted more like fifth columnists than like interns. Some social workers pursued the path of psychotherapy and personal growth in the private sector; some took the path of social change into the streets. Few stayed in the social services, often enduring the disdain of their co-professionals (Trattner, 1999).

By 1980 the left jab of the 1960s was followed up with a right cross from the Reagan administration that seemed to put the War on Poverty on permanent hold. Federal support for social work training dropped to between 50% and 75% of previous levels. Jobs in the public sector were cut, and many of the remaining jobs were declassified. The extent of the profession's disinterest in the public agencies was reflected in the relatively feeble response to the declassification of social work positions (see Chapter 4). In the 1970s and 1980s social work and the public social services observed a sort of cease-fire, but by the late 1980s the schools of social work, the professional organizations, and the public agencies began to talk again. What changed?

A MUTUAL CHALLENGE

The saying goes, "The enemy of my enemy is my friend." Certainly the profession, the schools, and the public agencies had endured a mutual attack from the right for 20 years. It is natural they might begin to recognize the advantages of an alliance. Those social workers who had gone into the public social services and stayed had been slowly moving up in the ranks. Like the New Dealers, they believed in the *social* in social work, and they believed the person-in-environment perspective makes social workers uniquely qualified to serve the multiproblem clients they were seeing. Unfortunately, they were having difficulty attracting and retaining MSW workers. In spite of the fact that child welfare settings were perceived as primary training grounds for social workers,

> following 1970 and throughout much of the 1990s, fewer than 10% of MSW students' primary field of practice or social problem concentration was child welfare (although slightly higher percentages were placed in child welfare field settings between 1985 and 1995). Thus, the unresponsiveness of MSW programs and the minimization of the importance of the MSW as a preferred professional degree for public child welfare in combination with other policy and practice events helped contribute to the de-professionalization of public child welfare in the United States. These events would have a compounded effect as the service demands placed on child welfare agencies/systems would dramatically increase in the 1970s and 1980s. (Perry & Ellett, 2008, pp. 152–153)

In California, Perry (2001) discovered that MSW students' interest in child welfare ranged from 10.2% in 1992, prior to the inception of the California Social Work Education Center (CalSWEC) program, to 15.6 % in 1996 by the time the program had begun.

Finally, in the 1980s the nation and the profession woke up to the plight of children and families. Characterized by epidemics of drug use in the inner cities, the 1970s and 1980s had seen a marked growth in the population requiring services. Resources had not even begun to keep pace. One source of alarm was the horrendous stories of neglect, abuse, and death occurring among children in placement.

In Illinois the courts had ordered the counties to train their workers, and based on this mandate, the counties had turned to the social work schools for help. The CB offered Title IV Section 426 grants (Social Security Act, Title IV, Section 426) to academic institutions for social work training.

An informal CalSWEC study of California county departments of social services in 1989 found 25% of child welfare workers were MSWs, and one third of the 58 counties had no MSW staff at all (Santangelo, 1993). The tremendous growth of immigrant and minority populations in California had created a special recruitment problem for agencies in that state. The total child population was 9.3% African American and 28% Hispanic. The percentage of emergency-response-to-abuse clients was 15.9% African American and 27.8% Hispanic. The proportion of children in foster care as of January 1990 was 37.9% African American and 20.6% Hispanic. Professional direct service staff ethnicity, however, was 19.3% African American and 16.6% Hispanic. Even fewer of those minority workers held MSWs. For African American staff it was 2.7% of all direct service staff; for Hispanics it was 2.2% (Santangelo, 1993).

Simply not enough social workers of color were being prepared by California schools of social work to staff public child welfare agencies. Administrators of the schools and the agencies recognized a common need to address this problem. There had been increasing concern in segments of the social work education community about the drifting away of the profession from its commitment to the poor. Applications to schools of social work were growing. The schools were eager to incentivize students to direct their energy to the public sector and the most disadvantaged families and children.

CREATION OF CALSWEC

CalSWEC was and still is one of the most ambitious state collaborations among schools of social work and state and county governments in the country.[1] Similar programs existed in Florida, New Mexico, Iowa, New York, and Illinois, but no other included all the accredited MSW programs in the state. The model for the center emerged from the experience of the Bay Area Social Services Consortium (BASSC), a coalition of the three San Francisco Bay Area social work schools and nine county departments of social services. Begun in 1987, BASSC had addressed regional policy and practice issues in pediatric AIDS, child welfare risk assessment, homelessness, and family support policies.

With BASSC as a backdrop, the formation of a child welfare committee of the California Chapter of the National Association of Social Workers (NASW) and renewed interest in child welfare at the California State University, Fresno and Long Beach, the county welfare directors and the deans met in 1988 to discuss state-level action. There were significant barriers. A state child welfare stipend program had ended 10 years previously because the directors of county social services felt the schools were not preparing students well for the work. Some agency directors were leery of the schools' new interest. BASSC had helped convince key Bay Area directors that the interest was sincere, but it took a while for others to commit. So prior to the start of the partnership, there was distrust: The academics felt the public social services were not good places to practice professional social work, and the county directors felt the schools offered education that was irrelevant and perhaps harmful to the client problems with which they dealt.

Funding was a key problem. An early effort to secure federal funds using a state match had died in 1989 in a state budget crisis. However, the structure of Title IV-E provided for the prospect of a program matched through university overhead. In this regard, federal Region 9 staff of the Administration of Children and Families played an indispensable role in demonstrating to the California Department of Social Services (CDSS) that the program could be created without a commitment of state funds.

As a show of good faith, the schools agreed to adopt, for the first time, a common statement of mission. The statement reads in part:

> The mission is the preparation of social workers for a wide range of pro-
> fessional leadership and practice roles addressing the needs of oppressed
> and disadvantaged persons and communities through publicly-supported
> services. . . . Priority recipients of direct social work services will be seen as
> the poor and the underserved. . . . The primary locus of practice will be in
> institutional systems supported by the public. . . . Essential modes of prac-
> tice will be those most relevant to these clients and systems . . . including
> but not limited to resource provision, case management, support and
> counseling, skill development, integration of services, administration and
> planning and empowerment strategies. (California Deans and Directors
> of Graduate Education for Social Work and Social Welfare, 1989)

Through the connections of Ed Nathan of the Zellerbach foundation, Specht learned that the Ford Foundation was looking to the social work profession to provide the staff required to implement new federal initia-tives in child welfare (Adoption Assistance and Child Welfare Act of 1980). In partnership with a group of local foundations including Zellerbach, Ford agreed to provide $1 million of startup funding for a center that would have three goals:

- provide significant financial aid to students, particularly those already employed in the public social services and members of ethnic and racial minority groups, who would upon graduation commit to a year of employment in public child welfare for each year of financial support;
- develop a competency-based curriculum for child welfare with the full involvement of faculty and agency personnel; and
- work to improve departmental service programs to enhance client outcomes and the desirability of long-term employment in public child welfare.

The center had start-up funding, and grant author Bart Grossman became the first director. At its first statewide conference in 1991, a stipend agreement in principle was signed by the president of the CalSWEC Board of Directors, the president of the California Chapter of NASW, the president of the California Welfare Director's Association (CWDA), and the deputy director for Children and Families of the California Department of Social Services (CDSS). However, the creation of a contract to provide stipends ultimately took 2 years of work between the schools, the state, the counties, and the Administration of Children and Families. During this period, the coalition of the CDSS— 58 counties, 3 universities, 10 schools of social work, and NASW—remained a fragile creature. Here, once again, the CB played a crucial role.

In 1998 the three accredited graduate social work schools in Los Angeles established a separate partnership with the Los Angeles Department of Social Services called the InterUniversity Consortium (IUC). The IUC is a nonprofit entity formed to provide short-term academy training to newly hired child welfare workers and 1-year stipends to employees of the Los Angeles County Department of Children and Families.

When the deans of the other schools of social work learned that Los Angeles had taken this step with no consultation, a great deal of dismay was expressed. At that moment it appeared the larger coalition might collapse. Eventually cooler heads prevailed, and a compromise was achieved whereby each school would receive a maximum of 20 full-time student stipends per year, but any Title IV-E stipends supplied through a different source would be subtracted from that school's total. The IUC was then seen as a precursor to CalSWEC, which set a precedent in the state. CalSWEC eventually negotiated a higher match rate on Title IV-E funding, and the three schools of social work later became CalSWEC subcontractors.

In 1991 CalSWEC was awarded a 5-year Title IV-E Section 426 Interdisciplinary Child Welfare Training Grant by the CB. It was the largest of 11 such grants throughout the United States. As the project emerged, the training program was designed to accelerate development of the central CalSWEC effort while allowing exploration of specialized education for interdisciplinary practice. The term *interdisciplinary* was interpreted in two ways:

- as a range of knowledge from a wide variety of disciplines (social work, law, mental health, medicine and public health, and management and public administration) required for effective professional social work practice in child welfare (diffusion of knowledge), and

- as a set of skills needed by social workers to effectively communicate with and link other professionals involved in serving child welfare clients (Grossman & McCormick, 2003).

The program provided an educational stipend of $8,000 to one 2nd-year student at each of the 10 MSW programs. This important recognition from the CB and the flow of stipends was a key demonstration of the power of a statewide consortium to attract funding and support the work of all the schools (Grossman & McCormick, 2003).

In addition to the funding provided, the CB brought the grantees and other state program leaders together annually and in special meetings, including a national meeting hosted by CalSWEC. These gatherings furthered the dissemination of best practices in education and service development. These CB efforts brought the schools of social work to the tipping point of change, moving toward an emphasis on public child welfare as a central direction in social work training. They also reinforced and in some cases created working partnerships between state child welfare agencies and the schools.

In 1992 the state of California and CalSWEC, under the auspices of the regents of the University of California, signed their first contract providing 20 two-year, full-time MSW stipends of $15,000 per year for each school. The contract supported faculty, staff, and necessary equipment to manage the program. In time, funds were added for research and evaluation to serve as the foundation for empirically based curricula and the creation of a child welfare library housed at California State University, Long Beach that serves as a central dissemination point for the empirically based curricula. The 10 deans and directors became principal investigators for their Title IV-E programs and the foundation of the CalSWEC board along with representatives from CDSS, CWDA, NASW, and private foundations. Because of the history of social work involvement with children and families, and in large part because of the supply of MSWs in California, the MSW is considered the entry-level professional practice degree; so until 2005 all the Title IV-E graduates in California were MSWs.

A strong supportive structure of project coordinators at each school who still meet regularly to attend to curriculum development was built into the CalSWEC subcontracts with all 10 accredited social work programs at California universities. The first project coordinators were mostly public child welfare agency field liaisons or instructors who came to the universities with strong public child welfare connections and experience. Lately, more project coordinators are Title IV-E graduates.

CURRICULUM DEVELOPMENT

Curriculum development for the Title IV-E child welfare project took a unique shape. Rather than create a lock-step curriculum for all the schools, CalSWEC undertook a highly collaborative approach to developing competencies (Clark, 2003). A very broad set of child welfare competencies was gleaned from a wide-ranging review of the literature. Staff added competencies that were deemed missing from the literature that applied to work in agencies and to California's diverse population. A committee of faculty and agency leaders reviewed and refined the competency list. The initial set of 76 core competencies was approved by the board in 1991, and each school was directed to formulate its own curricular model to meet the competencies. They were guided by a values statement drawn from NASW's ethical principles for working with families.

From the beginning the curriculum was evaluated using the curriculum snapshot instrument in which project coordinators documented progress on teaching the competencies, finding appropriate field placements, and ongoing efforts for county and university partnerships, such as committee membership, guest lecturing, and participation on the Title IV-E student admission committees. Other efforts to draw in faculty at the schools consisted of small curriculum development grants to address gaps in the public child welfare curriculum and to develop products that could be used by all member schools either in the classroom or in the field.

Curriculum development has continued with a unique mutual involvement of faculty, practitioners, and agency leaders. The CalSWEC board's Curriculum Committee oversees curriculum modification to address gaps noted in the schools' snapshots. Meetings with field faculty about how to apply the competencies in the field occur on a regular basis, and innovative field instruction curriculum development projects are supported throughout the state. At periodic statewide curriculum modification meetings, agency directors and child welfare directors are able to express their needs for specific knowledge and skills. The competencies have been modified in 1995, 2002, 2007, and in 2011. For some agency leaders, it was the first time they saw the social work education process not only as meeting their need for professional staff skills and knowledge but also as providing the most up-to-date and relevant education for new employees in the context of social work values for engaging families and children in the system. It may also have been the first time the social work educators were receptive to regular input from the practitioners themselves to develop curriculum for teaching social work students to work in agencies with disadvantaged families (Clark, 2003). The process continues to be highly collaborative and iterative.

In 2011 the curriculum competencies were aligned with the Council on Social Work Education's (CSWE's) 2008 *Educational Policy and Accreditation Standards*, a competency-based curriculum approach. The MSW competencies for public child welfare are integrated foundation and advanced competencies (CalSWEC, 2011a). The CalSWEC competencies also served as the basis for in-service training delivered by the regional training academies statewide in the common core curriculum for newly hired child welfare workers (Clark, 2003). The public child welfare competencies are consistent to provide a learning continuum for public child welfare workers from preservice through in-service training, whether or not the new worker has an MSW. Therefore, the social work curriculum is influencing public child welfare worker and supervisor practice statewide.

Distance Education

The rural northern and eastern parts of California are beautiful and isolated. When CalSWEC began in the 1990s, the closest school of social work to the northernmost part of the state was in Sacramento, at least 300 miles away and difficult to access. Consequently a part-time educational option was added in 1994, and distance education programs were created for underserved regions in the northern rural part of the state in 1995. These 3-year, weekend programs, administered by California State University,

Long Beach, used synchronous video technology to conduct classes at Humboldt State University and Chico State University, using Long Beach's curriculum. At the time, neither Chico nor Humboldt had an MSW program, but each did have an undergraduate BASW program. Field liaisons were hired by the two distance education sites with field instructors from the local communities. The project coordinators were based at Long Beach.

The evaluation indicated that this program was highly successful in terms of retention of students and number of graduates (Potts & Hagan, 2000). The students were all county employees who met every Saturday for 3 academic years, including summer block placements with field seminars. Each student had one field experience in a private nonprofit agency and one field placement in the county child welfare agency that was different from the student's job unit assignment, including in some instances when the students participated in indirect services, such as evaluation and program planning. Two cohorts of students went through this program before Chico and Humboldt were able to achieve candidacy from the CSWE and launch their own MSW programs.

Responding to the Need for BASWs

As early as 1995–1996, CalSWEC considered development of a baccalaureate option for child welfare stipends. Again, in certain areas of the state the need was for college-educated child welfare workers. A market study prior to implementation of the BASW program indicated the need for BASWs in the northern region and central region counties, which preferred BSWs to general baccalaureate degrees. Initially three schools of social work whose baccalaureate programs were already operational (including the two that had the distance education programs) were designated to have BASW student stipends and financial support for those seeking jobs in public child welfare agencies.

The Title IV-E BASW program was established in fiscal year 2004–2005 to meet county employees' needs for professional career paths and to meet the California State University system's needs for providing access to a college education for those who may not otherwise be able to complete college. Thirty-eight (63%) California counties responded to a CalSWEC needs assessment in 2004. County officials estimated that 200 BASWs could be hired over a period of 3 years. Officials of 34 counties indicated they would hire BASWs and provide field placements for them. Officials of 37 counties indicated they could provide release or flex time to employees to obtain their degree.[2] Central, Mountain Valley, and Northern CWDA regions' regional educational efforts led to the development of more agency-based field instructors and shared field instruction models in the rural areas to support BASW students. The needs assessment determined that in rural areas, BASW interns could expect to do home visiting, some case management, service plan development, and court assistance; provide transportation; and participate in foster home recruitment and licensing, data entry, information and referral, differential response, report generation, and interviewing (CalSWEC, 2005).

Challenges for the BASW program included the problem that county employees who were not in child welfare already might not be supported by their home departments, because upon graduation they would go to child welfare and not return to their home departments. Two academic issues were the lack of availability of general education classes in the community colleges to bring potential BASW students into a 4-year college and conflict between work and class schedules for part-time students.

Empirically Developed Curricula

As faculty at the participating universities learned more about CalSWEC, interest naturally grew with the possibility of research support for curriculum enhancement. Title IV-E would not pay for pure research, but Region 9 of the Administration of Children and Families staff accepted the concept of empirically based curriculum development projects that would employ research strategies to test practice and policy approaches and generate curricular modules based on best practices. Uniquely, through this vehicle the agencies were able to play a pivotal role in directing research and scholarship activities. Most of these projects' curricula and research reports are available at the California Child Welfare Library in Long Beach and online at the CalSWEC website (http://calswec.berkeley.edu/). Topics supported by the CalSWEC board's Research and Development Committee are generated through a mutually cooperative development process with CWDA's Children's Services Committee and five regional consortia.

Child Welfare In-Service Training

As the CalSWEC collaboration matured and stabilized, the state of California also began to see CalSWEC as a useful structure for a variety of other child welfare–related activities. In 1995 CalSWEC's Regional Training Academy project, mentored by Nancy Dickinson, supported the development of three new regional academies and incorporated two existing regional training entities to provide formative and ongoing training of agency staff. Three of the four regional training academies are administered directly by university schools of social work.[3] The Northern California Training Academy, a part of University of California, Davis Extension's Center for Human Services, had been operating for 20 years to provide short-term training to the northern part of the state (mostly rural and frontier counties). Although not attached to a school of social work, it is still part of a university and remains part of the CalSWEC coalition. The IUC of the Los Angeles County Department of Children and Families is also a full partner in the Regional Training Academy Project.

As a result of legislation, in 1998 the California Department of Social Services contracted with CalSWEC to develop a standardized core training program for all newly hired public child welfare workers to learn the "fundamental principles of good child welfare practice, and to recommend ways to deliver the curriculum to each new child welfare worker prior to assuming a full caseload" (California Social Work Education Center, 2000). The Common Core, as it is now called, is closely linked to the CalSWEC competencies, which provide a basis for the continuum of learning for all California public child welfare workers.

In 2002 CalSWEC, the California training academies, and the consortium began development of a statewide evaluation of common core training. This evaluation is part of the strategic plan for multilevel evaluation of child welfare training in California. The purpose of the plan is to develop rigorous methods to assess and report effectiveness of training so the findings can be used to improve training and training-related activities. Developers of the Common Core evaluations are following a rigorous process to ensure that test items reflect the competencies, learning objectives, and content of the curricula, and measure trainee learning as accurately and consistently as possible. Knowledge test plans, test items, and embedded skills assessment tools have been developed and critiqued. Early results indicated that trainee knowledge from pre- to posttest increased at a statistically significant level. CalSWEC Title IV-E MSW graduates scored significantly higher at pretest and posttest than trainees who had not participated in a Title IV-E program, regardless of educational level. CalSWEC Title IV-E MSW graduates scored significantly higher than non-Title IV-E MSWs in the topic modules Family Engagement in Case Planning and Case Management, Permanency and Placement, and Child Maltreatment Identification, Physical Abuse (CalSWEC, 2012a).

The Child Welfare Fellows Project

Connecting applied practice-oriented research with curriculum improvement has been a major goal of CalSWEC since its inception. The Child Welfare Fellows Project was promoted by Judith Jhirad-Reich at the CB and designed for tenured faculty at schools of social work across the country to conduct public child welfare practice research and apply the learning to one or more courses taught to undergraduate or graduate social work students. CalSWEC was awarded a 3-year 426(c) grant to accomplish this. From 1995 to 1999, 24 fellows, who received a small stipend matched by their universities, conducted research in collaboration with public and private child welfare agencies and with one tribal agency. Topics ranged from evaluating parenting programs to documenting disparities in rates of American Indian children in foster care to retention of IV-E graduates. Fellows attended three institutes at Berkeley to share their findings and curriculum applications with their cohorts. Their topics varied from evaluating parent education methods to forensic interviewing to determining retention factors in the workforce. A major part of the learning involved creating sustainable research partnerships with agencies and practitioners.

HOW DO WE EVALUATE SUCCESS?

Two tools that enable evaluation of the IV-E program in California are the CalSWEC Student Information System (CSIS), which is used to keep track of graduates' work obligations, and the evaluation framework. As part of the contractual arrangement between CalSWEC and member universities, a statewide database is kept at CalSWEC, which is updated monthly by administrative staff at the member schools. Using the CSIS, CalSWEC can track the completion and retention rate of CalSWEC students and gradu-. ates. The CSIS allows CalSWEC to generate graduates' contact information for evaluation surveys and interviews. This is accomplished with the oversight of the Center for the Protection of Human Subjects at Berkeley.

The integrated evaluation framework states:

> The purpose of the CalSWEC evaluation framework, which applies to all CalSWEC initiatives, is to assess the effects of CalSWEC's educational and training programs on increasing the quantity and quality of social workers in California who work with disadvantaged populations in public human services, including how well they are prepared (knowledge, skills, and values) and retained in their respective fields. Broad, systematic dissemination of results is intrinsic to CalSWEC's overall goals and supports the implementation of new policies, evidence-based practices, curricula, and new practice models for public human services. (CalSWEC, 2011c)

The CalSWEC evaluation is driven by state and federal regulations regarding education and training, which require evaluation that includes, at a minimum, scanning program elements, counting the program's participants and graduates' outcomes and the program's successes and challenges, listing needed resources, and disseminating results broadly. The evaluation framework is aligned with CalSWEC's mission and goals, which leads us to evaluate the extent to which CalSWEC's efforts have increased the numbers of professionally educated public sector social workers who work with the poor and disadvantaged and have diversified the professional workforce by creating access to higher education and in-service training.

The evaluation promotes efforts to increase and improve the workforce necessary for the improvement of client services. It includes the following activities, which CalSWEC is obligated to accomplish:

- tracking the count and diversity of the population of public human services social workers in California;
- monitoring the number and characteristics of students and graduates who apply for and who accept support through CalSWEC programs;

- tracking the numbers of graduates who complete their work obligations;
- evaluating pre-service and in-service curricula content, incorporating regular stakeholder review, with the goal of moving toward best practices in education and training for human services;
- identifying, promoting, and evaluating alternative educational and in-service training delivery models which prepare the public sector workforce;
- evaluating the student field experience, including the available opportunities, curriculum, and transfer of learning;
- comparing how well CalSWEC students and trainees are prepared to those who are not similarly prepared, including their impact on practice, policy, and program; and
- examining retention post-work obligation or training to determine factors that influence retention. (CalSWEC, 2010)

New Graduate Survey

As one means of evaluating the curriculum, about 6 months after graduation, CalSWEC staff sends a new graduate survey via e-mail to all MSWs who graduated from the Title IV-E program from all schools the previous spring. This survey grew out of focus groups Sherrill Clark conducted from 1995 to 1999. The main purpose is to gain their perspectives as newly hired workers on how well their schools' curricula prepared them for work in a public child welfare agency. A report for that year's cohort is presented for consideration to the school project coordinators, many of whom are responsible for the content in the field seminars. New graduates critique the quality of their field 1st- and 2nd-year placement, and the availability of classes and curriculum material that helped or would have helped them on the job. Aggregated summaries were provided to the project coordinators for the years 2004–2009. Mental health needs of child welfare families, content on substance use and its effects on children and families, and case management are frequently noted by the new graduates. Recent developments to address the new graduates' issues are field instruction improvement projects and webinars on the topics new graduates have noted for faculty to integrate into their classes.

The Entry-Graduation Study

As a baseline measure to determine if interest in public child welfare was succeeding, CalSWEC conducted the Time1-Time2 Study with all entering and graduating MSW students from 1992 (prior to the implementation of the Title IV-E stipend program) through 2003 to determine if the MSW program influenced their interest in working with the poor and disadvantaged. This study emphasized how important it was to recruit the right people for the public child welfare program (Perry, 2003) and that minority students had more desire to work with the poor than majority students (Limb & Organista, 2003), but as a whole, social work graduate school influenced most students in the direction of providing services to the poor as a priority (Clark, 2007).

Retention

Partners from CalSWEC member universities have studied their own graduates (Jones & Okamura, 2000), reporting positive retention of Title IV-E graduates. The Title IV-E graduates have a year-for-year work obligation for receiving graduate school support. Most of them are in school for 2 years. Consequently, we survey them postwork obligation. Our 3-year retention studies show that those who stay in child welfare differ significantly from those who leave shortly after their work obligation is completed (Benton, 2010). Worker characteristics (being of mixed ethnicity and cohort) and previous county employment (except when county differences were controlled for) predicted retention. Furthermore, at least one variable from each of these categories predicted retention: extrinsic job factors (salary, hours, and supervisor support), intrinsic job factors (level of success), and response-to-job factors (client-related stress). One worker characteristic (cohort) and two response-to-job factors (burnout/emotional exhaustion and visit-related stress) were significantly associated with leaving. Perceived supervisor support significantly increased the odds of several types of job satisfaction, except client-related job satisfaction. Peer support increased the odds of client-, growth-, office-, and salary-related job satisfaction (Benton, 2010).

A retrospective study of a sample ($n=415$) of graduates who graduated between 1993 and 2003 showed that the mean length of stay in the first job was 43 months; for the career in child welfare the median was 168 months. These graduates continue to serve children and families in public and related nonprofit agencies for at least 5 years after graduation. Support for licensure, additional on-the-job training, and becoming supervisors were correlated to retention (Clark, Uota, & Smith, 2010).

THE PROPORTION OF MSWS IN THE CALIFORNIA PUBLIC CHILD WELFARE WORKFORCE

The California Public Child Welfare Workforce Study, also known as the Workforce Study, conducted since 1992 prior to the start of the Title IV-E program, is a statewide study of the child welfare workforce. In collaboration with CWDA and CDSS, CalSWEC surveys the 58 counties and their child welfare staff members. The data gathered from these studies help ensure that the CalSWEC staff has the best information possible to guide resources for meeting the short- and long-term educational needs for all child welfare workers in California.

The Workforce Study is the only statewide attempt to glean a census of all California public child welfare staff, their positions, service assignments, and educational levels. It has been conducted, with researchers refining the methods along the way, every 3 years since 1992. Prior to the implementation of Title IV-E in California in 1993, the percentage of MSWs working in public child welfare agencies was estimated by the counties to be around 21% (Santangelo, 1993). Twenty years later the percentage of MSWs (39%) in county public child welfare agencies has nearly doubled, largely because CalSWEC created a growing supply of appropriately trained professionals (CalSWEC, 2012b). CalSWEC continues, now in its 22nd year, as a vibrant statewide partnership and a national leader in educating social work students for the public social services and the many nonprofit agencies that rely on public funding. There are now 21 member universities providing stipends to students for public child welfare practice. Even in tight state budget times, CalSWEC has continued to express the common vision of the schools and public agencies.

Had CB staff not initiated and supported the effort to unlock Title IV-E as a source of funding for MSW education, it is highly unlikely that CalSWEC would have survived its early years. Although California's economy has been badly damaged in the recession, and jobs for MSW social workers are tight, Title IV-E graduates continue to find employment in the state. So far 4,634 child welfare social workers have graduated through the CalSWEC Title IV-E program. In 2011, 475 students were enrolled in good standing. There were 358 graduates statewide in 2011 with a commitment to work in public child welfare services (CalSWEC, 2011b). In spite of poor economic conditions, by the end of September 2011, 79% of the 2011 MSW graduates had found appropriate jobs (D. Thoreson, personal communication, February 2, 2012).

Though most of the visionaries in the CB, in California social work education, and in the public agencies that created this program have retired and some, sadly. are deceased, CalSWEC continues to hold to their vision and should continue to influence social work education and child welfare practice in the state for many years to come.

REFERENCES

Adoption Assistance and Child Welfare Act, 94 Stat. 500 (1980).

Benton, A. (2010). *Why do they stay? Building a conceptual model to understand worker retention and turnover in public child welfare* (Unpublished doctoral dissertation). University of California, Berkeley.

Briar, K. H., Hansen, V. H., & Harris, N. (Eds.). (1992). *New partnerships: Proceedings from the National Public Child Welfare Training Symposium 1991.* Miami: Florida International University Press.

California Deans and Directors of Graduate Education for Social Work and Social Welfare. (1989). *Mission statement for the establishment of the California Social Work Education Center.* Long Beach, CA: Author.

California Social Work Education Center. (2000). *Common core curricula for child welfare social workers.* Retrieved from http://calswec.berkeley.edu/common -core-curricula-child-welfare-workers

California Social Work Education Center. (2005). *2004–2005 annual report.* Unpublished manuscript, University of California, Berkeley.

California Social Work Education Center. (2010). *The new evaluation framework.* Retrieved from http://calswec.berkeley.edu/files/uploads/updated _calswec_evaluation_framework.pdf

California Social Work Education Center. (2011a). *Integrated foundation and advanced competencies: For public child welfare in California.* Retrieved from http://calswec .berkeley.edu/CalSWEC/CW_Competencies_Revised_2011.pdf

California Social Work Education Center. (2011b). *Title IV-E stipend program final report: July 1, 2010-June 30, 2011.* Unpublished report, University of California, Berkeley.

California Social Work Education Center. (2011c). *The CalSWEC evaluation framework.* Unpublished manuscript, University of California, Berkeley.

California Social Work Education Center. (2012a). *Report to the CalSWEC board, February 2012: Secondary analysis of child welfare in-service training data comparing Title IV-E and non-Title IV-E graduates.* Retrieved from http://calswec.berkeley.edu /CalSWEC/TrainEval_IV-EReport_Feb2012_FINAL.pdf

California Social Work Education Center (2012b). *Preliminary analysis of the 2011 workforce study.* Unpublished report, University of California, Berkeley.

Clark, S. J. (2003). The California collaboration: A competency-based child welfare curriculum project for master's social workers. *Journal of Human Behavior in the Social Environment, 7*(1/2), 135–157.

Clark, S. J. (2007). Social work students' perceptions of poverty. *Journal of Human Behavior in the Social Environment, 16*(1/2), 149–166.

Clark, S. J., Uota, K., & Smith, R. J. (2010, October). *Sustaining specially trained child welfare workers over the long-term.* Paper session presented at the Council on Social Work Education 56th Annual Program Meeting, Portland, OR.

Council on Social Work Education. (2008). *Educational policy and accreditation standards.* Retrieved from http://www.cswe.org/Accreditation/Handbook.aspx

Grossman, B. F., & McCormick, K. (2003). Preparing social work students for interdisciplinary practice: Learnings from a curriculum development project. *Journal of Human Behavior in the Social Environment, 7*(1/2), 97–113.

Jones, L. P., & Okamura, A. (2000). Reprofessionalizing child welfare services: An evaluation of a Title IV-E training program. *Research on Social Work Practice, 10,* 607–621. Abstract retrieved from http://rsw.sagepub.com/content/10/5/607

Leiby, J. (1978). *A history of social welfare in the United States.* New York, NY: Columbia University Press.

Leighninger, L. (1987). *Social work: Search for identity.* Westport, CT: Greenwood Press.

Limb, G., & Organista, K. (2003). Comparisons between Caucasian students, students of color, and American Indian students on their views on social work's traditional mission, career motivations, and practice preferences. *Journal of Social Work Education, 39,* 91–109.

Perry, R. E. (2001). The classification, intercorrelation, and dynamic nature of MSW student practice preferences. *Journal of Social Work Education, 37,* 523–542.

Perry, R. E. (2003). Who wants to work with the poor and homeless? *Journal of Social Work Education, 39,* 321–341.

Perry, R. E., & Ellett, A. J. (2008). Child welfare: Historical trends, professionalization, and workforce issues. In B. White (Ed.), *Comprehensive handbook of social work and social welfare* (pp. 143–184). Hoboken, NJ: Wiley. doi:10.1002/9780470373705.chsw001012

Piven, F. F., & Cloward, R. (1971). *Regulating the poor: The functions of public welfare.* New York, NY: Pantheon.

Potts, M. K., & Hagan, C. B. (2000). Going the distance: Using systems theory to design, implement, and evaluate a distance education program. *Journal of Social Work Education, 36,* 131–145.

Santangelo, A. (1993). *The 1991 class of entering graduate students in California's ten schools and departments of social work* (Unpublished doctoral dissertation). University of California, Berkeley.

Social Security Act, Public Welfare Amendments, 76 Stat. 172 (1962).

Social Security Act, Title IV, Section Sec. 426.42 U.S.C. 626 (a)(1)(C)

Social Services Amendments of 1974, Pub. L. No. 93-647 (1974).

Specht, H., & Courtney, M. (1994). *Unfaithful angels: How social work has abandoned its mission.* New York, NY: The Free Press.

Trattner, W. I. (1999). *From poor law to welfare state: A history of social welfare in America* (6th ed.). New York, NY: The Free Press.

NOTES

1   Much of this history of CalSWEC is based on the recollections of the authors, who were both involved in its creation.

2   Los Angeles County officials did not respond, but the Los Angeles Department of Children and Family Services regularly hires BA workers.

3   Fresno State University administers the Central Training Academy and the Bay Area Academy, temporarily, and San Diego State administers the Southern Academy.

DISSEMINATION AND TECHNICAL ASSISTANCE
The Evolution of Resource and Training Centers

Anita P. Barbee

For almost 40 years, the Children's Bureau (CB) has been building and refining a dynamic training and technical assistance (T/TA) infrastructure to support states. National Child Welfare Resource Centers (NCWRCs) have consistently been charged with compiling information, providing T/TA, and building capacity in states, tribes, and courts. The CB has relied on social workers to staff many of these NCWRCs and forged partnerships with schools of social work to manage them. These NCWRCs increasingly rely on evidence-based practice to inform not only the practices they endorse but also how they provide technical assistance. This chapter reviews the key thrusts of funding announcements for NCWRCs, the awards that were made, and major developments of the T/TA Network, as well as the roles the social work discipline and other forces have played in those developments in six periods of time: initial foundation of NCWRCs, 1974–1985; beginning of the NCWRCs, 1985–1988; consolidation and change, 1988–1997; expansion of NCWRCs, 1998–2004; increased focus and coordination, 2004–2009; and overcoming barriers, 2008–2014. The chapter also focuses on the future and includes a proposed unifying framework for T/TA implementation and dissemination.

BACKGROUND

As noted in earlier chapters of this book, the CB was established by the U.S. Congress in 1912 and has primary responsibility for administering federal child welfare programs. The agency works to accomplish its mission through leadership, support for necessary services, and partnerships with all jurisdictions that manage child welfare services, which include states, tribes, territories, their communities, and courts (hereafter referred to as states/tribes). A primary focus is to help prevent and protect children from abuse in their families and to find permanent placements for children who cannot safely return home. For almost 40 years, the CB has been building and refining a dynamic T/TA infrastructure that provides support to states/tribes through continual innovation in response to the changing needs of child welfare agencies.

Knowledge development and transfer, leadership development, information management, dissemination of effective and promising practices, and capacity building have all been key objectives of the T/TA Network. Throughout the journey of providing T/TA, faculty and staff at schools of social work have received grants and contracts from the CB. These are not only for specific resource centers or implementation centers but also for training and demonstration grants that help shape the way these services are delivered and the interventions that are championed. In this second decade of the 21st century, the CB has taken the lead from the cutting-edge sector of social work research and begun to embrace evidence-based and evidence-informed practices, not only in the programs and practices brought to the attention of states/tribes, but also in the way T/TA is delivered and *how* programs are implemented. The first sections of this chapter review the key thrusts of announcements for NCWRCs, awards that were made, major developments of the T/TA Network across time, and the role the social work discipline and other forces have played in those developments. Organized chronologically, the six periods under discussion vary in length corresponding to times of rapid change. The second section of the chapter focuses on the future and includes a proposed unifying framework for T/TA implementation and dissemination.

INITIAL FOUNDATION: 1974–1985

The story of the CB T/TA Network is one of legislative changes and federal mandates for increased accountability, which over time has helped shape and modify the focus of T/TA efforts and how services have been provided. Dating from 1974, when the Child Abuse Prevention and Treatment Act was originally enacted, the federal role was established for supporting TA activities related to child protection. At the time the Child Abuse Prevention and Treatment and Adoption Reform Act of 1978 was enacted, a provision was made for the implementation of an adoption T/TA program. Thus, between 1974 and 1984 the CB funded regional resource centers that focused on particular areas of child welfare, including adoption, child abuse and neglect, and child welfare training. These regional centers were housed in state offices, nonprofit agencies, and 21 universities, including 17 schools of social work.[1] This was a time when the CB and schools of social work began to collaborate in earnest. By 1982 there were 30 regional centers around the country, which were later consolidated into 10 region-wide centers capable of providing assistance in multiple areas.

For example, Pam Day, who currently is director of the Child Welfare Information Gateway, directed an integrated regional center at the University of Washington. She hired a cadre of staff and doctoral students whose names are at the forefront of child welfare research and who are involved in the current T/TA Network.[2] Katharine Cahn recalled "going to child welfare related conferences around the region and taking calls at the center, helping people with just-in-time answers, resources, and connections, and convening regional meetings and conference calls around breaking issues" (K. Cahn, personal communication, January 28, 2012). Although most of those regional resource centers disappeared when funding ended in September 1984 in the final months of president Reagan's first administration (Department of Health and Human Services, 1985), the University of Washington kept its center active for another 15 years. Cahn recalled:

> Through a series of (sometimes overlapping) training grants, we exposed the tribal and state agencies in the Pacific Northwest to many new practices and ideas, including risk assessment, family centered (strengths-based and systemic) supervision, *Children Can't Wait* (promoting court/child welfare collaboration), family group conferencing, and *Supervising for Excellence*. One of the most impactful grants was the "Multi-disciplinary Training Grant" that supported the formation of Title IV-E partnerships

and social work curriculum reform to serve child welfare. I always thought there was a real strength in regional resource centers, as we knew everyone in child welfare in the Pacific Northwest. We knew the tribal leaders and cultures, the ongoing state initiatives and local regional cultures, and new and old execs as they came and went. We were able to connect them to one another and connect all with national resources when those were needed. We had our ear to the ground and could hear problems arising and could connect people to "just in time" knowledge.

A mechanism that led to the support of such training centers was the passage of the Child Welfare and Adoption Assistance Act of 1980, which set aside a portion of Title IV-E funds to support education and training in foster care and adoption services. These Title IV-E funds were intended to be used for professionalizing child welfare practice through agency-based training and social work degree education (Zlotnik, 2003). After the dismantling of the regional training centers and the creation of the integrated regional resource centers in the early 1980s, the CB developed two forms of support to states/tribes. One form of support is informational and consultational involving the federal CB T/TA Network. The second form of support is financial, including the provision of funds for education at institutions where social work students at the BSW and MSW levels specialize in child welfare, and the provision of funds for training to prepare new and veteran workers and supervisors to engage in best practices (Rheaume, Collins, & Amodeo, 2011; U.S. General Accounting Office, 2003; Zlotnik, 2003).

In the mid-1980s many schools of social work around the country established child welfare training centers similar to the one at the University of Washington. These were and continue to be supported by CB training and demonstration grants and sometimes national resource centers. Today there are over 100 child welfare training programs in schools of social work that administer Title IV-E stipends to students or deliver training to those already in the workforce (Barbee, Antle, Sullivan, Dryden, & Henry, 2012).[3] To support these training centers, as well as research, and as a result of the Medicare and Medicaid Budget Reconciliation Amendments in 1985 and

1986, funding was made available for the National Adoption Information Clearinghouse. This clearinghouse, in addition to the National Clearinghouse on Child Abuse and Neglect, served as key TA resources to support states/tribes and the child welfare field. The legacy of these early TA components has continued today, whereby both clearinghouses have evolved into the Child Welfare Information Gateway (see http://www.child-welfare.gov), which provides access to publications, websites, and online databases covering a range of topics such as child abuse and neglect, prevention, permanency, and adoption.

BEGINNING OF THE NCWRCS: 1985–1988

Starting in September 1985 six NCWRCs were funded for 3 years. They were tasked to focus on the areas of foster care, adoption, family-based preventive services,[4] youth services, child welfare program management and administration, and legal resources for child welfare. This was the beginning of NCWRCs as we know them today. The purpose of the NCWRCs was "to develop, expand, strengthen, and improve the capacity of State and local, public, and private child welfare agencies throughout the country to utilize exemplary methods and resources to provide effective services to children and families" (Department of Health and Human Services, 1985). Four of the NCWRCs were awarded to universities, two of which were in schools of social work (see Table 8.1 for the changing names of NCWRCs, the timing of funding, and the entities that received the awards in the past 30 years). So even though fewer universities and schools of social work were involved than when regional resource centers were in place, a critical interrelationship remained between the academic institutions and federal agencies focused on child welfare issues. Professionals with social work degrees served as directors or consultants for most of the NCWRCs.

CONSOLIDATION AND CHANGE: 1988–1997

Funding announcements between 1988 and 1990 could not be located, so it was not possible to examine the renewal of the original nine NCWRC contracts. A large announcement in 1991 for discretionary grants, however, referred applicants to use the expertise of the 10 national resource centers located across the country (Fiscal Year 1991 Coordinated Discretionary

Table 8.1   Evolution of Funding and Naming of National Child Welfare Resource Centers From 1981 to 2014

	1981–1984	1985–1990	1988–1995	1993–1999	1998–2004	2003–2009	2008–2014
Family-based prevention services[1] **Over 30 years**	●	●	● Family-based services	●	● Family-centered practice		● In-home services
Child abuse prevention and treatment[2] **30 years**		●	●	● Community-based family resource and support programs	●	● Community-based child abuse prevention	●
Foster care[3] **30 years**		●	●	●	● Foster care and permanency planning	● Family-centered practice and permanency planning	● Permanency and family connections
Adoption[4] **25 years**		●	●	●	●	●	●
Child welfare program management and administration[5] **30 years**		●	●	●	● Organizational improvement	●	●
Legal resources for child welfare[6] **30 years**		●	●	●	● Legal and judicial issues	●	●
Youth services[7] **30 years**		●	●	●	● Youth development	●	●
Child abuse and neglect treatment[8] **30 years**		●	●	● Child maltreatment	● Child protective services	●	●
Information technology[9] **15 years**					●	● Data and technology	●

1 A national resource center (NRC) for family-based prevention services was initially awarded to the University of Iowa School of Social Work in 1981 until 1999 when it was awarded to a nonprofit, then it was combined with permanency practice and awarded to Hunter College School of Social Work in 2004 until the present. Beginning in 2009 a new NRC for in-home services began and was awarded to the University of Iowa School of Social Work.

2 NRC for child abuse prevention treatment was initially awarded to the C. Henry Kempe Center, University of Colorado, Health Sciences Center in 1985, then changed its focus to community-based family resource and support programs in 1993 when it was awarded to the Chapel Hill Training-Outreach Project. The name changed to Community-Based Child Abuse Prevention in 2004, but it remained in the same location.

3 NRC for foster care was awarded in 1989 to Eastern Michigan University, School of Social Work, and finally was awarded to Hunter College School of Social Work in 1994, where it has remained, but its name and focus has changed three times.

4 NRC for adoption was initially awarded to Spaulding for Children in 1985 and has remained there to date.

5 NRC for child welfare management and administration was awarded to the University of Southern Maine Muskie School of Public Service in 1985 and has remained there to date with a name change in 1999 to NCWRC for Organizational Improvement.

6 NRC for Legal Resources for Child Welfare was awarded to the American Bar Association in 1985 and has remained there to date with a name change in 1999 to NRC for Legal and Judicial Issues.

7 NRC for youth services was awarded to the University of Oklahoma in 1985 and has remained there to date with a name change in 1999 to NRC for Youth Development.

8 NRC for child abuse neglect and treatment was initially awarded to the American Humane Association in 1985. In 1996 it was renamed NRC for Child Maltreatment and awarded to the Child Welfare Institute and ACTION for Protection. In 1999 the name changed to NRC for Child Protective Services and was awarded to ACTION for Protection, where it has remained to date.

9 NRC for information technology was awarded in 1999 to the Child Welfare League of America, where it has remained to date with a new name NRC for Data and Technology in 2004.

Funds Program, 1991). Therefore, 60% of the NCWRCs were located in universities, half of which were affiliated with schools of social work. The topics of these NCWRCs largely corresponded to the topics listed in the 1985 announcement (see Table 8.1). Their charge was to (a) identify, review, evaluate, and disseminate resource materials; (b) develop specific work plans for the needs of minority children and families in their area; (c) develop networking and coordination activities to establish linkages between agencies, organizations, and individuals serving children and families; (d) provide technical assistance, training, and consultation to promote use of resources and best practices related to child welfare services, including methods and techniques for program implementation and evaluation; and (e) develop innovative methods of appropriate materials to respond to and recognize deficiencies of resources in specific aspects of programs and emerging program needs (Department of Health and Human Services, 1985). Yet, as a result of two major shifts in federal legislation, the overriding focus of T/TA was about to change, even while retaining dissemination of resource materials, establishing linkages, and relying on best practices.

In 1994 the Social Security Act Amendments authorized the U.S. Department of Health and Human Services to review state child and family service programs to ensure conformity with the requirements in Titles IV-B and IV-E of the act.[5] These early reviews focused primarily on assessing state agencies' compliance with procedural requirements and did not offer states the opportunity to make improvements before imposing penalties. Then, in 1997 the Adoption and Safe Families Act was passed, which amended Titles IV-B and IV-E of the Social Security Act and required a focus on results and accountability in the child welfare system. The emphasis on results provided the federal government and its partners with an opportunity to reform child welfare services, leading to the Child and Family Services Review (CFSR) process, published as a final rule in the *Federal Register* in January 2000 and effective on March 25, 2000 (Title IV-E Foster Care Eligibility Reviews and Child and Family Services State Plan Reviews).

EXPANSION OF NCWRCS: 1998–2004

In 1998 there was an announcement for new NCWRCs to support statutorily mandated services on abandoned infants assistance (which was awarded to University of California, Berkeley School of Social Welfare) and community-based family resources and support. In 1998 the NCWRC for special needs adoption was refunded, and in 1999 the NCWRC announcements were for family-centered practice, foster care and permanency planning, organizational improvement, legal and judicial issues, youth development, and information technology (see Table 8.1 for movement of NCWRCs in 1999). Two schools of social work lost an NCWRC, and one gained a center, resulting in a net loss.

Those NCWRCs that were funded at the time of the first round of CFSRs focused the majority of their T/TA activities on responding to state needs related to the federal reviews and implementation of program improvement plans (PIPs). Another resource was added to the larger T/TA system in 2001 with the establishment of Regional Quality Improvement Centers and later in 2006 with National Quality Improvement Centers (QICs). The purpose of forming the QIC model was to promote the development of evidence-based knowledge about effective child welfare practices and ensure the dissemination of this information in a manner that informs and alters practice at the direct service level (Nolan & Brodowski, 2006). The QICs focused on such topics as engagement of tribes (University of Washington's School of Social Work), clinical casework supervision and privatization (both QICs at the University of Kentucky's College of Social Work), adoption, nonresident fathers, differential response, early childhood, and legal representation of children. While these centers used a research-based demonstration model, they provided needed information on special aspects of practice forming a deep knowledge base for the NCWRCs. Most centers were awarded to nonprofit agencies, such as the American Humane Association, but two were located in social work schools.

INCREASED FOCUS AND COORDINATION: 2004–2009

The findings that emerged from the first round of CFSRs, compiled in 2004, demonstrated the need for a more integrated and coordinated T/TA approach to assist states in meeting their PIP goals and other goals related to systems change. This integrated and coordinated approach to working with states/tribes on systems change efforts was included in the NCWRC program announcement in 2004 (National Child Welfare Resource Centers Cooperative Agreements, 2004), as was an emphasis on child welfare systems of care (SOC) principles and practice.[6] Thus, the CB expanded NCWRC meetings to include all members of the larger T/TA Network,[7] increased communication with states/tribes and encouraged them to use all parts of the T/TA Network to meet agency needs, and developed marketing materials that listed all these services as part of the larger T/TA Network of the CB (http://www.acf.hhs.gov/programs/cb/assistance). The CB also directed the NCWRCs to continue to focus the majority of their T/TA in response to the needs of the CFSRs and PIPs.[8] For example, when Louisiana and Mississippi were hit by Hurricane Katrina in 2005, all the NCWRCs successfully came together in a coordinated fashion to develop an integrated work plan for rebuilding the child welfare systems in both states.

In the funding announcement for an NCWRC for organizational improvement, additional funds were provided for the first evaluation of the NCWRCs. The evaluation used a longitudinal, multi-perspective, multi-method approach to assess processes and initial outcomes. The final report focused on (a) round one CFSR outcome data, (b) round two CFSR outcome data for 31 states, (c) data on the amount and type of T/TA provided, collected, and archived in the Technical Assistance Tracking Internet System (TATIS), (d) interviews with child welfare agency leaders, and (e) survey results from state respondents at two points in time. The following are several key findings that emerged from that evaluation that helped shape future work:

1 NCWRC involvement improved outcomes in states/tribes. The amount and type (planning, tool development, building capacity, facilitating organizational changes) of NCWRC involvement in states were significantly related to the degree of improvement in five out of seven CFSR outcomes in those states that improved their CFSR outcomes from the first to the second round of the CFSR.

2 Not all states used T/TA extensively or enacted recommendations. For states that engaged T/TA, consultations were rated as fairly

useful, practical, important, and increased knowledge, skills, and confidence of state staff. However, states varied in how much they facilitated the consultations and how much they followed through with recommendations at the conclusion of consultations. Change fatigue, budget cuts, and lack of capacity to implement projects and change efforts contributed.

3   Training in the form of regional roundtables, peer-to-peer meetings, and teleconferences were most appreciated by leaders. In these venues states/tribes learned more about issues, such as how to build an effective quality assurance system or training system, how to tackle disproportionality and disparities, helping youths to exit care to independent living successfully, and trans-state adoptions.

4   Initial assessments with states/tribes to meet needs and reach critical outcomes in a coordinated fashion were valued. Directors valued the way NCWRCs helped frame issues and questions rather than simply taking an initial request at face value. Coordination among multiple NCWRCs was positive, but often was overwhelming for states/tribes. By the end of the grant period, a new TA Planning Matrix, which coordinated the involvement of multiple NCWRCs in a state/tribe, assisted with that need. Leaders expressed a desire for more collaboration between NCWRCs and their own universities and private consultants, including the Annie E. Casey Foundation.

5   Several gaps were noted, including a need for an NCWRC exclusively focused on tribal issues and more information on the T/TA Network in general. Because of the constant turnover of state leaders (the average tenure is 2 years), some wanted more information on the NCWRCs, ways to access curricula and tools, and ways to meet with NCWRC associates at conferences and regional meetings (Barbee & Cunningham, 2009).

OVERCOMING BARRIERS: 2008–2014

Despite the level of T/TA that the CB has made available through the T/TA Network, several barriers have often prevented systemic change from occurring. For example, some child welfare agencies require enhanced levels of T/TA to successfully implement complex and widespread systems change. While states/tribes may strive to institutionalize new evidence-informed practices, they often lack the resources for such an implementation. This is compounded by budget cuts, staff turnover, shifting agency priorities, agency culture that resists new approaches, and high caseloads. NCWRCs have the resources to assist states/tribes with addressing changes that support enhancements in agency capacity, but the federal mandate to largely focus on the CFSR process sometimes has given NCWRCs less time to spend on helping agencies reorganize institutional structures that support changes in frontline practice. In general, the T/TA Network was not structured to provide the proactive, intensive, long-term TA that seems necessary for promoting and sustaining systemic changes in child welfare systems.

To enhance state/tribal systems change efforts, beginning in 2008 the CB funded five child welfare Implementation Centers (ICs) to complement the existing T/TA Network. The Northeast and Caribbean IC at the University of Southern Maine serves Regions 1 and 2. The Atlantic Coast Child Welfare IC at the University of Maryland School of Social Work serves Regions 3 and 4. The Midwest Child Welfare IC at the University of Nebraska serves Regions 5 and 7. The Mountains and Plains Child Welfare IC at the University of Texas at Arlington School of Social Work serves Regions 6 and 8, and the Western and Pacific Child Welfare IC at American Institutes for Research serves Regions 9 and 10. Social work faculty have a strong influence on how these centers were developed, operate, and are evaluated. ICs support and facilitate more intensive and longer-term communication and networking across state/tribal child welfare systems to leverage existing knowledge and expertise and foster collaborative problem solving. ICs focus on a particular problem in states/tribes, such as a practice-related challenge, and provide in-depth and long-term consultation and support to make substantial and lasting changes intended to improve the quality and effectiveness of child welfare practice.

A key advantage that enhances the ability of ICs to assist states/tribes is their regional proximity, which offers ICs frequent contact with state/tribal leaders, easy access to outcome documents and other available data, and opportunities to learn about available resources that can be shared with other states (e.g., strong university partners, consultants, or proven models).

This knowledge of the states/tribes they work with enables ICs to provide tailored interventions through (a) regional roundtables, (b) quarterly tele-conferences that focus on specific topic areas, (c) peer-to-peer teleconfer-ences, (d) monographs, and (e) other tools specific to the states/tribes' regions. IC leaders with this specific regional knowledge can serve as a bridge to the larger T/TA Network, broker services from the T/TA Network, and suggest specific TA providers to help states/tribes in build-ing organizational capacity.

As part of their operations ICs have been working with states/tribes that had not fully used the NCWRCs for T/TA. ICs provide funding to states/tribes through a request for proposals process and work intensively with the successful applicants for up to 3 years to address organizational factors that influence service delivery and practice, such as leadership; team-work; organizational structure, culture, and climate; workforce develop-ment; and administration and management of agency resources. The CB expects that the implementation projects established through partnerships between ICs and states/tribes will help facilitate systemic changes and suc-cessful institutionalization of child welfare principles, policies, and effective or promising models of practice, as well as foster changes in direct practice with children and families. With the addition of the ICs to the T/TA Network, the CB is returning to the use of a regional model and all the strengths it brings. In addition, these ICs bring more schools of social work into the T/TA Network.

Also in 2008 the National Child Welfare Workforce Institute (NCWWI) was funded and awarded to a partnership of schools of social work that had all received workforce recruitment and retention demonstration grants from the CB from 2003 to 2008. The institute's mission is to deliver training and cul-tivate leadership among professionals in child welfare.[9] Then in 2009 the NCWRCs' contracts were renewed. The NCWRC on organizational improvement was originally charged with systems change T/TA efforts in the 2004 program announcement, but now all NCWRCs share this responsibil-ity, and the coordination of TA is overseen by the T/TA Coordinating Center. In addition, two more NCWRCs were added: the NCWRC for tribes awarded to a nonprofit agency, and the NCWRC for in-home Services, which returned a center to the University of Iowa School of Social Work.

MOVING INTO THE FUTURE

The restructuring of the CB T/TA Network offers a propitious opportunity for states/tribes to further improve outcomes for children and families. In order for frontline practice to change and remain improved, new behaviors need reinforcement, the agency culture must permit frontline staff to use information they gather through improved practices, and other partners who serve children and families involved in child welfare must be involved in the move toward systemic change. Because there are so many schools of social work in the T/TA Network and so many social workers in the other agencies that house ICs and NCWRCs, there is a definite reliance on social work values, evidence-based and evidence-informed research and practices, and social work strategies for working in partnership with organizational entities to create change that enhances the lives of families and children.

The current cross-site evaluation of the T/TA Network by James Bell Associates and ICF International builds on the previous evaluation by Barbee and Cunningham (2009) and expands the evaluation to include the newly formed ICs. It continues to interview directors, survey all parties involved in T/TA, analyze on-site and off-site work recorded in the new information system (One Net), and uses enhanced document reviews. In addition, it adds a 3-year case study of five jurisdictions to gain better insight on how contextual variables affect the delivery and impact of T/TA. The cross-site evaluation is expected to provide critical information needed to enable the CB to identify whether and how the integration of T/TA through ICs and NCWRCs supports systemic change in child welfare services, fosters knowledge development about promising and effective practices in transforming organizations and child welfare systems, and promotes the dissemination and use of evidence-informed and evidence-based practices.

Over the past 40 years resource centers have continued to collect and disseminate information, provide T/TA, and build capacity in states/tribes. They also have grown to conduct thorough assessments of states/tribes, which lead to integrated work plans that encourage collaboration among all T/TA providers within and outside the CB T/TA Network. The addition of the ICs, QICs, the NCWWI, and other network members to the original NCWRC groups to help states/tribes implement complex changes and embed evidence-based practices to improve outcomes for families and children has been very positive. Expanding the cross-site evaluation of the T/TA Network is helping the CB build an evidence base of how T/TA works to build capacity in states/tribes, create organizational and systems change, and improve outcomes for children and families. All these efforts have been strengthened over the past 3 years since the CB has introduced the framework and findings of implementation science to the NCWRCs and ICs and adopted the National Implementation Research Network model to serve as a common framework for approaching work with states/tribes using evidence-based implementation strategies to help solve some of the most intractable problems facing child welfare systems (Fixsen, Naoom, Blase, Friedman, & Wallace, 2005).

THE INTEGRATIVE SYSTEMS FRAMEWORK (ISF) FOR DISSEMINATION AND IMPLEMENTATION

The emphasis on implementation science harkens to a framework developed by the Department for Violence Prevention of the Centers for Disease Control to translate research findings and facilitate capacity in organizations so that effective practices can be used in the field. The Interactive Systems Framework for Dissemination and Implementation (ISF; Wandersman et al., 2008) details the structures and functions that work bi-directionally to bridge science and practice. The ISF was created to incorporate the perspectives of multiple stakeholders, including funders, researchers, practitioners, and technical assistance providers. The ISF is designed to be applied toward any innovation including "information that could be useful to prevention or practice efforts in the field including programs, policies, processes, and principles" (Saul, Wandersman, Flaspohler, Duffy, Lubell, & Noonan, 2008).

The ISF includes three systems: the synthesis and translation system, the support system, and the delivery system. The function of the first system is to distill information about innovations and prepare them for implementation by end users, such as administrators (in the case of policies and processes) and practitioners (in the case of programs and principles). Synthesis tools, such as systematic and integrative reviews, meta-analysis, and state of the science reviews, analyze evidence at multiple levels. One goal of synthesis should be to identify key characteristics and core elements of programs, processes, principles, and policies so these key features can be replicated in the field and modified appropriately for unique needs and contexts of different agencies and at-risk populations. This is where the QICs, the Child Welfare Information Gateway, and CB research, training, and demonstration projects fall in generating new knowledge and synthesizing the knowledge they generate with findings from the growing child welfare literature.

The support system's function is to support the work of those who will put the innovations into practice, and it is involved in two activities. The first is innovation-specific capacity building. This is focused on a particular innovation, such as (a) providing information about a new idea before it is adopted (i.e., practice models), (b) providing training on how to carry out the innovation, (c) providing tools that operationalize the innovation, and (d) providing technical assistance while the innovation is being rolled out and embedded in the organizational delivery system. New research finds that developing and supporting the new skills for innovation through specialized training, monitoring of fidelity and adherence, coaching, and supervision are essential in this process (Fixsen et al., 2005). The second activity is general capacity building, which is intended to enhance infrastructure, skills, and motivation in an organization to support the implementation of innovations. This is where the NCWRCs, ICs, and university training centers contribute their expertise and assistance.

The delivery system is where implementation of innovations occurs in the field and where T/TA providers walk hand in hand with states/tribes. The organizations that carry out delivery of services have varying levels of existing capacity, including the ability and motivation to implement evidence-based or evidence-informed innovations (Aarons, 2004). These activities also include innovation-specific and general activities (e.g., workforce strength, leadership, partnerships).

The CB continues to strengthen all three ISF systems in partnership with social workers from many institutions, including schools of social work, through the federal T/TA Network and local child welfare education and training efforts. However, the support system can only be as strong as the research it stands on. The biggest challenge for the future is generating enough support for research and evaluation studies that can inform the support system. Then as the evidence base grows, it is necessary to hold T/TA providers accountable for using interventions with the most evidence in a way that is supported by the findings and strategies of implementation science. Identifying and implementing best practices will be an ongoing challenge for the T/TA Network, the CB, and the field of child welfare.

REFERENCES

Aarons, G. A. (2004). Mental health provider attitudes toward adoption of evidence-based-practice: The evidence-based practice attitude scale (EBPAS). *Mental Health Services Research, 6*(2), 61–74.

Administration for Children, Youth and Families Child Welfare, Research and Demonstration Grants Program. (26 January 1981). *Federal Register 46*, 8121.

Adoption and Safe Families Act, Pub. L. No. 105-89 (1997).

Barbee, A. P., Antle, B. F., Sullivan, D. J., Dryden, A. A. A., & Henry, K. (2012). Twenty-five years of the Children's Bureau investment in social work education. *Journal of Public Child Welfare, 6*(4), 1–14.

Barbee, A. P., & Cunningham, M. R. (2009). Evaluation of the Children's Bureau Training and Technical Assistance Network: A final 5 year analysis (2004–2009). Louisville, KY: Cunningham, Barbee, & RoBen Associates.

Child Abuse Prevention and Treatment Act, Pub. L. No. 93-247 (1974).

Child Abuse Prevention and Treatment and Adoption Reform Act, Pub. L. No. 95-266 (1978).

Child Welfare and Adoption Assistance Act, Pub. L. No. 96-272 (1980).

Department of Health and Human Services, National Resource Centers for Child Welfare Services, 50 Fed. Reg. 45962 (November 5, 1985).

Fiscal year 1991 coordinated discretionary funds program. (14 March 1991). *Federal Register, 56*, 10948.

Fixsen, D. L., Naoom, S. F., Blase, K. A., Friedman, R. M., & Wallace, F. (2005). *Implementation research: A synthesis of the literature.* Tampa, FL: University of South Florida, Louis de la Parte Florida Mental Health Institute, National Implementation Research Network.

Medicare and Medicaid Budget Reconciliation Amendments, H.R. 3290 (1985).

Medicare and Medicaid Budget Reconciliation Amendments, H.R. 5287 (1986).

National Child Welfare Resource Centers. (25 June 2004). Cooperative agreements. *Federal Register, 69*, 35860-918.

Nolan, C., & Brodowski, M. (2006, October). *The Children's Bureau Quality Improvement Centers on CPS and adoption: Lessons learned from the first four years.* Paper presented at the National Advisory Group Meeting of the Quality Improvement Centers on Privatization, Lexington, KY.

Rheaume, H., Collins, M. E., & Amodeo, M. (2011). University/agency IV-E partnerships for professional education and training: Perspectives from the states. *Journal of Public Child Welfare, 5,* 481–500.

Saul, J., Wandersman, A., Flaspohler, P., Duffy, J., Lubell, K., & Noonan, R. (2008). Research and action for bridging science and practice in prevention. *American Journal of Community Psychology, 41(3-4),* 165–170.

Social Security Act Amendments, Pub. L. No. 103-432 (1994).

Title IV-E foster care eligibility reviews and child and family services state plan reviews. (25 January 2000). *Federal Register, 65,* 40-4093 (to be codified at 45 C.F.R. pt. 1355–1357).

U.S. General Accounting Office. (2003). *HHS could play a greater role in helping child welfare agencies recruit and retain staff* (GAO-03-357). Washington, DC: Author.

Wandersman, A., Duffy, J., Flaspohler, P., Noonan, R., Lubell, K., Stillman, L. . . . Saul, J. (2008). Bridging the gap between prevention research and practice: The interactive systems framework for dissemination and implementation. *American Journal of Community Psychology, 41*(3–4), 171–181.

Zlotnik, J. L. (2003). The use of title IV-E training funds for social work education: An historical perspective. *Journal of Human Behavior in the Social Environment, 7*(1/2), 5–19.

NOTES

1 These include schools of social work at the University of Connecticut, Columbia University, Virginia Commonwealth University, University of North Carolina, University of Tennessee, University of Michigan, University of Illinois, University of Wisconsin-Milwaukee, University of Texas, Tulane University, University of Missouri, George Warren Brown at Washington University, University of Denver, University of California Los Angeles, University of Hawaii, Portland State University, University of Washington, Cornell University's College of Human Ecology, Howard University's Institute for Urban Affairs, University of Iowa's Institute of Child Behavior and Development, and California State University's Department of Special Education.

2 Rick Barth, Katharine Cahn, Nancy Dickenson, and Cathy Potter, to name a few.

3 For example, one of the oldest child welfare training centers was established
   in Kentucky in 1983. The University Training Consortium is led by Eastern
   Kentucky University in a collaborative of eight public universities to
   develop, execute, evaluate, and reinforce education and training programs to
   enhance the child welfare workforce.

4 In 1981 the first National Resource Center on Family Based Services was
   established by the CB (Department of Health and Human Services, 1981).
   The center was awarded to the University of Iowa and was eventually
   directed by Miriam Landsman, who today directs a new NCWRC on in-
   home services as a faculty member in the school of social work.

5 One additional NCWRC was added in the area of child maltreatment in
   1996, which was awarded for 5 years to the Child Welfare Institute and
   ACTION for Child Protection. This was followed by a cooperative
   agreement that ran from 2001 to 2004 with the same agencies and
   subsequent renewals noted in the following.

6 In 2003 nine communities received funding to develop an SOC approach in
   child welfare. The communities served as learning laboratories for the CB
   and the field. SOC in child welfare is a principle-guided process that
   emphasizes interagency collaboration, individualized strengths-based care,
   cultural competence, child and family involvement, community-based
   services, and accountability. To achieve effective systems change, these
   principles need to be embodied in agency infrastructure and values, in the
   day-to-day work of agency staff at all levels, and in the administration,
   policies, and practice of the agency. An SOC approach also involves crucial
   partnerships outside the agency—with other agencies, the community, and
   parents and children or youths themselves.

7 All of these NCWRCs were funded in 2004, with the exception of
   Collaboration to AdoptUsKids, which received its first funding in 2002 and
   its current funding in 2007, which will continue through 2012. In 2009
   AdoptUsKids was awarded an NCWRC for recruitment and retention of
   foster and adoptive parents. In addition, two NCWRCs consolidated.

8 Additional members of the CB T/TA Network include the Association of
   Administrators of the Interstate Compact on Adoption and Medical
   Assistance, Child Welfare Information Gateway, National Data Archive on
   Child Abuse and Neglect, National Technical Assistance and Evaluation
   Center for Child Welfare Systems of Care Grantees, Technical Assistance to
   State Legislators on the Child and Family Service Reviews, National Child

Welfare Leadership Institute, National Resource Center for Community-Based Child Abuse Prevention, National Quality Improvement Center on Non-Resident Fathers and the Child Welfare System, National Quality Improvement Center on the Privatization of Child Welfare Services, National Abandoned Infants Assistance Resource Center, National Resource Center for Community-Based Child Abuse Prevention, National Center on Substance Abuse and Child Welfare, and National Technical Assistance Center for Children's Mental Health.

9   The grant is housed at the University at Albany School of Social Work in partnership with the other former recruitment and retention grantees, eight from schools of social work, and one from a school of public service, including the University of Southern Maine, Fordham University, University of Maryland (formerly University of North Carolina, Chapel Hill), University of Michigan, Michigan State University, University of Iowa, and the University of Denver. Other partners include Portland State University and the National Indian Child Welfare Association.

9

THE REPROFESSIONALIZATION
OF CHILD WELFARE
Recruitment and Retention

Miriam J. Landsman

The decline in the professional stature of child welfare as a specialized area of social work practice has been well documented (Ellett & Leighninger, 2007; Lieberman, Hornby, & Russell, 1988; Pecora, Whittaker, Maluccio, & Barth, 2000). Such factors as inadequate funding to address the growth of public child welfare services and caseloads, elimination of social work degree requirements, and the emergence of private social work practice and other higher-status social work specializations all contributed to deprofessionalization in public child welfare and the accompanying problem of high turnover. This chapter examines the empirical literature on the child welfare workforce with an emphasis on retention and discusses efforts by the Children's Bureau (CB) to encourage schools of social work and child welfare agencies to collaborate toward reprofessionalization and improved retention in child welfare.

OVERVIEW OF RESEARCH ON CHILD WELFARE RETENTION

Research on the child welfare workforce has increased considerably over the past decades in response to long-standing concerns about the problem of retaining qualified and competent employees in child welfare agencies. This research is difficult to summarize succinctly because of the substantial variations in independent and dependent variables, use of theoretically based explanatory frameworks versus correlational approaches, and differences in samples. Because of the high volume of research in this area and the complexities of interpreting results, this review is limited to several key factors that have emerged across studies as significant in explaining retention in child welfare. These factors have also served as the foundation for the strategies used in current collaborations between the CB and schools of social work to improve child welfare retention. Specifically, we examine the research on supervision, agency work environment, personal motivation, and social work education. Demographic characteristics and various dimensions of burnout are not included.

Supervision

The support and competence of supervisors have emerged as important predictors of child welfare workforce retention across multiple studies. A meta-analysis of 27 studies on the effect of supervision on worker outcomes, though not exclusively focused on child welfare, concurred that effective supervision is associated with numerous positive worker outcomes (Mor Barak, Travis, Pyuna, & Xie, 2009). Specifically examining studies of the child welfare workforce, quantitative and qualitative approaches have identified supervision as key to worker retention.

Supervisors have a role in facilitating the learning process, especially important for new workers (Curry, McCarragher, & Dellmann-Jenkins, 2005), and strengthening workers' enthusiasm for their job (Scannapieco & Connell-Carrick, 2007). In one study of all new employees hired in a 3-year period, those who stayed reported receiving more guidance from their supervisors and feeling more attached to their supervisors compared to those who left (Yankeelov, Barbee, Sullivan, & Antle, 2009). Studies of the child welfare workforce in different states have found that supportive and competent supervision affects job satisfaction (Barth, Lloyd, Christ, Chapman, & Dickenson, 2008; Strand & Dore, 2009), intention to stay in the job (Landsman, 2001; Smith, 2005), and lower intention to leave (Dickinson & Painter, 2009). In one state, social support from supervisors and coworkers lowered child welfare workers' intentions to leave even in the face of high levels of organizational stress (Nissly, Mor Barak, & Levin, 2005). In still another state, supervisor support affected child welfare employees' attachment to the organization through two different pathways: their emotional satisfaction with the job and their appraisal of how the organization valued them and cared about them (Landsman, 2008). Supporting these findings, qualitative studies of the child welfare workforce have similarly identified supportive supervision as critical to retention (Rycraft, 1994; Westbrook, Ellis, & Ellett, 2006).

Studies of master's-level Title IV-E graduates—a special subgroup of the child welfare workforce population—have also identified an effect of supportive supervision on retention (Dickinson & Perry, 2002; Jacquet, Clark, Morazes, & Withers, 2007), as well as a role for supervisors in buffering the pressures of the work that might otherwise lead to turnover (Morazes, Benton, Clark, & Jacquet, 2010). One study, however, found that supportive supervision predicted retention only after the first year of employment (O'Donnell & Kirnker, 2009). By the end of the second year, this was no longer a significant predictor.

Agency Work Environment

This classification includes variables that have been examined in different studies of the child welfare workforce, sometimes classified as organizational factors (i.e., DePanfilis & Zlotnik, 2008), organizational conditions (Mor Barak, Nissly & Levin, 2001), or organizational climate (Glisson & James, 2002). This category may include agency support, workload, promotional opportunities, autonomy, decision making, role conflict, role ambiguity, agency fairness, job safety, physical working conditions, salary, job stress, and others. Because of the wide variation in organizational factors examined across studies, as well as differences in how these factors are measured, it is quite difficult to draw conclusions about which facets of the agency work environment are the best predictors of retention.

Workload. Workload has emerged as a factor across different studies, but findings from research are mixed. In one state, counties with low turnover rates had lower average caseloads than counties with higher turnover (Lawson et al., 2005), and the odds of turnover increased as caseload size increased (Smith, 2005). A study in a different state found the reverse, a positive association between caseload size and workers' length of stay (Curry et al., 2005). In a third study caseload size was not related to actual retention; those who were satisfied with the size of their caseloads were less likely to express an intention to leave, and those who felt their caseloads were too high were more likely to stay (Jacquet et al., 2007). In still another, caseload size had no effect, but having a full caseload too soon had an effect on leaving the job, though not on workers' expressed intention to leave (Weaver, Chang, Clark, & Rhee, 2007). In a study based on interviews with workers who left, high caseloads were noted as contributing to their departure (Gonzales, Faller, Ortega, & Tropman, 2009). Using a measure of work overload rather than caseload size, independent studies of the child welfare workforce in two different states found that in one case it negatively affected organizational commitment (Landsman, 2008), and in the other it increased organizational commitment and intention to stay (Landsman, 2001).

Salary. The research on the impact of salary on retention has yielded curious findings. A federal study on child welfare recruitment and retention noted low pay as an important factor related to turnover (U.S. General Accounting Office, 2003). However, many studies of the child welfare workforce do not include salary as a specific variable; those that include salary use different conceptualizations. For example, in studies that use satisfaction with salary as the measure for salary, there is no significant effect on retention (Smith, 2005; Strolin-Goltzman, Auerbach, McGowan, & McCarthy, 2008; Weaver et al., 2007). Whether salary was conceptualized as fairness of salary and benefits or actual salary, there was no effect on turnover (Dickinson & Painter, 2009; Landsman, 2001, 2008). Two studies that compare child welfare employees in public and private agencies noted that private agency salaries are much lower (Jayaratne & Faller, 2009; Auerbach, McGowan, Ausberger, Strolin-Goltzman, & Schudrick, 2010). Only in the latter study did the lower salaries of private workers have an effect on their intention to leave.

Role conflict and role clarity. These have been included in a number of child welfare workforce studies, again with mixed results. Higher role conflict was predictive of child welfare workers' leaving the job (Weaver et al., 2007) and of master's level Title IV-E trainees' not staying past their commitment at the end of 2 years (O'Donnell & Kirkner, 2009). Role clarity has been associated with lower intention to leave (Dickinson & Painter,

2009; Landsman, 2008), and in one state had a large effect on intention to leave, especially in systems that experienced relatively low turnover (Strolin-Goltzman, 2008). However, when role conflict and role clarity were included in another study, neither had a significant effect on retention (Cahalane & Sites, 2008).

Goodness of fit. Qualitative studies have noted that permitting employees to find the position they are best suited for contributes to retention. The importance of finding a position in the agency that matched one's skills and interests emerged through qualitative interviews with experienced workers as related to retention (Rycraft, 1994). A similar construct of finding one's niche in the agency was also noted in a later qualitative study (Westbrook et al., 2006).

Other organizational variables. Many other aspects of the agency work environment have been examined in workforce studies but without enough consistency to attempt to summarize results: job stress, agency fairness, involvement in decision making (Mor Barak, Levin, Nissly, & Lane, 2006), organizational support (Smith, 2005; Landsman, 2008), coworker support (Nissly et al., 2005), opportunities for growth and advancement (Dickinson & Painter, 2009), autonomy (O'Donnell & Kirkner, 2009), and work/family conflict (Nissly et al., 2005). Some studies combine individual variables into broader constructs (i.e., Collins-Camargo, Ellett, & Lester, 2012; Ellett, 2009), which makes comparisons across studies difficult.

Personal Motivation

Personal motivation has also been conceptualized and measured in different ways: as a mission, service orientation, or human caring. Although most workforce studies do not include this construct, those that do find it a potent predictor of employee outcomes. In a qualitative interview study, Rycraft (1994) identified a service mission as one of the key themes that led child welfare caseworkers to stay in their agencies despite the many demands and challenges of the work. In quantitative studies of the child welfare workforce in two states, a service orientation was a strong predictor of job satisfaction and organizational commitment (Landsman, 2008) as well as intention to stay in the agency (Landsman, 2001). A measure of human caring used in child welfare worker surveys in two states found a significant association with intentions to stay in child welfare work (Ellett, 2009). In yet another state child welfare agency, individuals whose values were consistent with the mission of the organization and its work demonstrated stronger commitment and intention to stay than those who took the job for external rewards (Chernesky & Israel, 2009). Qualitative studies conducted through focus groups (Westbook et al., 2006) and interviews (Mor Barak et al., 2006) have also identified a commitment to children and families as important in workers' desire to stay in their jobs.

Social Work Education

Research on the relationship between social work education and retention in child welfare has yielded mixed findings. Support for a positive effect of having a social work degree on the likelihood of remaining in child welfare is found in numerous studies of graduates of Title IV-E funded traineeship programs. In several states, 70% to 80% of Title IV-E traineeship participants were still employed with the agency after their contractual employment obligation expired (Fox, Miller, & Barbee, 2003; O'Donnell & Kirkner, 2009; Scannapieco & Connell-Carrick, 2003). In another state, more than half the trainees remained with their public child welfare agency well past the minimum requirement, and more than 90% continued employment in the child welfare field (Robin & Hollister, 2002). Child welfare workers who completed Title IV-E traineeships were more likely to remain employed compared to nontrainees (Jones & Okamura, 2000; Rosenthal & Waters, 2006).

Not all studies found a positive effect of social work degrees on child welfare retention. Smith (2005) concluded that employees with social work degrees are likely to leave child welfare positions unless they experience other positive attributes on the job. Studies of two different states' public child welfare employees found no effect of a social work degree on organizational commitment or intention to stay in the agency (Landsman, 2001, 2008), although in one, the degree was associated with a stronger intention to remain in the field of child welfare (Landsman, 2001). Some studies have noted a higher likelihood of turnover among MSW-level employees in public child welfare agencies (Curry et al., 2005; Yankeelov et al., 2009). In one state, MSW-level child welfare workers started to leave more rapidly than others 6 months into employment (Dickinson & Painter, 2009).

Together these studies suggest that providing students with a child-welfare focused social work education through Title IV-E traineeships that also include field placements in a child welfare setting and a contractual agreement to work in the child welfare agency upon graduation does appear to cultivate a commitment to child welfare and strengthen retention. In addition to providing a focused experience that builds the competencies needed for child welfare practice, the employment requirement may provide workers with the incentive to remain during the time they may be most vulnerable to premature turnover. The longer-term challenge to sustained retention is making sure agencies make the best use of highly trained workers (Hopkins, Mudrick, & Rudolph, 1999).

STRATEGIES TO IMPROVE RETENTION IN CHILD WELFARE

Specific initiatives encouraged or funded by the CB have been directed at strengthening recruitment and retention. These include collaborations funded by Title IV-E between schools of social work and child welfare agencies, recruitment and retention grants, and the National Child Welfare Workforce Institute (NCWWI) and Comprehensive Workforce projects.

Title IV-E Collaborations

Stipends to support students and child welfare employees to receive social work degrees, either at the BSW or MSW level, have been the primary focus of school and child welfare agency collaborations to improve retention. The Adoption Assistance and Child Welfare Act of 1980 created the Title IV-E program that supports training and education for the child welfare workforce including current and future employees. Schools of social work, in partnership with child welfare agencies, can receive Title IV-E funding for professional development of the child welfare workforce through student stipends, development of child welfare–focused curricula, distance education programs, field instruction, and research and evaluation of the program. Students who receive stipends are required to make a commitment to employment with the agency, usually for an equivalent length of time as their stipend. The number of university/child welfare partnerships funded through Title IV-E has increased considerably over time. A survey conducted in 1996 identified 29 states that were using Title IV-E funds for BSW and MSW education (Zlotnik & Cornelius, 2000), and later estimates note that more than 40 states are managing these partnerships (Zlotnik, 2003).

Recruitment and Retention Projects

In 2003 the CB funded eight university social work programs to develop, implement, and evaluate models for recruiting and retaining a committed and competent child welfare workforce. These 5-year projects, funded through the Title IV-B, Section 426 discretionary program, all involved collaborations between schools of social work and public child welfare agencies. They developed a unique, research-based approach to address the workforce needs in their states and engaged in efforts to strengthen recruitment of new workers as well as retention of the existing workforce.

Recruitment. Issues related to recruitment vary according to the needs of each state: ongoing difficulties in filling vacancies and high turnover among new employees, varying turnover rates in different areas, and challenges because of budget cuts and layoffs. Recruitment strategies devised by the recruitment and retention projects (R&R) were based on the needs of the state and workforce research.

The University of North Carolina developed and implemented tools to improve recruitment and selection of job applicants. To reach a broad audience, posters, brochures, and public service announcements were widely disseminated, and potential employees were provided with realistic information about the job. Employers used structured processes for evaluating candidates for their fit with the job, including interview guides and written exercises completed by applicants. The University of Southern Maine similarly focused on realistic recruitment and screening to help reduce turnover, especially among new hires.

Realistic job previews (RJP) were developed by four of the R&R projects to provide an accurate depiction of a position to job applicants, inform the process of decision making about whether the job might be a good fit, and to reduce premature turnover. RJPs can be used at different points in the application process—as the first step in applying for a position, after an initial screening, or prior to accepting a position. The RJP developed for North Carolina features interviews with various child welfare workers who provide candid descriptions of the challenges and rewards of their jobs. The University of Southern Maine and the University of Denver also produced RFP videos; in addition, the Maine project revised caseworker job descriptions to reflect current practices, revised the competency-based screening process, and developed performance standards and competencies for supervisors to use in recruitment and employee selection. Research on the use of these RJPs in Maine found a decline in cumulative turnover from 3.8% prior to the project to 1.9% after implementation (University of Southern Maine, 2008). The University of Michigan tracked newly hired workers and also found significantly lower turnover among those who had viewed an RJP that had been developed prior to the project (12%) compared to those who had not (21.7%; Faller et al., 2009).

Supervision. Consistent with the findings from previous research, each of the R&R projects included some emphasis on strengthening supervision. A survey by Fordham University of the workforce of the state child welfare agency in Connecticut found that supervisors were more dissatisfied than caseworkers with their jobs and with the supervision they received (Strand & Bosco-Ruggiero, 2010). In response, project administrators developed a mentoring program in which midlevel or upper-level managers were matched with supervisors who had at least 2 years on the job. The goals of the mentoring program were to build leadership capacity among supervisors, improve their ability to work in the agency and community, provide opportunities for professional and personal growth, and increase organizational commitment and retention. Evaluation results, though limited by incomplete data, found that mentees expressed a greater level of confidence and commitment to their jobs and to the agency and that mentors also derived personal benefits from providing mentorship (Strand & Bosco-Ruggiero, 2010).

The University of Iowa worked with the state to strengthen supervision among child welfare supervisors and midlevel managers. The project began shortly after the agency experienced reorganization and a substantial budget cut that resulted in the loss of a large number of management positions and training resources. No training program was in place for child welfare supervisors; these positions were filled almost completely through internal promotions of caseworkers. Iowa's R&R project worked closely with an inclusive statewide advisory committee, supervisors, and midlevel managers to develop, implement, and evaluate a model of child welfare supervision. To obtain maximum input from supervisors, project staff conducted focus groups in each of the state's eight service areas, with 78% of all supervisors participating and providing information about their challenges and successes as well as their ideas for needed content in a supervision training program (Landsman, 2007).

The training program, which was field-tested, revised, and implemented statewide, is based on a model that defines supervision as an intentional practice that uses a parallel process model of supervision teaching strengths-based supervision between supervisor and worker to facilitate strength-based practice between workers and families. Strength-based supervision relies more heavily on reflective questioning rather than directives. This model of supervision is also a developmental model in which supervisors help to facilitate workers' growth and development in autonomy, insight, and practice skills. As workers' skills and confidence increase, they are able to assume expertise in specific areas of practice and provide support to coworkers, and in so doing strengthen their own investment in the agency. The multiphased supervisory curriculum was designed to engage supervisors at all career stages in honing skills as reflective practitioners in organizational leadership and supervision. Evaluation results documented a high level of participation and knowledge gain. After 4 years, retention rates among those individuals employed at the beginning of the project ranged from 94% to 97%.

The University of Michigan collaborated with the Michigan Department of Human Services to develop training materials in specific areas of supervisory skills directed at worker retention, cultural humility, court work and legal ethics, and advanced implementation of the Indian Child Welfare Act (ICWA) of 1978. The supervisory skills training was developed from management literature and includes differential use of self in supervision based upon the supervisee's level of expertise, effective planning with a focus on the end goal, managing difficult people, and strategies for providing workers with feedback. Supervisors are asked to commit to trying at least one strategy in supervision over the following month, and when they return for the next training they assess their success at implementing the strategy and undertake problem solving if unsuccessful (University of Michigan, n.d.).

The cultural humility, legal, and advanced ICWA trainings were chosen to address areas that are challenging to workers and lead to frustration and premature turnover. Cultural humility is an approach to addressing cultural competency that, instead of teaching staff about different populations, teaches them how to learn from the diverse people they work with and how to develop respectful, collaborative relationships. The legal training evolved from the finding that workers' involvement in the court process was one of the most stressful and demoralizing parts of child welfare work and an important cause of turnover. This training uses case simulation exercises to improve perceptions and interactions between child welfare workers, families, and legal staff and to reduce the dissonance between social work and legal ethics. The advanced ICWA training, a one-day case-based training program, addresses practical implementation issues with ICWA and its interaction with other federal statutes.

Michigan State University developed a series of training workbooks focused on the supervisor's role and based on key principles emerging from the literature on child welfare retention, that is, retention can be strengthened by understanding and reinforcing the resiliency factors that lead people to choose this line of work. The relationship between the child welfare worker and supervisor is among the most important factors in retention, and because turnover tends to be heaviest during the first year on the job, supervision of new workers is especially important. Furthermore, a strength-based approach to supervision is important in modeling how staff should treat their own clients. Thus, the training reinforces that building on staff strengths is important for retention as well as for positive child and family outcomes (Michigan State University School of Social Work, 2007).

Organizational interventions. The review of research on specific agency work environment factors noted a high degree of variability in the areas studied and in their effects on retention. The R&R projects worked in different ways to facilitate organizational change in the specific factors found to be important in the projects' states. For example, the University of Denver's Western Regional Recruitment and Retention Project worked with state child welfare agencies in Colorado, Arizona, and Wyoming to address recruitment, selection, and retention in five rural and urban sites. The project team conducted comprehensive organizational assessments that guided a strategic planning process in each site, implemented site-specific strategies, and reassessed progress on an ongoing basis. The collaboration between the University of Denver and the public child welfare agency in each state was implemented through teams at each site composed of staff from both organizations (Potter, Comstock, Brittain, & Hanna, 2009).

As an example of what was accomplished in one site, in the first 2 years the team streamlined the vacancy and hiring processes; standardized the process for selecting staff, including developing an RJP video; restructured the on-the-job training program; and increased training opportunities in general. Toward the goal of improving organizational culture, the team openly addressed concerns about a culture of fear that had emerged strongly in the organizational assessment and made a commitment to move away from compliance-based management. In addition, the team conducted a workload study and implemented a variety of alternative work schedules that included telecommuting, part-time, flexible work schedules, and compressed workweeks. The team implemented a plan for rewarding and recognizing staff achievements and a communication plan to facilitate the transmission of information across the agency (Potter et al., 2009).

Using a different strategy, the University at Albany focused on improving organizational climate and retention through the use of design teams. Based on action theory, organizational learning theory, and the work of Argyris and Schon (1978) and Senge (1980), the design teams function as mechanisms for organizational learning and improvement. The design team intervention was implemented in four county agencies in upstate New York and one New York City borough that were experiencing problems with high turnover, defined as being 25% or higher for 2 consecutive years before the project began (Strolin-Goltzman, 2010). Each team was composed of staff from various levels (frontline workers, supervisors, managers) and units (child protection, foster care, etc.) of the public child welfare agency. Trained external facilitators worked with the design teams to identify priorities and help devise solutions to problems that were related to staff turnover and negative client outcomes (Caringi et al., 2008; Lawson et al.,

2006; Strolin-Goltzman et al., 2009). The design team intervention was characterized as data driven, solution focused, and action oriented, and the external facilitators worked to ensure fidelity to the intervention model through a carefully planned multiphased process (Strolin-Goltzman, 2010).

Through a quasi-experimental evaluation comparing the five intervention sites with seven other agencies that were assessed as high turnover sites, the intervention sites fared significantly better in job satisfaction, commitment to the agency, and intention to stay. The intervention sites also experienced a significantly greater decrease in intention to leave the agency over time than the comparison sites (Strolin-Goltzman, 2010).

NCWWI

Building on the accomplishments of the recruitment and retention projects, in 2008 the CB funded a 5-year NCWWI. The purpose of the NCWWI was to strengthen the capacity of the child welfare workforce nationally with a focus on improving outcomes for children and families. The scope of the NCWWI's work is broad. Several initiatives support leadership development in public agencies and in private agencies that provide case management under contract with the state as well as tribal child welfare systems. The specific activities include disseminating effective and promising workforce practices, development and sustaining national peer networks, coordinating traineeship programs at the BSW and MSW level, and developing leadership training for supervisors and middle managers. NCWWI is a member of the CB's Child Welfare Training and Technical Assistance Network (NCWWI, 2010a).

All activities of the NCCWI are based on developing leadership capacity for child welfare agencies to perform effectively. NCCWI developed a leadership competency framework that presents a conceptual model of leadership and specifies the competencies needed by staff at each level of the organization to lead positive change (NCWWI, 2010b). Based on the competing values approach (Preston, 2005; Quinn & Rohrbaugh, 1983), the framework proposes that the environment of the child welfare leader consists of four quadrants, each with a corresponding focus: internal flexibility (leading people/workforce development), external flexibility (leading in context/building collaborative relationships), internal control (leading for results/accountability), and external control (leading change/goal setting). Furthermore, the conceptual framework specifies five pillars of leadership that characterize the attributes of effective child welfare leadership: (a) being adaptive, the ability to learn new ways to respond to emerging challenges (Heifitz & Linsky, 2002); (b) being collaborative, the ability to engage with the surrounding community in a spirit of partnership (Lawson, 2008); (c) being distributive, in which leadership and decision making are instilled at all levels of the organization (Spillane, 2006); (d) being inclusive, the quality of encouraging participation of diverse groups in organizational processes (Ryan, 2006); and (e) being outcome-focused, the ability to use technical knowledge to analyze problems and use data to inform decisions that lead to desired measurable results (Lawson, 2008).

Leadership for middle managers. Middle managers play an important role in employee retention as they help to establish the organizational climate and the agency's external and internal relationships. To promote leadership development among middle managers, NCWWI created the Leadership Academy for Middle Managers, consisting of four components: pretraining work including readings, self-assessment, and completion of an introductory module; selection of a change initiative each individual works on throughout the academy; a 5-day in-person leadership academy; and peer networking activities including webinars, following the residential program to support trainees' implementation of their change initiative. Participants have been selected from each of the 10 federal regions with an explicit intention to recruit individuals from every state as well as tribal leaders from each region.

The leadership academy is not a substitute for basic management training; rather, it focuses on the leadership role of the child welfare manager. Participants learn how to identify their personal style of leadership and how to use it effectively. They learn the attributes of leadership and skills that are important to adaptive, collaborative, distributive, inclusive, and outcome-focused leadership. Participants learn how to lead change, how to lead people, how to lead for achieving results, and how to build collaborative relationships. The academy also focuses on how to work effectively within the cultural and policy environment, and how to build an organizational culture that strengthens partnerships with families. Using data to inform the change process and implementation science for sustained systems change are stressed. The in-person residential format provides opportunities for trainees to learn and practice skills, and follow-up coaching and mentoring provide participants with ongoing support when they return to their agency settings to work on implementing their change initiative.

Leadership for supervisors. Complementing the Leadership Academy for Middle Managers is a Leadership Academy for Supervisors (LAS), designed to develop leadership skills among experienced child welfare supervisors who are interested in leadership positions in their own units or managerial positions. The LAS is delivered in an online format that participants can complete at their own pace. To provide further support, webinar sessions are convened for each of the six core modules, allowing supervisor trainees to interact with peers (NCWWI, 2010a). The LAS was intended to be completed individually by supervisors across the country, but early experiences found that few supervisors were able to sustain their participation for the entire program because of heavy workloads, lack of time, competing demands, and lack of institutional support for their participation. However, several states wanted to provide leadership training to their supervisors through the LAS. In this *state-directed* approach, supervisors' participation is legitimized, and a team from the state helps implement the program and reduce barriers to participation that emerged in the individualized approach. States have also been able to adapt delivery of the curriculum in ways that best fit their needs.

Child welfare traineeships. A third important function of the NCWWI is administering child welfare traineeships that support child welfare social work programs at the BSW or MSW level with a particular focus on building leadership capacity. The CB had previously administered such traineeships directly, but administering these through NCWWI provides better coordination, increased support, and a consistent evaluation. The traineeships recruit diverse students and provide stipends to help support the costs of their education. Each program also offers an educational experience designed to prepare trainees for child welfare work through the development or innovation of child welfare curricula. All trainees are expected to have their field placements in child welfare agencies, complete all curricular requirements of the traineeship program, and work in child welfare agencies following graduation.

At the institutional level the traineeships are intended to build capacity among schools of social work, prepare students for culturally competent child welfare work, and prepare students as future child welfare leaders. Twelve schools of social work are currently participating in this traineeship program. Evaluation results thus far yield promising findings; in the first 2 years of these traineeships, over 150 students were awarded stipends, and more than 100 have already completed their social work degrees. Furthermore, all who completed their degree in the first year successfully obtained positions in child welfare agencies. The only ones who did not were a small number of BSW graduates who postponed their employment obligations in order to complete their MSWs (NCWWI, 2011).

COMPREHENSIVE WORKFORCE PROJECTS

During the same funding cycle as the NCWWI, the CB continued to support university–child welfare partnerships through child welfare comprehensive workforce grants. Six universities were funded through 5-year cooperative agreements to work collaboratively with one or more child welfare agencies. The scope of effort was broad, encompassing comprehensive assessment of the state's workforce practices; development and implementation of a plan to address recruitment, training, and retention; implementation of a traineeship program to strengthen professional education; and collaboration with the NCWWI and the CB's larger network of technical assistance and training providers.

Each comprehensive workforce project is designed to address the particular needs of the child welfare agency. For example, one project is focusing on the needs of the workforce in voluntary agencies under contract to the state, another is working with a group of community-based services providers and a tribal service provider, and a third is focusing on midcareer staff in a county-based child welfare system. The comprehensive workforce projects are each conducting site-specific evaluations and collaborating on a cross-site evaluation, but results are not yet available.

This chapter focuses on CB-sponsored initiatives to reprofessionalize child welfare. We note that individual states have implemented strategies such as modifying job classification systems, increasing educational requirements, and developing systematic recruitment approaches to better identify job candidates with a good fit for child welfare work. Space limitations preclude a comprehensive examination of each state's efforts in this area.

CONCLUSIONS AND IMPLICATIONS

Child welfare has long been considered to have a workforce crisis with high turnover, difficulties filling vacant positions, high levels of burnout, ineffective performance, and low status. Previous strategies to reprofessionalize child welfare focused primarily on providing opportunities for social work education, but the issues have proven to be more complex. Social work education has a role in child welfare recruitment and retention, but addressing systemic issues related to the practice setting and environment are equally if not more important in ensuring a competent and committed workforce. Research has strengthened our understanding of factors contributing to successful recruitment and retention of child welfare employees, but many questions remain unanswered.

Child welfare workforce research is abundant, but each study is site or state specific, uses a different sampling approach or different configurations of independent and dependent variables, and similar constructs are measured differently. The vast majority of these studies are conducted on the public sector workforce; we know little about the private sector workforce and how various aspects of child welfare work may affect retention differently across sectors. The National Survey of Child and Adolescent Well-Being (U.S. Department of Health & Human Services, 2003) collects some data relevant to the workforce, but has a limited focus on private sector workers and does not assess retention. A nationally representative study of the child welfare workforce across the public and private sectors is long overdue, one that includes the most salient constructs with well-validated measures. Such a study would help to sort through the confusing and sometimes contradictory findings gleaned from the existing research.

Building on the current knowledge base, the CB has spearheaded a host of new initiatives to support university–child welfare partnerships directed at creating systemic changes. These partnerships are implementing interventions to improve agency work environments, strengthen leadership and supervision, enhance opportunities for professional growth and development, and ensure that recruitment and selection of employees result in a good fit between the employee and the job. These efforts represent promising, comprehensive approaches to achieving the reprofessionalization of child welfare. Continued research on these and emergent initiatives will establish their long-term effectiveness in improving retention of a competent and committed workforce and ultimately whether strengthening the workforce will result in improved outcomes for children and families.

REFERENCES

Adoption Assistance and Child Welfare Act, Pub. L. No. 96-272 (1980).

Argyris, C., & Schon, D. (1978). *Organizational learning: A theory of action perspective.* Reading, MA: Addison-Wesley.

Auerbach, C., McGowan, B. G., Ausberger, A., Strolin-Goltzman, J., & Schudrich, W. (2010). Differential factors influencing public and voluntary child welfare workers' intention to leave. *Children and Youth Services Review, 32,* 1396–1402.

Barth, R. P., Lloyd, E. C., Christ, S. L., Chapman, M. V., & Dickinson, N. (2008). Child welfare worker characteristics and job satisfaction: A national study. *Social Work, 53*(3), 199–209.

Cahalane, H., & Sites, E. W. (2008). The climate of child welfare employee retention. *Child Welfare, 87*(1), 91–114.

Caringi, J., Strolin-Goltzman, J., Lawson, H., McCarthy, M., Briar-Lawson, K., & Claiborne, N. (2008). Child welfare design teams: An intervention to improve workforce retention and facilitate organizational development. *Research on Social Work Practice, 18*(6), 565–574.

Chernesky, R. H., & Israel, M. K. (2009). Job expectations and intention to leave in a state child welfare agency. *Journal of Public Child Welfare, 3,* 23–39.

Collins-Camargo, C., Ellett, C. D., & Lester, C. (2012). Measuring organizational effectiveness to develop strategies to promote retention in public child welfare. *Children and Youth Services Review, 34,* 289–295.

Curry, D., McCarragher, M., & Dellmann-Jenkins, M. (2005). Training, transfer, and turnover: Exploring the relationship among transfer of learning factors and staff retention in child welfare. *Children and Youth Services Review, 27*(8), 931–948.

DePanfilis, D., & Zlotnik, J. L. (2008). Retention of front-line staff in child welfare: A systematic review of research. *Children and Youth Services Review, 30,* 995–1008.

Dickinson, N. S., & Painter, J. S. (2009). Predictors of undesired turnover for child welfare workers. *Child Welfare, 88*(5), 187–208.

Dickinson, N. S., & Perry, R. E. (2002). Factors influencing the retention of specially educated public child welfare workers. *Journal of Health & Social Policy, 15*(3/4), 89–103.

Ellett, A. J. (2009). Intentions to remain employed in child welfare: The role of human caring, self-efficacy beliefs, and professional organizational culture. *Children and Youth Services Review, 31*(1), 78–88.

Ellett, A. J., & Leighninger, L. (2007). What happened? An historical analysis of the de-professionalization of child welfare with implications for policy and practice. *Journal of Public Child Welfare, 1*(1), 3–34.

Faller, K. C., Masternak, M., Grinnell-Davis, C., Grabarek, M., Sieffert, J., & Bernatovicz, F. (2009). Realistic job previews in child welfare: State of innovation and practice. *Child Welfare, 88*(5), 23–47.

Fox, S., Miller, V. & Barbee, A. P. (2003). Finding and keeping child welfare workers: Effective use of training and professional development. *Journal of Human Behavior in the Social Environment, 7*(1/2), 67–82.

Glisson, C., & James, L. R. (2002). The cross-level effects of culture and climate in human service teams. *Journal of Organizational Behavior, 23*, 767–794.

Gonzalez, R. P., Faller, K. C., Ortega, R. M., & Tropman, J. (2009). Exit interviews of child welfare workers. *Journal of Public Child Welfare, 3*(1), 40–63.

Heifetz, R., & Linsky, M. (2002). *Leadership on the line: Staying alive through the dangers of leading.* Boston, MA: Harvard Business School Press.

Hopkins, K. M., Murdock, N. R. & Rudolph, C. S. (1999). Impact of university-agency partnerships in child welfare on organizations, workers, and work activities. *Child Welfare, 78*(6), 749–773.

Indian Child Welfare Act, 93 Stat. 3071 (1978).

Jacquet, S. E., Clark, S. J., Morazes, J. L., & Withers, R. (2007). The role of supervision in the retention of public child welfare workers. *Journal of Public Child Welfare, 1*(3), 27–54.

Jayaratne, S., & Faller, K. C. (2009). Commitment of private and public agency workers to child welfare: How long do they plan to stay? *Journal of Social Service Research, 35*, 251–261.

Jones, L. P., & Okamura, A. (2000). Reprofessionalizing child welfare services: An evaluation of a Title IV-E training program. *Research on Social Work Practice, 10*(5), 607–621.

Landsman, M. (2001). Commitment in public child welfare. *Social Service Review*, 75 (3), 386–419.

Landsman, M. (2007). Supporting child welfare supervisors to improve worker retention. *Child Welfare, 86*(2), 105–124.

Landsman, M. J. (2008). Pathways to organizational commitment. *Administration in Social Work, 32*(2), 105–132.

Lawson, H. A. (2008). *A leadership/management matrix with relevant competencies and indicators of sustainable systems change.* Unpublished manuscript, University at Albany, State University of New York.

Lawson, H., Claiborne, N., McCarthy, M., Strolin, J., Briar-Lawson, K., Caringi, J., ... Sherman, R. (2005). *Retention planning to reduce workforce turnover in New York State's public child welfare systems.* Albany: New York State Social Work Education Consortium, University at Albany School of Social Welfare.

Lawson, H., McCarthy, M., Briar-Lawson, K., Miraglia, P., Strolin, J., & Caringi, J. (2006). A complex partnership to optimize and stabilize the public child welfare workforce. *Professional Development, 9*(2/3), 122–139.

Lieberman, A., Hornby, H., & Russell, M. (1988). Analyzing the educational backgrounds and work experiences of child welfare personnel: A national study. *Social Work, 33*, 485–489.

Michigan State University School of Social Work. (2007). *Staff retention in child and family services: The role of leaders. Workbook 1.* Retrieved from http://www.socialwork.msu.edu/outreach/docs/Workbook%201%20Role%20of%20Leaders%206-07-07.pdf

Morazes, J. L., Benton, A. D., Clark, S. J., & Jacquet, S. E. (2010). Views of specially-trained child welfare social workers. *Qualitative Social Work, 9*(2), 227–247.

Mor Barak, M. E., Levin, A., Nissly, J. A., & Lane, C. J. (2006). Why do they leave? Modeling child welfare workers' turnover intentions. *Children and Youth Services Review, 28*, 548–577.

Mor Barak, M., Nissly, J., Levin, A. (2001). Antecedents to retention and turnover among child welfare, social work, and other human service employees: What can we learn from past research? A review and meta-analysis. *Social Service Review, 75* (4), 625–661.

Mor Barak, M. E., Travis, D. J., Pyun, H., & Xie, B. (2009). The impact of supervision on worker outcomes: A meta-analysis. *Social Service Review, 83* (1), 3–32.

National Child Welfare Workforce Institute. (2010a, February). *Leadership Academy for Supervisors (LAS) implementation resource package.* Albany, NY: Author.

National Child Welfare Workforce Institute. (2010b). *Leadership competency framework.* Albany, NY: Author.

National Child Welfare Workforce Institute. (2011). *NCWWI's child welfare traineeships: Twelve comprehensive program and innovation summaries.* Albany, NY: Author.

Nissly, J. A., Mor Barak, M. E., & Levin, A. (2005). Stress, support, and workers' intentions to leave their jobs in public child welfare. *Administration in Social Work, 29*(1), 79–100.

O'Donnell, J., & Kirkner, S. L. (2009). A longitudinal study of factors influencing the retention of Title IV-E master's of social work graduates in public child welfare. *Journal of Public Child Welfare, 3,* 64–86.

Pecora, P. J., Whittaker, J. K., Maluccio, A. N., & Barth, R. P. (2000). *The child welfare challenge: Policy, practice, and research* (2nd ed.). Hawthorn, NY: Aldine de Gruyter.

Potter, C. C., Comstock, A., Brittain, C., & Hanna, M. (2009). Intervening in multiple states: Findings from the Western Regional Recruitment Project. *Child Welfare, 88*(5), 169–185.

Preston, M. S. (2005). Child welfare management training: Towards a pedagogically sound curriculum. *Administration in Social Work, 29*(4), 89–111.

Quinn, R. E., & Rohrbaugh, J. (1983). A spatial model of effectiveness criteria: Towards a competing values approach to organizational analysis. *Management Science, 29*(3), 363–377.

Robin, S. C., & Hollister, C. D. (2002). Career paths and contributions of four cohorts of IV-E funded MSW child welfare graduates. *Journal of Health and Social Policy, 15*(3/4), 53–67.

Rosenthal, J. A., & Waters, E. (2006). Predictors of child welfare worker retention and performance: Focus on Title IV-E-funded social work education. *Journal of Social Service Research, 32*(3), 67–85.

Ryan, J. (2006). *Inclusive leadership.* San Francisco, CA: Jossey-Bass.

Rycraft, J. R. (1994). The party isn't over: The agency role in the retention of public child welfare caseworkers. *Social Work, 39*(1), 75–80.

Scannapieco, M. & Connell-Carrick, K. (2003). Do collaborations with schools of social work make a difference for the field of child welfare? Practice, retention, and curriculum. *Journal of Human Behavior in the Social Environment, 7*(1/2), 35–51.

Scannapieco, M., & Connell-Carrick, K. (2007). Child welfare workplace: The state of the workforce and strategies to improve retention. *Child Welfare, 86*(6), 31–52.

Senge, P. (1980). *The fifth discipline: Art and practice of learning organizations.* New York, NY: Doubleday/Currency.

Smith, B. (2005). Job retention in child welfare: Effects of perceived organizational support, supervisor support and intrinsic job value. *Children and Youth Services Review, 27*(2), 153–169.

Spillane, J. (2006). *Distributed leadership.* San Francisco, CA: Wiley.

Strand, V. C. & Bosco-Ruggiero, S. (2010). Initiating and sustaining a mentoring program for child welfare staff. *Administration in Social Work, 34*(1), 49–67.

Strand, V. C., & Dore, M. M. (2009). Job satisfaction in a stable state child welfare workforce: Implications for staff retention. *Children and Youth Services Review, 31*, 391–397.

Strolin-Goltzman, J. (2008). Should I stay or should I go? A comparison study of intention to leave among public child welfare systems with high and low turnover rates. *Child Welfare, 87*(4), 125–143.

Strolin-Goltzman, J. (2010). Improving turnover in public child welfare: Outcomes from an organizational intervention. *Children and Youth Services Review, 32*, 1388–1395.

Strolin-Goltzman, J., Auerbach, C., McGowan, B. G., & McCarthy, M. L. (2008). The relationship between organizational characteristics and workforce turnover among rural, urban, and suburban public child welfare systems. *Administration in Social Work, 32*(1), 77–91.

Strolin-Goltzman, J., Lawrence, C., Auerbach, C., Caringi, J., Claiborne, N., Lawson, H., ...Shim, M. (2009). Design teams: A promising organizational intervention for improving turnover rates in the child welfare workforce. *Child Welfare, 88*(5), 149–168.

University of Michigan School of Social Work. (n.d.). *Recruitment & retention of child welfare professionals program: Project evaluation.* Retrieved from http://www.ssw.umich.edu/public/currentProjects/rrcwp/finalReport.pdf

University of Southern Maine. (2008). *Final report: Recruitment and retention of child welfare staff.* Retrieved from http://www.cwti.org/RR/R%20&%20R%20Final%20Report/FINAL%20RE PORT%2012-31-08.pdf

U.S. Department of Health & Human Services, Office of Planning, Research and Evaluation. (2003). *Child, family, and caseworker constructs, their rationale and the source in NSCAW data collection.* Retrieved from http://www.acf.hhs.gov/sites/default/files/opre/nscaw_data_collection.pdf

U. S. General Accounting Office. (2003). *HHS could play a greater role in helping child welfare agencies recruit and retain staff* (GAO-03-357). Washington, DC: Author.

Weaver, D., Chang, J., Clark, S.., & Rhee, S. (2007). Keeping public child welfare workers on the job. *Administration in Social Work, 31*(2), 5–25.

Westbook, T. M., Ellis, J., & Ellett, A. J. (2006). Improving retention among public child welfare workers: What can we learn from the insights and experiences of committed survivors? *Administration in Social Work, 30*(4), 37–62.

Yankeelov, P. A., Barbee, A. P., Sullivan, D., & Antle, B. F. (2009). Individual and organization factors in job retention in Kentucky's child welfare agency. *Children and Youth Services Review, 31*, 547–554.

Zlotnik, J. L., (2002). Preparing social workers for child welfare practice: Lessons from an historical review of the literature. *Journal of Health and Social Policy, 15* (3/4), 5–21.

Zlotnik, J. L. (2003). The use of Title IV-E training funds for social work education: An historical perspective. *Journal of Human Behavior in the Social Environment, 7*(1/2), 5–20.

Zlotnik, J. L., & Cornelius, L. (2000). Preparing social work students for child welfare careers: The use of Title IV-E training funds in social work education. *Journal of Baccalaureate Social Work, 5*(2), 1–14.

10

CHILD WELFARE RESEARCH
The Neglected Mandate

Crystal Collins-Camargo

After its creation in 1912 to perform essentially a research function, a series of statutory, organizational, and funding changes gradually led to the Children's Bureau (CB) relinquishing its internal research capacity and fulfilling its research mission through contracting and grants to university researchers and others. Over the years, methodology and funding lagged behind that of other federal agencies. As evidence-based practice has emerged as an important standard for social work, little is known about effective interventions in child welfare. With additional support, the CB is in an excellent position to provide leadership in promoting an integrated approach to child welfare research.

THE ORIGINAL RESEARCH MISSION

Julia Lathrop (1912), the first chief of the CB, described its legislated mandate as to

> investigate and report . . . upon all matters pertaining to the welfare of
> children and child life . . . , and shall especially investigate the questions
> of infant mortality, the birth rate, orphanage, juvenile courts, desertion,
> dangerous occupations, accidents and diseases of children, employment,

legislation affecting children in the several states and territories. (CB Act of April 6, 1912)

The term *investigate* certainly implied a research function with dissemination to follow. Lathrop noted that this mandate was "without boundaries," but that it would hopefully "offer a satisfying career to increasing numbers of young people of education and high social ideals." This hints at the origins of what would come to be a close connection between higher education and the CB.

The agency's second chief, Grace Abbott (1923), said that with the creation of the CB it was hoped it "would undertake on a national scale much-needed scientific research in the whole field" (p. 1). She described Lathrop's task to make a "beginning in this vast field of social research, which would establish respect for the scientific quality of the work of the bureau and at the same time make the conclusions reached available to the individual" (p. 2). Prior to 1925, the CB's work was focused primarily on research into the well-being of children, since its only administrative responsibilities were to enforce the Child Labor Laws in 1917–18 (Tobey, 1974). This focus was to change drastically, and the initial approach of conducting research internally was not to be sustained.

Following the passage of the Social Security Act of 1935, the CB's research was partially set aside to focus on recovery from the Depression and on development of Social Security programs. This refocusing on programs began a path that continues today. However, studies conducted during this period examined foster care placement, juvenile delinquency, infant and maternal mortality, and child labor, the latter significantly influencing the passage of the Fair Labor Standards Act in 1938 (Bradbury, 1962). During the early 1940s, however, any research that was not seen as contributing to the war effort was suspended. Bradbury observed that "never since the war years has the Bureau recovered its research programs" (p. 54).

A NEW POSTWAR DIRECTION

After recovery from the Second World War, the CB was moved to the Federal Security Agency (without the CB's child labor programs, which had been a primary research area) and focused on federal–state grants in aid programs. In 1951 CB administrators reviewed all previously published studies and research activities and considered recommendations from researchers, publishing *A Research Program of the Children's Bureau*. This report concluded that its studies should "focus on children whose health and welfare were in jeopardy" (Bradbury, 1962, p. 77). The report analyzed the investigative function, articulating two objectives: to gather facts to inform the nation on matters negatively affecting the welfare of children (which was attributed to its originating legislation) and to determine effective approaches to assisting children and families (which it drew from the rearticulation of the CB's responsibilities under Title V of the Social Security Act). The publication linked these objectives as forming the basis for an integrated research program, specifically noting the CB's responsibility to stimulate external research identifying research questions and methods and assisting others engaged in research (Bradbury, 1962).

Building on its earlier research collaborations with the School of Social Administration at the University of Chicago, the CB brought researchers together to collaborate on juvenile delinquency research and collected data from a representative national sample of juvenile courts, an important step forward in its own research (Bradbury, 1962). Reports were made to Congress on child welfare services, juvenile delinquency, and children in migrant families. There was a focus on developing program evaluation methods and compiling statistical data from state agencies on services for children. In 1960 the CB conducted perhaps one of the first studies on the topic, "Salaries and Working Conditions of Social Welfare Manpower," which included staff in public assistance, child welfare, and other settings, and noted an increase in professional social work positions by 74% over a 10-year period. The study observed a proportional decrease in workers with a graduate degree in social work (Bradbury, 1962), giving further support to the CB's long-lasting interest in funding workforce education in social work and other professions related to its mission.

This era also marked increased emphasis on child welfare research within the social work profession. In 1956 the Social Work Research Section of the National Association of Social Workers (NASW) sponsored the Conference on Research in the Children's Field, recognizing the relatively small body of research in this field of practice, which particularly focused on foster care and adoption. In 1963 NASW and the Child Welfare League of America cosponsored the Institute on Child Welfare Research to acknowledge the expansion of child welfare scholarship. The papers presented were published in a compendium, *The Known and Unknown in Child Welfare Research: An Appraisal* (Norris & Wallace, 1965).

FROM PRIMARY RESEARCHER TO PROMOTING AND SUPPORTING RESEARCH

In 1961 the CB convened university researchers and other experts to advise the agency regarding the 1962 amendments to the Social Security Act that would enable the CB to make grants for research and demonstration projects. Participants discussed challenges to service effectiveness and innovative prevention and treatment methods that should be tested through demonstration projects. A summary of these discussions, published in *Research in Child Welfare* (CB, 1961), emphasized that the CB must play a leadership role by prioritizing topics and providing technical assistance on design and data analysis to grantees. Basic and applied research should be supported through grants to universities and cooperative or contractual agreements. The CB was advised to support continuity through funding studies around a topical area of interest over time as opposed to individual, unrelated projects. The need for development of competent researchers in child welfare was also recognized (CB, 1961).

The 1962 amendments allocated $275,000 to the CB to make grants for "(1) special research and demonstration projects in the field of child welfare which are of regional or national significance, and (2) special projects for the demonstration of methods or facilities which show promise of substantial contribution to the advancement of child welfare" (Bradbury, 1962, p. 120). Institutions of higher education, agencies, and organizations engaged in research or child welfare services were eligible to apply. CB chief Katherine Oettinger asserted that CB research should be done

in a way that makes use of both the wider perspectives and the increased research resources of the 1960's. In addition to conducting its own investigations, the Bureau might well become a center for collecting and analyzing and correlating all relevant research. (Bradbury, 1962, p. 130)

The course for the CB's approach to research over the subsequent 50 years was in many ways set at this critical point, and the role of universities became extremely important in building the evidence base for programs. *It's Your Children's Bureau* (CB, 1964), echoed this new sentiment, noting the CB's emphasis was on fact gathering and disseminating findings from external research, conducting internal research only rarely.

In *The Children's Bureau's Job Today* (CB, 1969), it was observed that the number of children and youths in the United States nearly equaled the total population in 1912, and that knowledge about children and youths had grown significantly. Additional amendments to the Social Security Act in 1967 gave the CB authority to financially support demonstration projects regarding innovative service provision. Particular attention was paid in this publication to child welfare traineeships supported through Title IV-B (CB, 1969).

During the 1960s the CB was moved into the Welfare Division of the Department of Health, Education, and Welfare. While continuing to follow its initial mission, the CB was placing special emphasis on "making grants for research and acting as a spokesman on behalf of children" (Green, 1972, p. 6). With this organizational change, child health and crippled children's services were moved to the Public Health Service. The passage of the Child Abuse Prevention and Treatment Act in 1974 created a separate agency, the National Center on Child Abuse and Neglect (NCCAN), which took over most of the child welfare research funding. During this period, studies were funded that proved critical to the field related to permanency planning. The Oregon Project tested casework approaches toward permanency planning for children and the adjustment of children in placement (Lahti et al., 1978) and laid the foundation for legislation in this regard. The Child Welfare Act of 1980 provided incentives for states to collect data on children in foster care, develop management information systems, review cases of children in out-of-home care every 6 months, and provide placement prevention and reunification services (CB, 1987). Bureau-funded research focused on intensive family services that could serve such a prevention function (e.g., Fraser, Pecora, & Haapala, 1991; Nelson & Landsman, 1992). Both pieces of federal legislation responded to and served as benchmarks for research in child welfare.

These statutory changes paved the way for secondary analysis of large data sets through the CB-funded National Data Archive on Child Abuse and Neglect, established in 1988. This is the repository for the National Child Abuse and Neglect Data System, the Adoption and Foster Care Analysis and Reporting System, and data from some CB-funded research to make it accessible to researchers (Waldfogel, 2000).

RESEARCH OVER THE PAST 20 YEARS

In 1991 the Task Force on Social Work Research, funded by the National Institute of Mental Health and, with a few exceptions, composed of representatives from schools of social work across the country, found that "Federal agencies with responsibility for child abuse and neglect, and services to low-income families do not have a research development strategy or means for systematically supporting research training and development" (p. 66). Similar concerns have been expressed by others (e.g., Johnson, Wells, Testa, & McDonald, 2003; National Association of Public Child Welfare Administrators [NAPCWA], 2005; U.S. General Accounting Office, 2003). Around the same time, the Administration on Children Youth and Families (ACYF) asked the National Academy of Science to convene the Panel on Research on Child Abuse and Neglect. University scholars assessed the status of research and recommended a research agenda (National Research Council, 1993). This landmark report noted fragmentation of research and researchers, including those supported through federally funded fellowships, funding of child abuse and neglect-related research across at least 28 federal agencies, and a lack of infrastructure to support a comprehensive approach. Wide-ranging recommendations subsequently influenced the CB and universities (National Research Council, 1993).

For many years NCCAN, an entity separate from the CB, supported child welfare research and demonstration programs designed to prevent, identify, and treat child abuse and neglect. NCCAN funded 948 grants from its inception in 1974 through 1997. In fiscal year 1995, over $8.7 million was allocated across 23 research (as opposed to demonstration) grants, with 13 of those awarded to universities. In contrast, in fiscal year 1997, 10 research grants were funded totaling about $4.7 million, with eight awarded to universities (NCCAN & CB, 1998). After a reauthorization of the Child Abuse Prevention and Treatment Act eliminated NCCAN, the CB was reorganized to encompass its successor, the Office on Child Abuse and Neglect, in 1998. Catherine Nolan, office director, observed that with this reorganization very little research funding remained in the CB budget (C. Nolan, personal communication, January 20, 2012).

Sally Flanzer, director of the CB's Division of Data, Research and Innovation during the 1990s and the early years of 2000, characterized the CB's approach to research as influenced by three dynamic tensions:

- The tension between "leading the field and seeding the field," that is, by selecting topics of study based on staff or federal priorities versus funding investigator-initiated research. Bureau-selected topics enable the agency to build on prior results but may not be most responsive to the field. Researcher-initiated topics can yield innovative research but can be harder to synthesize into generalizable knowledge than clusters of projects funded around an identified topic with a cross-site evaluation or synthesis of findings.
- The tension between systemic research such as organizational processes, financing, and the workforce, and research focused on direct practice—what works best for which family and why.
- The tension between research on prevention and research on treatment. (S. Flanzer, personal communication, December 16, 2011)

Flanzer recalled that pressures within the federal government caused the CB to upgrade its research program:

What happens with the knowledge that the public is paying for? It isn't enough to grow knowledge—what happens to it? We began to build a feedback loop—by baby steps—requiring evaluation, focusing on the quality of the knowledge being developed. . . . We tried to use some funds to grow new researchers in the field. . . . Grantee meetings used to be the feds talking to the field—this is what we want you to know. . . . Little by little we tried to get to half the time where grantees were telling us what they were learning.... We funded contractor-based external evaluations around topic areas. This was an important step forward to look across very heterogeneous grantees [to identify] the threads which are reliable enough to use in the field. (S. Flanzer, personal communication, December 16, 2011)

Jack Denniston, a child welfare program specialist working as a contractor in the CB's Division of Program Innovation, provided me with copies of all discretionary grant announcements funded by the CB from 1995 through 2011. Denniston's position was established to assist in developing funding announcements, promote consistency in knowledge development, and serve as a liaison with the Child Welfare Information Gateway to facilitate dissemination. He noted that emphasis over the past 8 years has been to improve the quality of knowledge developed by providing clear expectations related to evaluation of demonstration projects, evaluation of technical assistance to grantees, and increased rigor, such as encouraging the use of comparison designs or rigorous alternatives (J. Denniston, personal communication, January 5, 2012).

The tensions Flanzer noted can be observed as playing out over time in these funding announcements. Grant and cooperative agreement amounts, length, topics, and eligible applicants vary over time and by funding source (such as adoption opportunities). At times, the CB has published compendiums of its discretionary grant projects (e.g., ACYF, 2003). Nolan explained that "funding decision-making is based on the administration's agenda, legislative mandate or suggestion, what staff feel has been learned from previous projects and can build on, and what the field wants" (C. Nolan, personal communication, January 20, 2012).

Some funding opportunities such as professional education training programs and faculty and doctoral fellowships programs were only available to institutions of higher education with accredited social work programs, while others—even those with very specific research purposes—were available to a wide range of parties including public and nonprofit agencies, such as the 2001 investigator-initiated Research Advancing the State of the Art in Child Abuse and Neglect grant. The CB's emphasis on providing training and technical assistance through national resource centers has been a longstanding commitment. Other grants focused on creating capacity in the field, such as the Building Analytical Capacity for Child Welfare Programs in State Systems demonstration projects in 2001 and Tribal Title IV-E Plan Development grants in 2009. While over time, demonstration grants tended to require evaluation and the setting aside of a portion of funding for that purpose (Brodowski, Flanzer, Nolan, Shafer, & Kaye, 2007), the majority of grants fund program innovation as opposed to research.

Federally funded research has evolved through collaborative, multisite, and longitudinal research conducted primarily by university scholars. The National Survey of Child and Adolescent Well-Being is a longitudinal, nationally representative study on the functioning of children and families served by the child welfare system (Webb, Dowd, Harden, Landsverk, & Testa, 2010). Longitudinal Studies of Child Abuse and Neglect, a consortium of five coordinated longitudinal research studies, began examining the antecedents and consequences of child maltreatment in 1990 (Runyan et al., 1998).

In 2001 the CB launched an experiment in knowledge development by funding regional Quality Improvement Centers (QICs), some of which were housed in university social work programs. QICs are funded for 5 years to manage a cluster of competitively bid upon research and demonstration projects in a topical area. The QICs provide technical assistance, conduct cross-site evaluations, and disseminate results (Brodowski, Flanzer, Nolan, & Kaye, 2003). Following a national evaluation of this research mechanism (see Hafford, Brodowski, Nolan, & Denniston, 2006), the CB funded the first national QIC on the Privatization of Child Welfare Services in 2005. National QICs have the additional responsibility of facilitating nationwide information-sharing on promising practices and the emerging evidence base (Collins-Camargo et al., 2007). QICs hold promise for conducting clusters of collaborative, multisite research to fill knowledge gaps through more intensive technical assistance and ongoing dissemination than federal agencies can provide. The CB has also used this mechanism to support doctoral dissertations as opposed to directly funding grants for this purpose.

This QIC approach could be expanded in a number of ways, including funding universities to become national research centers to provide the national resource and implementation centers currently funded by the CB with evidence-informed knowledge to support their training and technical assistance efforts. The CB funded a National Child Welfare Research Center at the University of California, Berkeley in the 1990s, but this type of support for research infrastructure, unfortunately, was not sustained.

THE CURRENT POSITION OF RESEARCH

The current vision of the CB's position is outlined in a brochure titled "A Legacy of Service . . . a Vision for Change" (2011). Its subheadings hint at its vision, priorities, and strategy: partnership with states, tribes, other federal agencies; a Training and Technical Assistance Network to support states, tribes, communities, and professionals; matching funding of child welfare services from a number of legislative sources; supporting innovative research and program development through discretionary grants; monitoring outcomes through Child and Family Services Reviews (CFSRs), IV-E Foster Care Eligibility Reviews, and federal and state reporting systems; and sharing results, including Adoption and Foster Care Analysis and Reporting System reports, child welfare outcomes reports, and its user manual series (Children's Bureau, 2011).

Today the CB operates in a larger and more complex federal government than it did originally, and child welfare research is funded by several federal agencies. In fiscal year 1996, for example, the Interagency Research Committee (1997) published a report that encompassed child abuse and neglect-related research through the Department of Education, Department of Justice, and numerous agencies in the Department of Health and Human Services, including the Centers for Disease Control and Prevention, the Maternal and Child Health Bureau, and the National Institutes of Health in addition to ACYF. A total of 122 studies were included with only 6 housed in the CB.

Jan Shafer, director of the former Division of Data, Research and Innovation, now the Division of Program Innovation, noted that the CB has had little true research funding for two decades.

> The Department has over time reorganized, and there has been an ebb and flow of centralization and decentralization, and with it the research function has not remained with the Bureau. . . . A lot of our research is done in partnership with the Office of Planning, Research and

Development (OPRE) in the Administration for Children and Families and the office of the Assistant Secretary for Planning and Evaluation (ASPE). My division is primarily responsible for discretionary grant work, some of which is research-related. . . . Some other federal agencies are more mission-focused on research where we are mission-focused on programs. (J. Shafer, personal communication, January 6, 2012)

To illustrate the relative role of research in the CB's overall mission, Shafer noted that under $200 million of an almost $8 billion budget funds research and demonstration projects.

Shafer said the CB has benefited from research expertise in OPRE and the office of the assistant secretary for planning and evaluation, housed elsewhere in the Department of Health and Human Services. Mary Bruce Webb, director of child and family development in OPRE, stated that while her agency was originally focused on welfare and employment research, the CB now funnels funding to OPRE to oversee legislatively mandated research, such as the National Incidence Study, much of which is conducted through universities (M. B. Webb, personal communication, January 6, 2012). OPRE's mission very clearly outlines a research function: "In collaboration with ACF [Administration for Children and Families] program offices and others, OPRE is responsible for performance management for ACF, conducts research and policy analysis, develops and oversees research and evaluation projects to assess program performance and inform policy and practice" (OPRE, 2011, para. 3). Past events underscore efforts to focus the CB on program innovation, including the December 28, 2011, reorganization that moved CB and Family and Youth Services Bureau research staff up to report to the ACYF commissioner. The "Division of Program Innovation still provides leadership and direction in program development, innovation, and research, and recommends areas for research, demonstration and evaluation" (U.S. Department of Health and Human Services, 2011, p. 81506).

However, the CB is working to closely link its program administration, technical assistance, and evaluation functions, and universities play a key role in that. For example, after the first round of CFSRs documented a deficit in the completion of comprehensive assessments in states, the Training and Technical Assistance Network was tasked to develop tools on this topic, and the CB funded a cluster of demonstration projects on comprehensive family assessments. One of these projects was a partnership of the Ramsey County Community Human Services and the University of Minnesota School of Social Work.

The CB's website includes a searchable discretionary grants library, national child welfare statistics, reports to Congress, and briefs on federally funded research such as the Longitudinal Studies of Child Abuse and Neglect and the National Survey of Child and Adolescent Well-Being. In addition, in 2009 and 2011 the agency sponsored Child Welfare Evaluation Summits—knowledge dissemination conferences focusing on showcasing research in the field, evidence-based practice, and innovative methodology. Shafer described these summits as

> bringing together practitioners, researchers, evaluators . . . to discuss the nitty-gritty issues of evaluation in child welfare. I think this has helped to move the field. . . , and the issues associated with translating research to practice. Research is often completed and published, but not translated into implications for practice change. (J. Shafer, personal communication, January 5, 2012)

LOOKING TO THE FUTURE

After 100 years of investment, the evidence base in child welfare is hardly sufficient. Unlike some other fields, evidence-based practice is in an early stage of development, particularly in terms of practice techniques and programs that are well documented as producing desired outcomes (Barth, 2008; NAPCWA, 2005). Child welfare workers are struggling to address complex problems in partnership with the families they serve without sufficient evidence of effective practices or ways to adapt existing evidence to their own local context (Mullen, Bledsoe, & Bellamy, 2008).

The need to address this issue is well documented, such as Testa and Poertner's (2010) results-oriented approach to building accountability in the field, and Lindsey and Schlonsky's (2008) strategy for using technology to put knowledge from practice research in the hands of frontline staff. As the evidence grows, avenues for making evidence-based practice information accessible are appearing, such as the California Evidence-Based Clearinghouse for Child Welfare, which rates programs using a scientific scale. Although not federally funded, these examples reflect university leadership in child welfare research and its application. While the CB has supported identification of evidence-based practices, such as an OCAN-sponsored study to identify exemplary prevention programs based on the level of evidence to support them (Thomas, Leicht, Hughes, Madigan, & Dowell, 2003), there may never have been a more important time for the CB to lead the field in partnership with academia to address the research questions to enhance the field's ability to intervene effectively.

As Flanzer said, we need to make the case for

> how important it is to individual children—the mythic abused child who will bounce through foster homes, and lights fires to get a disruption before rejection, . . . who will run from [the system at 18, and] yet at 21 realizes that he needs to find that one social worker that really made a difference in his life. How do you tie research to those stories? We aren't doing research that will cure cancer, but we should think about our research in just that way: curing maltreatment. (S. Flanzer, personal communication, December 16, 2011)

CONCLUSIONS AND RECOMMENDATIONS

Once a free-standing unit with a chief in a presidential Cabinet-level position, the CB's organizational home has shifted several times, and its purview has narrowed. Once focused on the whole child, many of its original foci such as child labor and juvenile delinquency have shifted to other federal agencies (Zigler & Muenchow, 1985). Some have recommended the CB once again become the source and clearinghouse of information on children and families by promoting research and innovation, not program administration (Zigler & Muenchow, 1985).

It may not be necessary or even appropriate for the CB to redevelop the internal capacity for research as was originally envisioned. This is a complex field, and research expertise exists in universities. University social work programs, in particular, and the CB have common aims. But there is a need for the development and execution of a well-thought-out plan to build the evidence base in well-defined areas through longer-term lines of research and careful integration of what is learned. This is an important role for the CB, and much could be learned from other federal agencies regarding how to approach research questions in an intensive, integrated manner. A clear barrier to this, of course, is the level of funding allocated to the CB for research. The CB has improved knowledge development through funding clusters of research projects, cross-site evaluations, and emphasis on rigor. However, much funding still goes to demonstrations, and even within grant clusters, the variance across projects limits what can be learned. This is just a beginning, and the CB need not undertake this mission alone.

Although partnerships between social work education and child welfare agencies have historically focused on education and training through the Title IV-E program (Zlotnick, 2010), there has been growing emphasis on research collaborations, and the results of the federal CFSRs have demonstrated a tremendous need for improving child welfare direct and organizational practice (Institute for the Advancement of Social Work Research [IASWR], 2008). The use of federal training funds through Titles IV-B and E resulted in a significant increase in professional social workers in child welfare (Barth, Lloyd, Christ, Chapman, & Dickenson, 2008). Similar investment in building the evidence base is needed. This is an area where the CB could demonstrate leadership through structuring its discretionary grant program and through a purposeful partnership with social work education's National Association of Deans and Directors (NADD). In 2009 NADD conducted an electronic survey regarding child welfare research being conducted in schools of social work, revealing a wide range of topics and methodology. A significant amount was funded by federal sources, primarily the CB. A wide range of dissemination activities was reported (Nelson & Springer, 2009). Although a child welfare research mentoring program was discussed, it has not been implemented. Clearly the foundation exists in schools of social work, and periodic discussions have been initiated by CB staff with NADD. It may be time to revisit the CB's 1950s strategy to bring university researchers to the table to examine the CB's approach to fulfilling its research mission and chart a course that will efficiently and effectively build the child welfare evidence base.

However, social work education has not always been persistent in its commitment to child welfare research or documented the assets it brings to the table (Collins-Camargo & Hoffman, 2006). Universities must step up to the plate as well. An assessment funded by Casey Family Programs, which led to the development of a detailed toolkit for university–child welfare agency research partnerships, found that about 30 schools of social work had child welfare research centers or formal child welfare research partnerships (IASWR, 2008). However, this work is not coordinated into an integrated strategy to increase the child welfare direct and organizational practice evidence base. Much of the work in university research centers is funded through private foundations (IASWR, 2008). High university indirect cost rates also present a barrier.

According to the NAPCWA (2005), "The level of federal and state resources focused on important child welfare research questions and available for sophisticated research studies have long suffered from the relatively low priority legislative bodies have placed upon research" (p. 5). The $110 million allocated to knowledge development reported by the CB (Brodowski et al., 2007) pales in comparison to that of the National Institutes of Health's (2001) budget for research grants of $2.17 billion in 2007. The National Institute of Mental Health and the National Institute on Drug Abuse still support field-initiated research, as the CB did in the past (IASWR, 2008). Such approaches could be supported as long as they fit within the integrated strategy for building the evidence base to address critical gaps identified through CB/researcher collaboration.

The occasion of the centennial anniversary of the CB presents an opportunity to revisit its research mission and develop just such a strategy. The focus on service delivery and program administration needs to at least be shared with the critical role of leading the field of child welfare research. IASWR's (2008) toolkit related to child welfare–university partnerships to enhance child welfare research recommended a "home and funding stream for child welfare research at the federal level" (p. 41), including reinvigorating the research mission of the CB, reinstating Title IV-B 426 Discretionary Research Grant appropriation, allocating funding to support the CB's research priorities (e.g., CB, 2006), and learning from the model of other agencies, such as the National Institutes of Health, in building a research program.

The need to create a larger and stronger cadre of child welfare researchers remains, and the CB has supported dissertation and research fellowships through various mechanisms. However, the CB also needs to establish a network of researchers to identify research questions in need of study and synthesize and disseminate the knowledge developed. The CB has made progress in strengthening research expectations including funding multisite and longitudinal research, sponsoring Child Welfare Evaluation Summits highlighting cutting-edge research and methods, and requiring more rigorous demonstration project evaluations. In partnership with universities, a strategy could and should be developed that will close the gaps in the evidence base in child welfare long before the 125th-year anniversary is celebrated. Children, families, and child welfare workers in the United States deserve nothing less.

REFERENCES

Abbott, G. (1923). *Ten years' work for children*. Washington, DC: Children's Bureau.

Administration on Children, Youth and Families. (2003). *Compendium of discretionary grant projects funded in FY 2003*. Washington, DC: Author.

Barth, R. P. (2008). The move to evidence-based practice: How well does it fit child welfare services? *Journal of Public Child Welfare, 2*(2), 145–171.

Barth, R., Lloyd, C., Christ, S., Chapman, M., & Dickinson, N. (2008). Child welfare worker characteristics and job satisfaction: A national study. *Social Work, 53*, 199–209.

Bradbury, D. E. (1962). *Five decades of action for children: A history of the Children's Bureau*. Washington, DC: U.S. Department of Health, Education, and Welfare.

Brodowski, M., Flanzer, S., Nolan, C., & Kaye, E. (2003). Quality Improvement Centers on child protective services and adoption: Testing a regionalized approach to building the evidence base—a federal perspective. *Professional Development, 6*(1/2), 10–16.

Brodowski, M., Flanzer, S., Nolan, C., Shafer, J., & Kaye, E. (2007). Children's Bureau discretionary grants: Knowledge development through our research and demonstration projects. *Journal of Evidence-Based Social Work, 4*(3/4), 3–20.

Child Abuse Prevention and Treatment Act, Pub. L. No. 93-247 (1974).

Children's Bureau. (1961). *Research in child welfare*. CB Publication No. 389—1961. Washington, DC: U.S. Department of Health, Education, and Welfare.

Children's Bureau. (1964). *It's your Children's Bureau: The bureau's current program*. Washington, DC: U.S. Department of Health, Education, and Welfare.

Children's Bureau. (1969). *The Children's Bureau's job today.* Washington, DC: U.S. Department of Health, Education, and Welfare.

Children's Bureau. (1987). *The Children's Bureau at 75: 1912–1987 The commitment continues.* Washington, DC: U.S. Department of Health, Education, and Welfare.

Children's Bureau. (2006). Children's Bureau proposed research priorities for fiscal year 2006–2008. *Federal Register, 71*(23), 5856–5858. Retrieved from http://edocket.access.gpo.gov/2006/E6-1480.htm

Children's Bureau. (2011). *The Children's Bureau: A legacy of service . . . A vision of change.* Washington, D.C.: Author.

Children's Bureau Act of April 6, 1912, C. 73, 37 Stat. 79, 42 U.S.C. 191–194 (1976).

Collins-Camargo, C., Hall, J., Flaherty, C., Ensign, K., Garstka, T., Yoder, B., & Metz, A. (2007). Knowledge development and transfer on public/private partnerships in child welfare service provision: Using multi-site research to expand the evidence base. *Professional Development: The International Journal of Continuing Social Work Education, 10*(3), 14–31.

Collins-Camargo, C., & Hoffman, K. (2006). University/child welfare agency partnerships: Building a bridge between the ivory tower and the state office building. *Professional Development: International Journal of Continuing Social Work Education, 9*(2/3), 24–37.

Fraser, M. W., Pecora, P. J., & Haapala, D. (1991). *Families in crisis: The impact of intensive family preservation services.* New York, NY: Aldine de Gruyter.

Green, F. (1972). Sixty years of service to children: Children's Bureau 1912–1972. *Children Today, 1*(2).

Hafford, C., Brodowski, M. L., Nolan, C., & Denniston, J. (2006). The Children's Bureau quality improvement centers: Knowledge development through research collaborations in child welfare. *Professional Development, 9*(2), 12–23.

Institute for the Advancement of Social Work Research. (2008). *Strengthening university/agency research partnerships to enhance child welfare outcomes: A toolkit for building research partnerships.* Washington, DC: Author.

Interagency Research Committee. (1997). *Fifth forum on federally funded child abuse and neglect research.* Washington, DC: Author.

Johnson, M., Wells, S., Testa, M., & McDonald, J. (2003). Illinois's child welfare research agenda: An approach to building consensus for practice-based research. *Child Welfare, 82*(1), 53–75.

Lahti, J., Green, K., Emlen, A., Zendry, J., Clarkson, Q. D., Kuehnel, M., & Casciato, J. (1978). *A follow-up study of the Oregon Project: A summary*. Portland, OR: Portland State University Regional Research for Human Services.

Lathrop, J. C. (1912). The Children's Bureau. In *Proceedings of the National Conference of Charities and Corrections*. Washington, DC: Children's Bureau.

Lindsey, D., & Schlonsky, A. (Eds.). (2008). *Child welfare research: Advances for practice and policy*. New York, NY: Oxford University Press.

Mullen, E. J., Bledsoe, S. E., & Bellamy, J. L. (2008). Implementing evidence-based social work practice. *Research on Social Work Practice, 18*(4), 325–338. doi: 10.1177/1049731506297827

National Association of Public Child Welfare Administrators. (2005). *Guide for child welfare administrators on evidence-based practice*. Retrieved from http://www.aphsa.org/Home/doc/Guide-for-Evidence-Based-Practice.pdf

National Center on Child Abuse and Neglect & Children's Bureau. (1998). *Compendium of discretionary grants: Fiscal years 1975-1997*. Washington, DC: Author.

National Institutes of Health. (2011). *Mechanism detail: Actual obligations*. Retrieved from http://officeofbudget.od.nih.gov/pdfs/FY12/NIH%20Wide %20Mechanism%20Summary%20FY%201983%20-%202010%20 %28Updated%2010312010%20Value%20Only%29.pdf

National Research Council. (1993). *Understanding child abuse and neglect*. Washington, DC: National Academy Press.

Nelson, K. E., & Landsman, M. J. (1992). *Alternative models of family preservation: Family-based services in context*. Springfield, IL: Charles C Thomas.

Nelson, K., & Springer, C. (2009). *Summary of findings: NADD Child Welfare Task Force study*. (Unpublished report). Portland, OR: Portland State University.

Norris, M., & Wallace, B. (Eds.). (1965). *The known and unknown in child welfare research: An appraisal*. New York, NY: Child Welfare League of America and the National Association of Social Workers.

Office of Planning, Research and Evaluation. (2012). *About OPRE*. Retrieved from http://www.acf.hhs.gov/programs/opre/about_opre.html

Runyan, D. K., Curtis, P. A., Hunter, W. M., Black, M. M., Kotch, J. B., Bangdiwala, S., ...Landsverk, J. (1998). LONGSCAN: A consortium for longitudinal studies of maltreatment and the life course of children. *Aggression and Violent Behavior, 3*(3), 275–285.

Social Security Act. Pub. L. No. 74-271 (1935).

Social Security Act. Pub. L. No. 87-543 (1962)

Task Force on Social Work Research. (1991). *Building social work knowledge for effective services and policies: A plan for research development.* Retrieved from http://www .socialworkpolicy.org/wp-content/uploads/TFRonSWRNov1991_opt.pdf

Testa, M., & Poertner, J. (Eds.). (2010). *Fostering accountability: Using evidence to guide and improve child welfare policy.* New York, NY: Oxford University Press.

Thomas, D., Leicht, C., Hughes, C., Madigan, A., & Dowell, K. (2003). *Emerging practices in the prevention of child abuse and neglect.* Washington, DC: Caliber Associates.

Tobey, J. A. (1974). *The Children's Bureau: Its history, activities and organization.* New York, NY: AMS Press.

U.S. Department of Health and Human Services. (2011). Administration on Children, Youth and Families: Statement of organization, functions and delegations of authority. *Federal Register, 76*(249), 81505–81508.

U.S. General Accounting Office. (2003). *Child welfare: Enhanced federal oversight of Title IV-B could provide states additional information to improve services.* Retrieved from http://www.gao.gov/new.items/d03956.pdf

Waldfogel, J. (2000). Child welfare research: How adequate are the data? *Children and Youth Services Review, 22*(9/10), 705–741.

Webb, M. B., Dowd, K., Harden, B. J., Landsverk, J., & Testa, M. F. (2010). *Child welfare and child well-being.* New York, NY: Oxford University Press.

Zigler, E., & Muenchow, S. (1985). A room of their own: A proposal to renovate the Children's Bureau. *American Psychologist, 40*(8), 953–959.

Zlotnick, J. L. (2010). Fostering and sustaining university-agency partnerships. In M. F. Testa & J. Poertner, *Fostering accountability: Using evidence to guide and improve child welfare policy* (pp. 328–356). New York, NY: Oxford University Press.

11

DEVELOPING A BETTER FUTURE FOR CHILDREN AND FAMILIES IN THE UNITED STATES
Toward a Shared Vision for Child Welfare

Alberta Ellett

The emergence of formal graduate university social work education occurred only a few years prior to the establishment of the U.S. Children's Bureau (CB) in 1912 (Perry & Ellett, 2012). At that time the country was responding to a severe economic depression, a shift from an agrarian to an industrial economy, an undeveloped infrastructure, large numbers of immigrants, huge wealth and income disparities, dangerous child labor, limited free public school education, and a large proportion of children living in impoverished conditions (Costin, 1983; Costin, Karger, & Stoesz, 1996; Phillips, 2002). CB efforts to pass child labor laws resulted in greater access to free public school education (Trattner, 1970), and in 1935 the Social Security Act included provisions for states to provide child welfare services (Ellett & Leighninger, 2007).

In 2012 the United States finds itself in conditions similar to those of a century earlier, with a slow, jobless recovery from the Great Recession, a shift from an industrial to an information/service economy, a crumbling infrastructure, large numbers of immigrants, huge wealth and income disparities, inferior public education, and 15% of the population with 22% of children living in poverty in 2010 (Addy & Wright, 2012). Sadly, it seems, history has a way of repeating itself. Without a vision for the future and a reallocation of resources, maltreated children and their families will predictably experience poorer physical and mental health, remain undereducated, lack job skills, and remain dependent on an increasingly politicized society. Nevertheless, since its inception, the CB has remained a strong voice for the creation of environmental conditions that enable improved outcomes for kids and families.

This chapter begins with a brief overview of historical milestones framing the evolution of the relationship between the CB and graduate social work education focused on child welfare practice.[1] This overview is followed by some observations about the current status of child welfare as a field of social work practice and inquiry. Included is a discussion of concepts, issues, and controversies pertaining to the professionalization of the child welfare workforce. The final section describes the roles of the CB and schools of social work in establishing the vision of a better future for children and families in the United States.

SOCIAL WORK EDUCATION, CB, AND CHILD WELFARE PRACTICE: A HISTORICAL CONFLUENCE

Child welfare services in the United States emerged from private charitable societies that from the mid-1800s until the early 1900s provided child welfare services when need outstripped private societies' abilities to cover costs. Counties and local governments then became involved, and all states participated following the passage of the Social Security Act in 1935, with child welfare being a public–private partnership for the past century. The CB had approved 44 states' child welfare programs by 1938, with 709 employees working in public child welfare units by 1939 (CB, 1940). Concomitantly, there were 34 schools of social work in 1930 offering at least 1 year of graduate social work education. From its beginning, the CB believed in and endorsed employing trained MSWs for child welfare casework (Lundberg, 1926; Willard, 1930), including CB staff to set an example (Bradbury, 1956). Following passage of the Social Security Act, the CB funded educational leave for child welfare workers to attend graduate schools of social work. The CB was especially gratified that by 1939 256 caseworkers had attended graduate schools of social work (CB, 1940). In 1950, 54.3% of public and 66% of private child welfare employees had 1 or more years of graduate social work education (U.S. Bureau of Labor Statistics, 1952). This figure fell to only 30% by 1961 (Coll, 1995) and further declined to 28% with either a BSW or MSW degree in 1987 (Lieberman, Hornby, & Russell, 1988). This trend reversed in 2002 when the National Survey of Child and Adolescent Well-Being found that 39.5% of child welfare workers had a BSW or MSW degree (Barth, Lloyd, Christ, Chapman, & Dickinson, 2008).

By 1960 more MSWs were employed in public and private child welfare agencies than other social work practice areas. There was a collaborative working relationship between child welfare agencies and schools of social work with some child welfare content in social work curricula. Interestingly, schools gave greater emphasis to social work preparation for psychiatric services, only placing 13.8% of MSW students in child welfare internships (Perry & Ellett, 2012). The ebb and flow of child welfare inclusion in BSW and MSW education curricula appear tied to the intermittent availability of federal funding for child welfare employees and BSW and MSW education (Zlotnik, 1998). Currently, few states require a social work degree for child welfare employment, and although federal legislation highly regulates child welfare practice, currently no minimum qualifications are set forth in federal law.[2]

Social work has been the only profession to claim child welfare as a practice area that prepares graduates with the complex set of knowledge, skills, abilities, and values requisite for child welfare practice. The effects of child maltreatment have been identified, leading to passage of state and federal child welfare legislation to prevent, assess, protect, and ameliorate the effects of child abuse and neglect. However, the numbers of child welfare professionals needed to protect children, support families in acquisition of the knowledge and skills to parent, and achieve permanence and well-being has grown without adequate and commensurate funding for workforce retention and client resources. Concomitantly, from the earliest days of schools of social work, there has been insufficient capacity to educate the numbers of social work graduates to fill child welfare positions (Perry & Ellett, 2012).

The CB supported and championed the passage of the Adoption Assistance and Child Welfare Act of 1980, which established Title IV-E under the Social Security Act. This 1980 legislation is intended to help states maintain their respective foster care and adoption programs for poor children whose parents are eligible for Aid to Families with Dependent Children. It was not until the late 1980s and early 1990s that a provision allowing state and university partnerships to claim funding for the education and training of public child welfare employees and potential employees came to light. Administrators of state child welfare agencies and BSW and MSW programs eagerly worked in partnership to improve the child welfare work force to better serve children and families.

The Adoption Assistance and Welfare Act, was passed during the Carter administration. However, the appropriations bill introduced during the Reagan administration provided insufficient operational funding and thus restrained the CB from issuing regulations. This negatively affected efforts to educate and train child welfare employees.

The advent of the Clinton administration brought renewed attention to children, and the CB was able to promote and rapidly expand the Title IV-E Child Welfare Agency/Education Partnerships during the last decade of the 20th century. Nevertheless, the CB was able to exercise only limited oversight of the programs through its 10 U.S. regional offices, which has led to various and ever-changing interpretations of allowable expenses and matching funds. Regrettably, there has been no systematic or uniform implementation or evaluation of the Title IV-E child welfare education programs. Zlotnik (2006) determined that over 40 states were participating in Title IV-E partnerships at the time of her study.

A century ago the CB recognized the need for child welfare staff to have graduate social work education to effectively work with families who have complex needs and challenges. An irony of current Title IV-E legislation and antiquated regulations is that child welfare training funds are disallowed for imparting knowledge and skills on treatment, services, or conducting child protection investigation to ameliorate the effects of child maltreatment. This issue needs to be addressed for a better future for children and families receiving child welfare services.

Policy makers and the public's unwritten standards and expectations for infallible decision making and actions on the part of child welfare employees continue to increase the need for an educated and professional workforce. State public agencies have been subjected to an increasing number of oversight mechanisms, including (a) juvenile courts, (b) judges appointing guardian ad litem or court-appointed special advocates for children in state custody, (c) 6-month review and permanency court hearings, (d) citizen review panels, (e) the media, (f) child advocates, (g) congressional legislation increasing federal requirements, and (h) CB child and family services reviews (CFSRs; Perry & Ellett, 2012).

The history and evolution of child welfare readily demonstrates the convergence between the CB and BSW and MSW education as advocates for, and agents of, change. However, the case can be made that a complex sociopolitical environment has at times interfered with efforts to strengthen and improve child and family safety, permanence, and well-being. The following section provides some observations about the current environment of child welfare in the United States.

SOME PERSPECTIVES ON THE CURRENT STATE OF CHILD WELFARE

Following publicity and public outrage about battered child and shaken baby syndromes, Congress passed the Child Abuse Prevention and Treatment Act of 1974.

However, the scope of the problem was unknown, resulting in insufficient funding for the exponential growth in child abuse and neglect reports that followed. The numbers of children removed from their families likewise grew rapidly, and by 1980 over a half million children were in out-of-home care. The magnitude of maltreatment reports, families served in child protective services, foster care, and adoption programs continued to rise until 2002. Since then the number of children and families served in child protective services and foster care programs has gradually declined, whereas the number of children adopted from foster care has gradually increased (CB, 2011a, 2011b); even during the prolonged economic downturn, positive CFSR outcomes for the struggling child welfare system are improving.

Many factors contribute to the declining number of maltreatment reports and decreasing numbers of children in foster care, which likely include (a) public awareness; (b) multiple congressional acts focused on safety, permanence, and well-being; (c) focus on accountability including state child and family service reviews; (d) improved court processes; (e) evidence-based child abuse and neglect prevention programs; (f) evidence-based parental education programs; (g) performance-based contracting; (h) alternative or differential response to maltreatment reports; (i) early engagement and diligent search for parents including fathers, extended family, and kin in planning, intervention, and guardianship when appropriate; (j) systems-of-care and interagency collaboration; (k) family-focused intervention, including family team meetings; (l) trauma-informed practice; (m) clinical supervision; (n) increased education and training of the child welfare workforce; (o) leadership training for midlevel managers; and (p) an increased number of employees with social work degrees in the child welfare system. The CB continues to provide partial funding for many of the aforementioned programs and supports through Title IV-B, Title IV-E, and demonstration grants. The CB's efforts have helped generate empirical evidence for effective child welfare practice. At the same time, BSW and MSW education programs have placed increased emphasis on emerging CB-supported evidence-based practices in child welfare courses.

Research on child welfare practices and the workforce is creating an evidence base for improved practice to enable more successful outcomes. The National Association of Social Work (NASW) 2004 workforce study identified an impending shortage of social workers (Whitaker, Weismiller, & Clark, 2006). The U.S. Bureau of Labor Statistics (2010) predicted that the growth of the social work profession will not keep pace with demand, and there is already an insufficient cadre of social workers to meet the escalation in the number of individuals in need of such services. More detailed analyses and recommendations to prepare and improve the child welfare workforce have been published in the past few years. Even with employment opportunities, attracting and retaining social work employees has become challenging because of high student loan debt, high stress, and low wages even with a college degree (Zlotnik et al., 2011).

In response to increasing accountability, child welfare agencies placed emphasis on task supervision to the neglect of mentoring and professional development of employees. CB administrators recognized the importance of quality supervision for improving child welfare practice to also include clinical aspects and funded the Quality Improvement Center on Child Welfare Clinical Supervision. The center included comparative evaluation of treatment groups with control groups of supervisors, which adds evidence of the importance of the clinical role in effective supervision. Given the complexities of the child welfare work environment, quality/competent supervision and worker–supervisor relationships are important for the recruitment and retention of child welfare workers (Collin-Camargo, 2005). Child welfare supervision needs to become less compliance oriented and more professionally reflective and practice oriented (Collins-Camargo, Sullivan, Washeck, Adams, & Sundet, 2009). According to Perry and Ellett (2012), research on supervision shows that quality supervision in child welfare makes important contributions to (a) organizational culture, (b) strengthening beliefs about making a positive difference in client outcomes, (c) strengthening professional commitment and employee retention, and (d) enhancing worker knowledge, critical thinking, and self-reflective learning.

With rapid expansion of privatization of child welfare services, the CB later funded the Quality Improvement Center on the Privatization of Child Welfare Services "to determine the extent to which states had shifted decision-making authority to the private sector" (Collins-Camargo, 2012, p. 1). Three states that had largely privatized their child welfare systems participated in the quality center evaluation effort. The findings identified shared risk, integrated quality assurance processes, data-driven reporting and decision making, and effective communication strategies as essential elements for successful performance-based contracting. Successful public–private partnerships require constant collaboration on all aspects of contract development, refinement, monitoring, and practice improvements designed to enhance outcomes for children and families (Collins-Camargo, 2012).

Other evidence has been accumulating to identify personal and organizational factors empirically related to child welfare employee retention and turnover (Ellett, Ellett, & Rugutt, 2003; Ellis, Ellett, & DeWeaver, 2007; Landsman, 2001; Mor Barak, 2001; Westbrook, Ellett, & DeWeaver, 2009; Zlotnik, DePanfilis, & Daining, 2005). Some findings suggest that (a) MSW students attain better outcomes with clients than those with bachelor's degrees, (b) Title IV-E stipend recipients are more knowledgeable and skilled in child welfare practice than non-IV-E graduates, and (c) social work–educated workers remain employed in public child welfare longer than others (Perry & Ellett, 2012).

During implementation of demonstration grants funded by the CB, rigorous evaluations have been impeded by the ever-changing political appointments of leaders (agency heads) at federal, regional, and state levels. Many heads of state organizations are bright and well-meaning but may have little or no child welfare experience or social work education. Thus, they find themselves on a steep learning curve. Frequent changes in agency leadership create instability, employee anxiety, and unpredictable work environments. CB administrators recognized that midlevel managers and supervisors were more stable than agency heads and subsequently initiated the National Child Welfare Workforce Institute to improve the workforce. One key element of the institute was the leadership academy, designed to provide professional development for midlevel managers and supervisors to develop leadership skills to sustain evidence-supported practices (National Child Welfare Workforce Institute, 2012).

It is beyond the scope of this chapter to describe in detail the many changes and innovations that have occurred in child welfare over the past century and those that currently pervade greater professionalization and a move toward enhanced evidence-based practice. The changes and innovations described previously document the plethora of issues and controversies surrounding child welfare systems. To date, there are few standardized processes and procedures for carrying out child welfare practices. For example, no standardized evaluation system exists for CB-funded Title IV-E child welfare BSW and MSW education programs. The following section provides some possibilities and recommendations to move child welfare toward a vision of a better future for children and families. Some of the recommendations are empirically based, whereas others are derived from professional experiences in child welfare practice and schools of social work.

TOWARD A VISION OF A BETTER FUTURE FOR CHILDREN AND FAMILIES

Professional child welfare has contributed much to U.S. children and families through the years at the national, state, and local levels. However, much remains to be done to accomplish the goals of safety, permanency, and well-being for our most vulnerable children and families. It is unlikely that states will be able to meet desired CB and CFSR outcomes without a competent and stable workforce to achieve collaboration among children, families, and communities. Explicating a comprehensive vision for the future of child welfare would encompass many elements with the long-term goal of improving child welfare outcomes for children and families. This vision might be framed by a larger concern for the increased professionalization of the child welfare workforce and continued collaborative work between the CB, schools of social work, and state and local agencies. Increasing professionalization includes many elements, extending from the content and focus of BSW and MSW curricula through the application of evidence-based practices to accomplish positive outcomes with children and their families. Between BSW and MSW education and evidence-based practices are many components that have implications for greater professionalization, such as (a) employee recruitment, (b) employee selection, (c) supervisory mentoring and support, (d) compensation and benefits, (e) work/caseload, (f) leadership, (g) continuing education and professional development, (h) career paths, (i) organizational culture, (j) research and evaluation, (k) adequate funding, (l) public relations and advocacy, (m) eliminating bureaucratic impediments, and (n) community collaboration. The following sections identify elements of the larger context any vision for child welfare is situated in and needs to be addressed if outcomes for children and families are to be accomplished. The primary focus is on issues pertaining to the increased professionalization of the child welfare workforce.

PROFESSIONALIZING AND IMPROVING CHILD WELFARE

As the size and complexity of the general population grow, the challenges for public child welfare will certainly increase. Vulnerable children and families will continue to be confronted with substance abuse, mental illness, cognitive deficits, teen parenthood, and incarceration, conditions that typically need multiple social services. Therefore, accurate assessments and the ability to communicate with and actively engage family members in planning and implementing evidence-based interventions will remain critical elements of child welfare practice (Perry & Ellett, 2012). Furthermore, the increasing racial and ethnic diversity in the United States virtually guarantees that BSW and MSW graduates' knowledge and skills in working with these groups will continue to grow in importance.

Child welfare agencies are embedded within a sociopolitical environment over which they have little control; for example, the courts, funding, media, and client problems and needs are outside agencies' control. However, the variables they usually can control are hiring procedures and the professional development of the workforce. A committed and competent workforce is essential to the professionalization and improvement of child welfare. Moving toward a professional child welfare practice model requires attention to personal, organizational, and work context variables.

Collaboration and partnerships between BSW and MSW programs and child welfare agencies through Title IV-E child welfare education and training have been important to enhancing the professionalization of child welfare. These partnerships have served to (a) strengthen advocacy and develop a stronger voice for child welfare, (b) improve child welfare practice, (c) develop greater leadership capacity, (d) increase the number of child welfare employees with social work degrees, and (e) increase the number of knowledgeable and experienced child welfare university faculty. The next sections provide some general comments on important means to continue the professionalization of the child welfare workforce with the long-term vision of accomplishing positive outcomes for children and families.

Employee recruitment, selection, and retention. In developing the child welfare workforce, not enough attention has been given to the importance of targeted employee recruitment, selection, and retention, and how these contribute to high rates of child welfare employee turnover. Considerable attention has been given in the extant literature to the reasons child welfare employees leave employment, including being overworked and underpaid, with few promotional opportunities, and poor supervision. Employee turnover is costly to the agency (preservice and on-the-job training, recruiting, and selecting) and, most important, to children and families. An important and notable national finding from the 2001–2004 CFSRs was the strong association between the frequency of quality child welfare worker contact and visits with parents and their children to attain the desired outcomes of safety, permanence, and child well-being (Administration for Children and Families, 2004). For example, Flower, McDonald, and Sumski (2005) found that 75% of children in foster care with one worker over an 18-month period achieved permanency, whereas only 17.5% of those with two workers achieved permanency. High employee turnover rates suggest that greater attention needs to be placed on targeted employee recruitment, careful employee selection, and other work force issues pertaining to the enhanced professionalization of child welfare.

Child welfare has never been adequately funded or staffed to meet the needs of children and families. Little attention has been given to hiring new child welfare staff members who have the requisite knowledge, skills, abilities, and values needed for successful practice. Identifying these attributes and more strongly addressing them in credentialing hiring practices would likely save considerable human and financial investments in new employees and perhaps improve outcomes for children and families as well. To this end, personal characteristics that enhance employee retention and strengthen the child welfare workforce have been identified through research (Ellett et al., 2003; Zlotnik et al., 2005). Using this information, better employee selection protocols might be used to select child welfare employees and Title IV-E students who possess the core knowledge and skills needed to survive and be successful in child welfare (Ellett, Ellett, Ellis, & Lerner, 2009; Ellett, Ellett, Westbrook, & Lerner, 2006). Clearly, recruitment, selection, and retention of employees need greater attention to increase the professionalization of child welfare and to accomplish the long-term vision of enhanced outcomes for children and families.

Career concerns and credentialing. Child welfare is a field of practice that has failed to adequately link professional and education requirements with the realities of practice. This seems clear when examining the large percentage of child welfare employees who do not possess an academic degree in social work (Barth et al., 2008). Given the difficulties of child welfare work and the frequency of child welfare employee turnover, policy makers have typically implemented a business rather than a professional model with a goal of bureaucratic efficiency rather than professionalism. For example, moving from casework to case management with little opportunity for professional advancement has been at the foundation of administrative practices. Research studies have shown that such management perspectives rather than a more professional perspective contributes to child welfare employee turnover (Ellett et al., 2003; Westbrook, Ellis, & Ellett, 2006). In such models, opportunities for professional advancement with clear career opportunities are lacking. Although assignment to another program (e.g., child protective services, foster care, adoptions) offers new learning, few promotional opportunities beyond supervisory positions (with limited earnings) are available. National salary comparisons between child welfare workers and other professional work such as teaching, nursing, and so on, show that child welfare employees continue to lag behind in beginning and average salaries (American Public Human Services Association, 2005).

What seems needed to further professionalize child welfare is rethinking and redesigning child welfare in a way that (a) provides a professional career path; (b) accommodates individual interests, knowledge, and skills; (c) provides differentiated pay for differentiated work; (d) includes merit-based and bonus-based pay; (e) values, encourages, and rewards attainment of the MSW rather than the BSW degree; (f) designates clear qualifications and levels of renewable licensing and professional certification in positions; (g) provides mentoring and close supervision for new employees; (h) assigns reasonable case/workloads balanced with other job responsibilities; and (i) implements a valid and reliable job performance evaluation system.

Each of these redesign elements for the profession would be included in a new plan for child welfare that targets better education, practice, credentialing, professional development, supervision, compensation, retention, and, ultimately, improved services and outcomes for children and families.

Our society values professional credentials and expects the various professions to credential and sanction members to communicate a level of competence, expertise, and accountability. Though a credential does not an effective practitioner make, professionals who hold state licenses or national credentials typically reap greater monetary investments and rewards and generate greater public confidence, respect, and prestige than those who lack or hold only minimal credentials. The public places strong value and trust in the credentials in high-paying, prestigious professions such as medicine and law. Although not guaranteeing competent practice, possessing a professional credential sends the public the message of professional accountability and expertise. Interestingly and as previously stated, for the first 60 years of the CB, the MSW was considered the appropriate entry-level credential for child welfare work; however, few states currently require a social work degree as an entry-level credential (Child Welfare League of America, 1999; Lieberman et al., 1988; Perry, 2006). Although discussion about social work degrees ensuring competent practice remains ongoing, most agencies prefer to hire BSW and MSW graduates of the Title IV-E programs because they have acquired child welfare knowledge and skills.

Without a professional degree as an initial social work credential, child welfare has many obstacles to overcome. First, the message is sent to the public that anyone with a bachelor's degree can do this complex work. Second, the lack of a social work degree requirement suggests there is no body of specialized knowledge that is important to include in college and university curricula. Third, and perhaps most important, a signal is sent to the general public and to policy makers that child welfare work is not professional work and is not worthy of increased monetary investments. Thus, those employed in child welfare are viewed as case managers in a business conception of child welfare, not as professional, highly credentialed experts who can work effectively with our most vulnerable children and families. From this perspective one approach to enhancing the positive public perception of child welfare as professional work may be the development of a national credentialing board for child welfare (perhaps patterned after the National Board of Professional Teaching Standards [NBPTS]) designed to implement a professional assessment and credentialing system based on what accomplished child welfare professionals ought to know and be able to do. This kind of national credentialing system for teachers has been successfully developed and implemented by teachers (not states). The work of the NBPTS in nationally credentialing some 100,000 teachers to date strongly signals the public that teachers are competent professionals and that teaching is a profession. Importantly, the NBPTS credential has been negotiated in many states and school districts for increases in base teacher salaries.

High turnover rates in child welfare leadership positions at federal, regional, and state levels create ever-changing child welfare philosophies, laws, and policies; instability; employee anxiety; and unpredictable work environments. Federal legislation with minimum social work degree qualifications for worker, supervisor, management, and administrator child welfare positions at federal, regional, state, and local levels could elevate public respect, trust, and confidence that a professional child welfare workforce is vital to our society. Administrators, managers, and supervisors could actively work to implement a professional organizational culture and climate, perhaps through developing professional learning communities that value professional development for all members of the organization, open communications and collaborations, and leadership capacity building.

Realizing a vision for child welfare will not be an easy task, and it will require considerable resources and support from social work professionals as well as from child welfare organizations, policy makers, the general public, and perhaps strategic champions who will advocate for the professionalization of child welfare as the means to achieve improved outcomes for children and families. From 1912 to the 1970s, the CB provided leadership and support for BSW and MSW education as the desired credential for child welfare employees. Subsequently dropping social work degrees as a minimal or expected qualification led to the rapid deprofessionalization of child welfare. Federal legislation specifying minimum qualifications for all child welfare positions (grandfathering in current employees) might well move states to professionalize the child welfare workforce.

ADVOCACY FOR STABLE, FLEXIBLE FEDERAL FUNDING

No other social work specialization is so driven and dominated by law and policy as child welfare. Accountability in public and private child welfare agencies is needed. However, alleviating the multiple layers of oversight might permit more time and resources for actual work with children and families. The federal funding structure is confusing at its best, and undermines practice at its worst.

States would seemingly benefit if there were one flexible funding stream delinked from parent Aid to Families With Dependent Children eligibility when children enter foster care that could be used for all child welfare programs and clients. Federal and state laws require serving maltreated children and families without regard to income. Multiple child welfare programs serve the same children and families, just at different points in time. Although the Child Abuse Prevention and Treatment Act provided states with funding for child maltreatment report and response systems, little capital has been provided for prevention and treatment. Title IV-B discretionary funds periodically provide education stipends. Title IV-B (child protective and in-home services) and Title IV-E (foster care and adoption) constrict training and education. For example, Title IV-E disallows training funds for treatment, services, and maltreatment investigations content knowledge and skills to ameliorate child maltreatment in families. Social work and child welfare professional organizations need to strategize and advocate with the CB for stable, flexible federal funding for child welfare programs as well as for education and training of child welfare employees. Such advocacies are important elements of developing and carrying out a future vision for child welfare shared by the CB and schools of social work.

EVALUATION AND RESEARCH

The CB has funded evaluation and research with schools of social work, but the levels of funding are small compared to other federal agencies, such as the National Institutes of Health. The funded projects have often been for periods of 2 to 5 years for a few demonstration grants with evaluation components. Once these projects end, there is a push for dissemination of the results, with little additional money to support expansion of practices with demonstrated successful client and workforce outcomes across states. In response to child fatalities and other critical incidents, child welfare systems work to identify promising practices, often implementing them statewide, but often with no evaluation or research evidence to see if the change leads to desired outcomes. Perhaps the CB could require states to work with schools of social work to evaluate implementation of new programs and practices, for example, visitation programs for pregnant women and new mothers, trauma-informed practice, differential/alternative response, and family team meetings, to name a few. Evaluation of practice changes would more quickly build evidence or highlight the lack thereof for particular child welfare practices. Sound evaluation and research findings that support CB child welfare program improvements are important components of any future vision for child welfare. Including funding for evaluation of demonstration grants should be a scholarly requirement to inform new or continuing research and evaluation efforts to improve child welfare practice.

EXPANSION OF SOCIAL WORK EDUCATION

Because of the shortage of health care workers, the U.S. Department of Health and Human Services through the Health Resources and Services Administration created a Bureau of Health Professions to develop its workforce (Zlotnik et al., 2011). The U.S. Department of Labor Statistics (2010) and NASW (Zlotnik et al., 2011) have likewise determined that the demand for social worker employment outstrips BSW and MSW availability, and this demand will only increase in the years ahead. Schools of social work, in collaboration with the CB, could advocate for an Institute of Child Welfare Professionals within the CB. Schools of social work have never been able to meet the labor demands of child welfare, which is one reason the social work positions began to be declassified, and the social work degree requirement was dropped in the 1970s. The Council on Social Work Education (CSWE), along with other social work and child welfare professional organizations, should advocate for funding to expand BSW and MSW programs. Social work programs need to increase the capacity to graduate more social workers to meet the rising demands in multiple practice areas such as child welfare, substance abuse, domestic violence, gerontology, and physical and mental health. No profession other than social work allows individuals without the requisite academic degree or degrees to call themselves doctors, attorneys, psychologists, and so on. There is an apparent need for NASW and CSWE to zealously guard appropriate professional credentials and title protection for social work.

The Title IV-E child welfare social work education programs have increased social worker employment in public and private child welfare agencies and leadership capacity, as child welfare employees with MSW degrees are often promoted. The Title IV-E agency–university partnerships have also increased child welfare employee enrollment in social work degree programs, including doctoral programs, and social work faculty with child welfare experience and expertise have increased concomitantly. Because child welfare content in social work curricula varies with federal funding, a program similar to the Hartford Geriatric Social Work Faculty Scholars Program that develops gerontology faculty could be pursued to develop faculty with child welfare expertise. Establishing and maintaining special interest groups in social work professional organizations, such as the CSWE and the Society for Social Work and Research, is one means of keeping child welfare visible and institutionalized. A means to preserve child welfare in social work curricula and field education is needed to prevent elimination of child welfare if federal funding for education evaporates. Also, NASW and

CSWE could more aggressively promote title protection and social workers in child welfare positions at all levels.

The CB and some agencies have noted that many BSW and MSW programs do not adequately prepare students with requisite child welfare knowledge, skills, abilities, and values, for example, child development, working with involuntary clients, family-focused practice, and systems of care. If schools of social work do not include child welfare content and practice in curricula, the CB will likely turn to other higher education disciplines such as nursing, counseling, and psychology to practice in what has traditionally been a social work practice area (Mitchell et al., 2012). This is an issue that CSWE could possibly address through standards for future reaccreditation of BSW and MSW programs. The CB has been promoting public and private interagency, community support and collaboration, through systems-of- care responsive to social work's study of the person-in-environment. Social work and child welfare organizations may need to better communicate with the CB that social work remains the discipline best suited to prepare graduates for child welfare practice.

Research on child welfare practices and the workforce is creating an evidence base for improved practice to enable more successful child welfare outcomes. It seems imperative that BSW and MSW programs teach and promote evidence-based practices with students and practicum internship agencies.

THE CB AND SOCIAL WORK EDUCATION: A SHARED VISION

The continuing growth of the evidence base in public child welfare practice will eventually necessitate an alliance between the CB, institutions of higher education, and our professional organizations, such as CSWE, NASW, and the Society for Social Work and Research, and a shared vision for professional child welfare practice should emerge. Developing this shared vision will require considerable communication and discussion among the principal actors. The importance of including other stakeholders (e.g., families, policy makers, state and local agencies, community representatives) is recognized but not discussed here. These discussions might begin with the mission statement of the CB: "The Children's Bureau seeks to provide for the safety, permanency and wellbeing of children through leadership, support for necessary services, and productive partnerships with States, Tribes, and communities" (CB, 2012). Mitchell and CB colleagues (2012) reported on a broad vision for the future of child welfare,

> focusing on the goals of reducing maltreatment and achieving optimal health and development of children and families through comprehensive seamless service delivery, collective impact strategies to leverage social change, policy and finance reform, and initiatives to strengthen and support the child welfare workforce. (p. 551)

For example, although reports and substantiation rates of sexual and physical abuse have been declining since 1992, the proportion of neglected children and the absolute number of child fatalities have increased. With the focus on community maltreatment prevention and child well-being, the CB is turning more attention and effort to reduce child maltreatment, especially neglect (Mitchell et al., 2012). Likewise, the CB is expanding its vision for the child welfare workforce to include (a) careful employee recruitment and selection of employees with a professional commitment to child welfare, (b) developing child welfare knowledge and skills, and (c) developing positive organizational culture, climate, and leadership at all levels to foster employee retention (Mitchell et al., 2012).

Recognizing that child maltreatment often has detrimental lifelong physical and mental health effects, attention is shifting to an integrated and coordinated community systems-of-care approach with families. Given the current value placed on evidence-based practices in child welfare and the previous observations, it will be necessary in the near future for the CB and its community and professional partners to use research and outcome data to establish a shared child welfare practice framework. Implementation and maintenance of this jointly developed framework will by necessity include policy formulation and the monitoring of an increasing body of empirically grounded practices to make more informed decisions on behalf of clients.

For this vision to have meaning in the future, five developmental factors are essential: a close professional alliance between key stakeholders (e.g., the CB and schools of social work), close professional communication and collaboration among stakeholders to attendant policies and practices, commitments on the part of stakeholders to the reprofessionalization of child welfare (to include differential credentialing), a strong grassroots effort to support child welfare professionals and the children and families they serve, and development of a comprehensive, systematic national database on characteristics of those working in child welfare and the children and families they serve.

Given the expected shift to primary child maltreatment prevention, stronger coordinated community collaborations, and the growing trend in family participation in service decisions, social work education remains the discipline best suited to prepare its graduates for public and private child welfare practice.

Finally, building the political will to provide effective services for children and families in need requires that we speak in one clear, uniform voice. This voice can propel important changes in social work education and in CB programs and efforts to ensure a better future for children and families in the years ahead. Developing a clearly stated, thoroughly discussed, and professionally endorsed and shared vision for child welfare is a necessary first step in improving the professional status of child welfare and services to our most vulnerable children and families.

REFERENCES

Addy, S., & Wright, V. R. (2012), *Basic facts about low-income children, 2010.* Retrieved from http://www.nccp.org/publications/pdf/text_1049.pdf

Administration for Children and Families. (2012). *Compiled results of the fiscal years 2001–2010 federal child and family services review.* Retrieved from http://www.acf.hhs.gov/programs/cb/resource/cfsr-compiled-results-2001-2010

Adoption Assistance and Child Welfare Act, 96 U.S.C. § 272 (1980).

American Public Human Services Association. (2005). *Report from the 2004 child welfare workforce survey: State agency findings.* Washington, DC: Author.

Barth, R. P., Lloyd, E. C., Christ, S. L., Chapman, M. V., & Dickinson, N. S. (2008). Child welfare worker characteristics and job satisfaction: A national study. *Social Work, 53,* 199–209.

Bradbury, D. E. (1956). *Four decades of action for children: A short history of the Children's Bureau.* Washington, DC: U.S. Department of Health, Education, and Welfare.

Children's Bureau. (1940). *Child welfare services under the Social Security Act, Appendix: Text of the sections of the Social Security Act relating to grants to states for child welfare services* (Publication No. 257). Washington, DC: U.S. Department of Labor.

Children's Bureau. (2011a). *Adoption and foster care statistics.* Retrieved from http://www.acf.hhs.gov/programs/cb/research-data-technology/statistics-research/afcars

Children's Bureau. (2011b). *Child maltreatment.* Retrieved from http://www.acf.hhs.gov/programs/cb/research-data-technology/statistics-research/child-maltreatment

Children's Bureau. (2012). *CB fact sheet.* Retrieved from http://www.acf.hhs.gov/programs/cb/aboutcb/about_cb.htm

Child Welfare League of America. (1999). *Minimum education required by state child welfare agencies, percent, by degree type. State child welfare agency survey.* Washington, DC: Author.

Coll, B. (1995). *Safety net: Welfare and Social Security, 1929–1979.* New Brunswick, NJ: Rutgers University Press.

Collins-Camargo, C. (2005). *A study of the relationship among effective supervision, organizational culture promoting evidence-based practice, worker self-efficacy, and outcomes in public child welfare* (Unpublished doctoral dissertation). University of Kentucky, Lexington.

Collins-Camargo, C. (2012). Introduction: Special issue on performance-based contracting and quality assurance systems within public–private partnerships. *Journal of Public Child Welfare, 6,* 1–12.

Collins-Camargo, C., Sullivan, D. J., Washeck, B., Adams, J., & Sundet, P. (2009). One state's effort to improve recruitment, retention, and practice through multifaceted clinical supervision interventions. *Child Welfare, 88*(5), 87–107.

Costin, L. (1983). *Two sisters for social justice: A biography of Grace and Edith Abbott.* Urbana: University of Illinois Press.

Costin, L., Karger, H., & Stoesz, D. (1996). *The politics of child abuse and neglect in America.* New York, NY: Oxford University Press.

Ellett, A. J., Ellett, C. D., Ellis, J. I., & Lerner, C. B. (2009). A research-based child welfare employee selection protocol: Strengthening retention of the workforce. *Child Welfare, 88,* 49–68.

Ellett, A. J., Ellett, C. D., & Rugutt, J. K. (2003). *A study of personal and organizational factors contributing to employee retention and turnover in child welfare in Georgia.* Athens: University of Georgia, School of Social Work.

Ellett, A. J., Ellett, C. D., Westbrook, T. M., & Lerner, B. (2006). Toward the development of a research-based employee selection protocol: Implications for child welfare supervision, administration, and professional development. *Professional Development: International Journal of Continuing Social Work Education, 9*(2/3), 111–120.

Ellett, A. J., & Leighninger, L. (2007). What happened? An historical analysis of the de-professionalization of child welfare with implications for policy and practice. *Journal of Public Child Welfare, 1*(1), 3–34. doi: 10.1300/J479v01n01_02

Ellis, J. I., Ellett, A. J., & DeWeaver, K. (2007). Human caring in the social work context: Continued development and validation of a complex measure. *Research on Social Work Practice, 17,* 66–76.

Flower, C., McDonald, J., & Sumski, M. (2005). *Review of turnover in Milwaukee County private agency child welfare ongoing case management staff.* Urbana: Children and Family Research Center, University of Illinois.

Landsman, M. J. (2001). Commitment in public child welfare. *Social Services Review, 75,* 386–419.

Lieberman, A., Hornby, H., & Russell, M. (1988). Analyzing the educational backgrounds and work experiences of child welfare personnel: A national study. *Social Work, 33,* 485–489.

Lundberg, E. O. (1926). *The county as a unit for an organized program of child caring and protective work* (Children's Bureau Publication No. 160). Washington, DC: U.S. Department of Labor.

Mitchell, L., Walters, R., Thomas, M. L., Denniston, J., McIntosh, H., & Brodowski, M. (2012). The Children's Bureau vision for the future of child welfare. *Journal of Public Child Welfare, 6,* 550–567.

Mor Barak, M. E., Nissly, J. A., & Levin, A. (2001). Antecedent to retention and turnover among child welfare, social work, and other human service employees: What can we learn from past research? A review and meta-analysis. *Social Service Review, 75,* 625–661.

Perry, R. (2006). Do social workers make better child welfare workers than non-social workers? *Research on Social Work Practice, 16,* 392–405.

Perry, R., & Ellett, A. J. (2012). Child welfare and social work practice. In C. N. Dulmus & K. M. Sowers (Eds.), *Fields of social work practice: Historical trends, professional issues, and future opportunities* (pp. 1–54). Hoboken, NJ: Wiley.

Phillips, K. (2002). *Wealth and democracy: A political history of the American rich.* New York, NY: Broadway Books.

Social Security Act, 42 U.S.C. 301 et seq. (1935).

Trattner, W. I. (1970). *Crusade for the children: A history of the National Child Labor Committee and Child Labor Reform in America.* Chicago, IL: Quadrangle Books.

U.S. Bureau of Labor Statistics. (1952). *Social workers in 1950.* New York, NY: American Association of Social Workers.

Westbrook, T. M., Ellett, A. J., & DeWeaver, K. (2009). Development and validation of a measure of organizational culture in public child welfare agencies. *Research on Social Work Practice, 19,* 730–741.

Westbrook, T. M., Ellis, J., & Ellett, A. J. (2006). Improving retention among public child welfare staff: What can we learn from the insight and experiences of committed survivors? *Administration in Social Work, 30*(4), 37–62.

Whitaker, T., Weismiller, T., & Clark, E. (2006). *Workforce study.* Washington, DC: National Association of Social Workers.

Willard, D. W. (1930). Public welfare, state agencies. In F. S. Hall (Ed.), *Social work yearbook, 1929* (p. 375). New York, NY: Russell Sage.

Zlotnik, J. L. (1998). *Historical analysis of the implementation of federal policy: A case study of accessing Title IV-E funds to support social work* (Unpublished doctoral dissertation). University of Maryland, Baltimore.

Zlotnik, J. (2006). No simple answers to a complex question: A response to Perry. *Research on Social Work Practice, 16,* 414–416.

Zlotnik, J. L., DePanfilis, D., Daining, C., & Lane, M. M. (2005). *Factors influencing retention of child welfare staff: A systematic review of research.* Washington, DC: Institute for the Advancement of Social Work Research.

Zlotnik, J. L., McCroskey, J., Gardner, S., Gibaja, M., Taylor, H., George, J., Lind, ...Taylor-Dinwiddie, S. (2011). *Report from a think tank symposium.* Washington, DC.: National Association of Social Workers.

NOTES

1 More detailed discussions of some of the content in this chapter are included in preceding Chapters 1–4 and 6.

2 For an analysis of the deprofessionalization of child welfare, see Ellett & Leighninger, 2007.

12

CREATING A HOUSE OF CARDS
The Struggle to Create Community Partnerships
Across Difference in a Child Welfare Context

Debora M. Ortega and Colleen J. Reed

B y their nature, community partnerships are developed from complicated organisms created from interdependent relationships that exist in historical contexts. They require the negotiation of power dynamics among members and can span multiple cultural and knowledge frameworks. Under the best conditions, and because the relationships with individual members and communities continuously shift and change, these partnerships are as easy to maintain as a house of cards that threatens to fall in response to the slightest breeze.

Our continually developing knowledge about human relationships in the context of community partnership is, in part, because of the Children's Bureau's (CB's) commitment to engage and its expectation that child welfare systems across the country will become involved with a variety of identity community representatives. Over its history and to its credit, the CB has worked with diverse communities and strived for successful partnerships despite difficulties in sustaining complex multidynamic community relationships. Inevitably the success and demise of community partnerships are influenced not just by individual actors, but by the politics, policies, and the depth of understanding about the nature of cultural, ethnic, and racial (as well as other identity) communities. Many of these communities exist in realities based on a history of inequity and injustice and have been the objects of policies that have disempowered and therefore created distrust of governmental organizations and their representatives.

It is nearly impossible to consider the future of community partnerships without appearing to become retrospectively critical of previous relationship-building efforts and activities (or lack thereof). It is imperative, however, to critically analyze these attempts at building relationships, because the knowledge that will be the foundation of the next generation of community partnerships will be built on the skeletons of our history together.

Our professional history as child welfare social workers at all levels includes successes and failures in involving cultural communities. But over time our efforts have enabled community partnerships and more appropriate interventions. The failures, perhaps even more than the successes, have created rich opportunities to create permanent community relationships, based not only on mutual areas of concern (i.e., disproportionality) but on mutual goals (i.e., the increased equity for and well-being of all children and families in all communities).

The shared history of social work education and the CB illustrates that caring for children requires support from many complex systems. This realization brings us full circle, because contained in this realization is the appropriateness of the whole child perspective, promulgated long ago and described by Stuart and Simon in Chapters 1 and 2. Community partnerships, in the broadest terms, include not only our connection to larger organized groups, but also those connections to friends, relatives, and others who share an interest in our well-being and the well-being of those around us. This chapter investigates the history of community partnerships in the context of child welfare. It explores the concept of community partnerships, looks at the complex history of community partnerships in child welfare, explores the process of reconciliation and healing of community relationships, and investigates approaches to reengage communities (especially communities of color).

KINSHIP CARE AS AN EXPRESSION OF COMMUNITY PARTNERSHIP

Kinship care predates the creation of the CB as communities created their own natural process of care for children. Born of necessity out of personal or community strife, kinship care has become an established, institutionalized practice, rooted deeply in the experience of many immigrants as well as the indigenous and enslaved. This type of care is an exemplar of organic community partnership, designed to provide support to a family, care for a child, and foster a healthy community.

Despite the efficacy of this once-informal model of community care, the growth of the foster care system continued apace for decades, with children removed and placed at a rather alarming rate. In fact, families have felt less supported by current welfare policies, such as the Adoption and Safe Families Act of 1997, which reduced the time available to parents to complete services so they can be reunited with their children at the same time as it increased incentives for adoption (Ayón, 2009; Harris & Skyles, 2008). Care for children apart from their parents in either foster care or kinship care creates different levels of financial support for children. Kinship care providers typically receive $200 monthly from the Temporary Assistance for Needy Families program based on the number of children in their care. Foster families receive $356 to $531 per month based on the age and need of each child in their care (Hill, 2006). These differences highlight a seemingly irrational policy structure that has an effect on community support for families.

Kinship families, many of which include economically challenged grandparents, experience different kinds of economic burden. Ironically, nonkin foster families have a higher socioeconomic status than their kinship care-providing counterparts. About 50% of kinship foster families live at 200% below the poverty line compared to 23% of their nonkin foster parent counterparts. Furthermore, kinship care is used at greater rates in the African American community (Macomber, Geen, & Main, 2003). Clearly the cost of raising a child remains consistent, whether one is a kinship care provider or a foster parent. The difference in financial support between kinship care and foster parents is just one example of the treatment of family and family-supported services (Harris & Skyles, 2008) that results in complicating the relationships in communities of color, leaving many partners feeling disrespected or devalued.

The complexity of this issue extends further when considering that although grandparents providing kinship care may be more likely to care for sibling groups and to foster connections to their culture for children, they face significant frontline challenges in maneuvering through the child welfare and other supportive systems (Stowell-Ritter, 2004). Kinship care families receive less-supportive services than foster families, who may not be a part of the child's community (or culture). Ultimately, kinship care becomes the "cheaper" child welfare option used by families who are committed to caring for their community's children regardless of the socioeconomic hardships involved.

In past decades community partnerships designed for the purpose of advocating and caring for vulnerable children and families seem to be like an Orphan Train that has run off the rails. Our well-meaning child welfare system, in all its various historical forms, has careened forward thoughtfully but frustratingly, while steeped in its own culture of power and domination. Outcomes for children in the care of the state, especially for those children who age out of foster care systems, leave some advocates wondering if we (child welfare workers and advocates) should remove foster children from ourselves. Child welfare researchers have suggested that the child welfare system has yet to assume sufficient responsibility for providing youths with the basic levels of well-being necessary for functioning adulthood (Poertner, McDonald, & Murray, 2000). Many of these young people aging out of the foster care system are youths of color who are overrepresented in the system. Most of them are from socioeconomically challenged communities and families. Consequently, the relationships with communities of color and poor families are at best frazzled and at worse seen as a threat to the survival of the unique characteristics and values of cultural communities.

LEARNING THE LESSONS OF HISTORY

The historical relationship of community partnerships in child welfare is filled with a mixed bag of successes and failures. One of the most famous of these mixed bags is the Orphan Trains. Although not necessarily thought of traditionally as a community partnership effort, the Orphan Trains most certainly engaged communities in the care of children. Orphan Trains, which ran from 1853 to about 1930, were misnamed, as very few of the children transported from New York to states across the country (including the Midwest, Texas, California, and the South) were in actuality orphans (Cook, 1995). Rather, the Orphan Train children and their families were predominantly immigrants who were victims of poverty (Cook, 1995). The stories told by these impoverished children include tales of family generosity and loving homes as well as experiences as slave farm labor and of abuse (Scheuerman, 2007). This is a poignant example of how our conceptualization of child welfare underpinned the development of an intervention, perhaps laced with anti-immigrant sentiment, aimed at individuals in response to what was actually the structural problem of poverty. Although the beginning of Orphan Trains predates the creation of the CB by more than 50 years, the Orphan Train experience provides insight into the beginning of the cultural and social class clash that repeats itself throughout the development of community partnerships in the 20th century.

Another mixed bag and less well-known history of child welfare work in community partnerships developed during World War II. Social workers, including child welfare workers, were involved in being "both the protector of the [Japanese] Nikkei and the instrument of their delivery into incarceration" (Park, 2008, pp. 455). Social workers participated in the assessment and registration of some of the 120,000 Japanese who were incarcerated in internment camps. Conversely, they also used members of the Japanese community as translators, sought treatment for disabled children, provided family counseling, and negotiated the return to communities after incarceration (Park, 2008). In this way, whole communities experienced social workers, many of whom were child welfare workers, as intrusive and coercive.

Later the partnerships created by collocating child welfare services within the dynamic context of family support centers have held some promise as neighborhood service settings caring for families. In these settings, social workers and affiliated human service workers aimed to serve whole-family constellations and the greater community. Still, too often these services fall short of cultural responsiveness, focus narrowly on individuals and families, and are often provided by outside professionals who do not engage in the necessary community capacity building that could produce lasting change to those served by the child welfare system and family support centers (Austin, 2005). Although these centers bring together services in a centralized location for families, they have yet to bring whole communities to the task of caring for children.

These examples are by no means exhaustive, but they do start to enable a connection of the dots between our past and present as they relate to the organization of community partnerships. First, historically in the United States those who work, study, do research, and have been committed to the child welfare system have, not surprisingly, infused the primary American cultural value of individualism into the child welfare system, a value that does not have primacy in all cultures (Marsiglia & Kulis, 2009). If the design, modification, and implementation of child welfare interventions occur to best match the value of American individualism, it is not likely to be fully understood or adhered to by clients whose communities of origin may be different. Second, historical events, like the involvement in internment camps and the removal of American Indian children from tribal people, have actively added to the traumatic experiences of already traumatized communities.

Members of the social work education community and those in the CB have come to recognize the role this disconnect has played in their shared history as they work with diverse communities to elevate the interests of children, families, and communities.

THE ROAD AHEAD

Community partnerships, not unlike many relationships, can be difficult to negotiate in the best of circumstances. Given the history of child welfare in communities of color, the key element is not about building relationships. Rather, it is about acknowledging our historical relationships and addressing the healing process. The steps toward healing must include an acknowledgment of the fundamental, and often traumatizing, experiences of families of color in the child welfare system. Cross (2008) described in detail a process of reconciliation based on the Truth and Reconciliation Movement of South Africa. These steps are a bold approach as they incorporate elements of restorative justice at a community and organizational level. The steps specifically require retelling the harmful experiences of broken trusts and trauma, acknowledging the far-reaching consequences of detrimental helping, creating structures that will reduce the opportunity for the reoccurrence of harmful helping, and creating an opportunity to invest in a new kind of community relationship. In addition, the reconciliation process, as Cross describes it, inherently contains a cultural power and domination analysis. It is in the acknowledgement of the failed partnerships that the emergence of new partnerships, built on mutuality and equity of relationship, can occur.

Almost as important as the steps to reconciliation is the experience of witnessing and healing from a collectivist perspective. The use of interventions designed from positions of power and infused with the values of individualism have been the basis for most of our child welfare interventions. These interventions (especially when categorizing child removal as an intervention) are redolent of the Orphan Trains, as most families who come in contact with child welfare services reflect a circumstance of poverty. Poverty continues to be a great threat to the welfare of our nation's children. The imposition of our nation's adherence to beliefs about individualism and hard work as the greatest keys to success, with little attention to conditions at the macro level, have left the children we raise in our foster care system isolated, economically disadvantaged, and educationally disengaged (O'Hare, 2008). This comes from and is reinforced by another unspoken double standard. Youths in the developmental phase of emerging adulthood are often exploring the larger world, identifying what matters most to them, and identifying and accomplishing goals (Arnett, 2007). Youths from economically stable families can return home to receive emotional and financial support from their families. They are even given a special name, the *boomerang generation*. In contrast, poor youths are expected to live independently, without a safety net, in a way that economically stable families do not expect of their own children.

Despite the overarching stamp of individualism in child welfare, a number of promising interventions have emerged from indigenous communities over the past years. These interventions reflect a collectivist perspective used in shaping the understanding of the problem and the resulting interventions. Collectivist cultures provide a perspective about human behavior whose centerpiece is interrelationships among people. Many collectivist cultures originate from communities whose histories of survival depended on interdependence. Their decision-making processes, social engagements, and business transactions are rooted in the dynamics of relationships (Marsiglia & Kulis, 2009). This sort of group orientation is valued and reinforced (social consequences and punishments) through social group norms. It is this collectivist cultural environment that was the foundation for family group conferencing imported to the United States as an innovative intervention in the late 1980s and early 1990s from New Zealand. The process in its original format allowed for family members (defined in the broadest possible context) to be empowered to create viable plans, assume responsibility, assign responsibility, rally support, and take steps that supported child welfare families to remain intact.

Since its original implementation family group conferencing has been used in most states across the United States. As it has spread across the country, it has changed in format, leaving the spirit of family (broadly defined) as optional with the actual power of decision making shifted from families back to professional helpers. Some of the exciting successes that occurred early in the adoption of family group conferencing have been less exciting or less successful (Berzin, Cohen, Thomas, & Dawson, 2008) as adoption has turned to adaptation. Many of the adaptive models reflect less of the collectivist nature and more of the individual values associated with U.S. culture.

It is perhaps in the domination of an individual values approach to the caring for children, which is by definition a collectivist activity, that we lose great possibilities for dynamic and successful community partnerships. Historically, we have made well-meaning attempts at creating community partnerships. At times we have made efforts to include communities of color in partnership by creating advisory boards (or perhaps advice boards) so that community leaders can be present in the conversation about the needs of children. All these attempts lack a deep and meaningful relationship with the community to correct not only the trauma of the past but the everyday traumas that continue to put poor families and families of color at great risk.

CONCLUSION

Creating viable dynamic community partnerships requires child welfare workers and advocates to use critical thinking about their own values and the value assumptions interventions are designed from, and to seek information beyond U.S. (or individually) culturally based systems. Expanding exposure beyond interventions developed on U.S. cultural values allows for individualistic value-based interventions to be challenged and provides fresh thinking about the creation of relationships with communities that have experienced a history of being slighted, misunderstood, or devastated by well-meaning individuals and institutions. Inherent in expanding tools beyond individually based systems requires workers and advocates to assess their own positions as people with power (educational, class, and positional) as they begin to involve themselves with identity communities.

In the end the question is about working in productive community partnerships for the express purpose of improving the lives of vulnerable children and families. From a collectivist perspective, improving the natural and social environments of those who are vulnerable will necessarily also improve the environments of those who are not vulnerable.

Ultimately, our personal and professional perspectives about our responsibility for vulnerable people in our communities affect our policy decision-making processes. From a collectivist perspective, every person is responsible for the most and least vulnerable people in our communities. We manifest this responsibility through our decisions about supporting tax initiatives that increase the quality of those things that support children and families, including schools, human services, and even infrastructures such as roads and emergency services. In the end, every child who experiences abuse, neglect, or poverty is our responsibility, for it no longer takes a village to raise a child, it takes a nation.

REFERENCES

Adoption and Safe Families Act, Pub. L. No. 105-89 (1997).

Arnett, J. J. (2007). Emerging adulthood: What is it, and what is it good for? *Child Development Perspectives, 1*(2), 68–73.

Austin, S. (2005). Community-building principles: Implications for professional development. *Child Welfare, 84*(2), 105–122.

Ayón, C. (2009). Shorter time-lines, yet higher hurdles: Mexican families' access to child welfare mandated services. *Children and Youth Services Review, 31*, 609–616.

Berzin, S. C., Cohen, E., Thomas, K., & Dawson, W. C. (2008). Does family group decision making affect child welfare outcomes? Findings from a randomized control study. *Child Welfare, 87*(4), 35–54

Cook, J. F. (1995). A history of placing-out: The Orphan Trains. *Child Welfare*, 74(1), 181–197.

Cross, T. (2008). Disproportionality in child welfare. *Child Welfare*, 87(2), 11–20.

Harris, M. S., & Skyles, A. (2008). Kinship care for African American children: Disproportionate and disadvantageous. *Journal of Family Issues*, 29, 1013–1030.

Hill, R. B. (2006). *Synthesis of research on disproportionality in child welfare: An update*. Seattle, WA: Casey-CSSP Alliance for Racial Equity in the Child Welfare System.

Macomber, J. E., Geen, R., & Main, R. (2003). *Kinship foster care: Custody, hardships and service*. Washington, DC: Urban Institute.

Marsiglia, F. F., & Kulis, S. (2009). *Diversity, oppression and change: Culturally grounded social work*. Chicago, IL: Lyceum.

Nelson, K. E. (1997). Family preservation: What is it? *Children and Youth Services Review*, 19, 101–118.

O'Hare, W. P. (2008). *Data on children in foster care from the Census Bureau: A working paper*. Baltimore, MD: Annie E. Casey Foundation.

Park, Y. (2008). Facilitating injustice: Tracing the role of social workers in the World War II internment of Japanese Americans. *Social Service Review*, 82, 447–484.

Poertner, J., McDonald, T. P., & Murray, C. (2000). Child welfare outcomes revisited. *Children and Youth Services Review*, 22, 789–810.

Scheuerman, D. (2007). Lost children: Riders on the orphan train. *Humanities*, 28(6), 44–48.

Stowell-Ritter, A. M. (2004). *AARP New York report on barriers to successful kin caregiving of children*. Washington, DC: American Association of Retired Persons.

INDEX

ABOUT THE AUTHORS

Anita P. Barbee, MSSW, PhD, is professor and distinguished university scholar at the Kent School of Social Work at the University of Louisville. She has worked in the field of child welfare for the past 21 years. Her major focus has been on workforce development, including employee selection, preservice and in-service education and professional development, and training and its evaluation. She has also studied the effects of supervision, organizational culture and climate, and adherence to and outcomes of the integration of casework practice models on child welfare outcomes systems. Barbee has served as a consultant for the National Child Welfare Resource Center for Organizational Improvement and the Northeast and Caribbean Child Welfare Implementation Center. For the past 9 years she has led and then participated in evaluating the overall effects of the Children's Bureau Training and Technical Assistance Network in collaboration with James Bell Associates.

Joel Blau, DSW, teaches at the Stony Brook University School of Social Welfare, where he is professor of social policy and director of the doctoral program. He is the author of many articles and three books on social policy, including (with Mimi Abramovitz) the textbook, *The Dynamics of Social Welfare Policy* (Oxford University, 2014) now entering its fourth edition.

Sherrill Clark, LCSW, PhD, research specialist at the California Social Work Education Center (CalSWEC), University of California Berkeley, School of Social Welfare conducts the evaluation of the CalSWEC effort to reprofessionalize child welfare services in California through the Title IV-E program. This includes study of the career paths of MSW child welfare social workers: BASW, new graduate, 3- and 5-year retention studies of specially trained title IV-E MSW public child welfare workers. She also conducts the Public Child Welfare Workforce Study every 3 years, which describes the population of child welfare staff in California, their educational levels, and related factors. Her primary research areas include professional development, preparation and retention of the child welfare workforce, and evaluation of child welfare social work education and training.

Crystal Collins-Camargo, MSW, PhD, teaches at the University of Louisville Kent School of Social Work and conducts research in the areas of child welfare, organizational interventions, and juvenile court systems. She was formerly clinical assistant professor at the University of Kentucky, College of Social Work, and was engaged in a variety of grant-funded research, education, and service projects in child welfare. Through this work she has overseen a number of evaluations related to the college's service and outreach programs and has mentored doctoral and master's students in research and evaluation projects designed to influence public policy and frontline practice. Collins-Camargo conducted several Children's Bureau-funded research projects, including directing the National Quality Improvement Center on the Privatization of Child Welfare Services and the Southern Regional Quality Improvement Center for Child Protection. She has been principal investigator for several studies regarding the Kentucky court system's effectiveness in responding to abused and neglected children and their families. Before coming to the University, she was program director for Prevent Child Abuse Kentucky and worked in the public child protection system as a worker, supervisor, and statewide specialist.

Alberta J. Ellett, PhD, is associate professor at the University of Georgia, School of Social Work, having joined the faculty in 2000. She received the 2010 Council on Social Work Education Distinguished Recent Contributions in

Social Work Education Award and is nationally known as a leader in several professional organizations through her contributions to promoting the continued professionalization of child welfare. Ellett is secretary of the Society for Social Work and Research editor-in-chief of the *Journal of Public Child Welfare*. Her research interests and specializations center on developing child welfare organizations and strengthening their holding power in ways that retain and promote the development of competent child welfare staff. Ellett received her PhD in social work with a minor in industrial and organizational psychology from Louisiana State University in 2000. She has more than 25 years of direct practice and administration in child welfare in Georgia and Louisiana at all organizational levels. She has been the principal investigator of several research/evaluation and instructional grants/contracts including a 2003 statewide study in Georgia of child welfare staff retention and turnover. Ellett's scholarly child welfare publications include refereed journal articles, book chapters, and book reviews 2000 and she has presented evaluation and research papers at national child welfare and social work conferences and professional meetings.

Bart Grossman, PhD, is adjunct professor emeritus at the University of California at Berkeley School of Social Welfare. He was founding director of the California Social Work Education Center and for 30 years was director of field education. Grossman has published extensively on field education and child welfare training in social work. He continues to teach at Berkeley and to consult with charities in the field of child abuse prevention and treatment.

Miriam J. Landsman, PhD, MSW, is associate professor of social work and executive director of the National Resource Center for Family Centered Practice at the University of Iowa. Her research interest focuses on the child welfare workforce, family-centered child welfare practice, and the intersection of these two areas. Professor Landsman is principal investigator for the Children's Bureau-funded National Resource Center for In-Home Services and a university partner of the National Child Welfare Workforce Institute. She has conducted workforce studies on improving recruitment and retention in public child welfare and on improving outcomes for youth in transition, both involving interventions with child welfare supervisors. Landsman has conducted research and evaluation across the continuum of child welfare services, including family support, family preservation, child welfare mediation, family reunification, intensive family finding, residential treatment, and permanency planning. She has published and presented on the child welfare workforce and on family-centered child welfare practices. At the University of Iowa she teaches courses on child welfare policy and practice, research, and organizations.

Alice Lieberman, PhD, is Chancellor's Club Professor of Teaching at the University of Kansas, chair of the BSW program, and the principal investigator on several current and past projects funded by the Children's Bureau, including the Kansas Workforce Initiative, a collaborative agreement with the Children's Bureau. She has either written or edited several books, including the New Directions in Social Work series (Routledge), *Women in Social Work Who Have Changed the World* (Lyceum), and *The Social WorkOut Book* (Pine Forge Press). She is the recipient of numerous awards, including (with Michelle Levy) the Academic Excellence Award from the American Public Human Services Association for the KU Child Welfare Scholars Program (2005), and several awards for teaching within the university.

Ruth G. McRoy, PhD, became the first holder of the Donahue and DiFelice Endowed Professorship at Boston College Graduate School of Social Work in 2009, having served as visiting research professor and consultant 2005–2009. McRoy was previously a faculty member at the University of Texas at Austin School of Social Work for 25 years, where she served as the director of the Center for Social Work Research, director of the Diversity Institute, and associate dean for research. A practitioner, academician, researcher, trainer, and lecturer in the field for more than 30 years, McRoy has focused her work on such topics as open adoptions, racial identity development, transracial adoptions, family preservation, older child adoptions, and postadoption services. She has served as principal investigator or co-principal investigator on numerous federal, foundation, state, and local research and evaluation projects. McRoy has published numerous articles and books, including *Transracial and Inracial Adoptees: The Adolescent Years* (with L. Zurcher);

Special Needs Adoptions: Practice Issues; *Openness in Adoption: Family Connections* (with H. Grotevant); *Challenging Racial Disproportionality in Child Welfare* (with Deborah Green, Kathleen Belanger, and Lloyd Bullard); and *Intersecting Child Welfare, Substance Abuse and Family Violence: Culturally Competent Approaches* (with R. Fong, and C. Ortiz-Hendricks).

Kristine Nelson (deceased) was professor emerita and, until 2011, dean of the School of Social Work at Portland State University. She died April 22, 2012. Nelson's career consisted of a series of leadership roles and some significant "firsts": She was the first female dean of the School of Social Work and led the effort to implement a bachelor of social work program. Her leadership was felt most keenly in the field of child welfare: She began her career as a family social worker in Harlem and was director of research for the National Resource Center on Family-Based Services at the University of Iowa before joining Portland State University in 1993. During her long academic career she authored or co-authored numerous articles, book chapters, and monographs on child welfare history, family preservation, child neglect, and evidence-based practice. In 2010 Nelson was awarded the Oregon National Association of Social Workers Lifetime Recognition Award, which is given to a social worker "who has demonstrated a lifetime commitment to the practice of social work and service to the community."

Debora M. Ortega, PhD, MSW, is the founding director of the University of Denver Latino Center for Community Engagement and Scholarship and is associate professor at the University of Denver Graduate School of Social Work. Her scholarship reflects an interest in culturally responsive practice and social justice for vulnerable people in the areas of child welfare, parenting, and immigration. Ortega has designed several child welfare curricula, including "Working With Hispanic Families, Partnering for Success: Youth Transitioning from Foster Care. " In partnership with Fundación Azteca America, she published *Agenda Latina: The State of Latinos 2008* and *Agenda Latina: Immigration*. Her current research focuses on the experience of queer Latino parents as they navigate multiple cultural identities. Ortega is co-editor-in-chief of *Affilia: Journal of Women and Social Work*.

Colleen J. Reed, PhD, MSW, received her MSW from Portland State University and her PhD from the University of Kansas. She received the Hartford Doctoral Fellow award in 2004. Her academic work focused on social support and older adults.

Barbara Levy Simon, PhD, has taught at Columbia University's School of Social Work since 1986. In 1987 Simon published *Never Married Women* (Temple University Press); in 1994 she published *The Empowerment Tradition in American Social Work: A History* (Columbia University Press), which has been available electronically since 1999. She and colleague Warren Green co-edited the *Columbia Guide to Social Work Writing* (2012). Simon's scholarly interests include the history of social work, social welfare, and urban professions. She relates frameworks of analysis from women and gender studies to applied professional settings and postcolonial contexts of social work practice. Her current research focuses on continuities and changes in the neighborhood center movement (a.k.a., settlement house) since the 1880s in the United States and the United Kingdom. Simon earned her MSS and PhD degrees in social work from Bryn Mawr College's Graduate School of Social Work and Social Research.

Paul H. Stuart is professor in the Robert Stempel College of Public Health and Social Work at Florida International University in Miami, where he teaches courses in social welfare policy and services in the undergraduate, master's, and doctoral programs. He earned an MSW at the University of California, Berkeley, and an MA in history and a PhD in history and social welfare at the University of Wisconsin, Madison. He has worked as a social worker in public welfare, recreation services, health care, and community mental health and served as a clinical social worker in the Indian Health Service, U.S. Public Health Service, on the Pine Ridge Indian Reservation in South Dakota. Stuart has more than 35 years of teaching experience. His research has focused on the history of Indian–White relations in the United States, the history of social welfare, and the history of the social work profession. He is the author of several books, including *The Indian Office: Growth and Development of an American Institution, 1865-1900* (UMI Research Press, 1979) and *Nations Within a Nation: Historical Statistics of American Indians* (Greenwood

Press, 1987), in addition to numerous articles and chapters in books. He co-edited the *Encyclopedia of Social Welfare History in North America* (SAGE, 2005) with John M. Herrick. He has been active as a reviewer and editorial board member for scholarly journals and is currently archives editor for the *Journal of Community Practice*.

Joan Levy Zlotnik, PhD, ACSW, has focused on forging academic/agency partnerships and on strengthening the bridges between research, practice, policy, and education. She currently serves as the director of the National Association of Social Workers' think tank, the Social Work Policy Institute. Zlotnik is an internationally recognized expert on workforce issues and author of numerous publications and monographs, including works on accessing federal funding, child welfare partnerships, competencies, and evidence-based practice. She has studied the history and policy affecting the use of Title IV-E funds in social work education and has taught child welfare practice and child welfare policy. She currently serves on the Institute of Medicine's Committee on Child Maltreatment Research, Policy and Practice for the Next Decade; the Dual Eligible Beneficiaries' Workgroup of the National Quality Forum's Measure Application Partnership; the CDC Knowledge to Action Think Tank on Child Maltreatment Prevention; and the National Advisory Committee for the National Child Welfare Workforce Institute. Zlotnik has been a consultant to the Children's Bureau and to the National Institutes of Health and led several foundation-funded projects on interprofessional education and practice, university/agency research partnerships, and competencies for family-centered care. She received a BA from the University of Rochester, an MSSW from the University of Wisconsin-Madison, and a PhD in social work from the University of Maryland, Baltimore. She is an NASW Social Work Pioneer and was the 2012 alumni of the year for the University of Maryland School of Social Work.